Sci コ

KU-429-045

Twelve Galton Lectures

Francis Galton when about 50 years of age
From Karl Pearson's biography "The Life, Letters and Labours of
Francis Galton"

Twelve Galton Lectures

These Lectures, which were delivered between 1914 and 1982, have been selected to commemorate the Centenary of The Galton Institute in 2007

Edited by

Steve Jones and Milo Keynes

The Galton Institute
19 Northfields Prospect
London SW18 1PE

1907 – 2007

British Library Cataloguing in Publication Data

I.   Twelve Galton Lectures

II. Jones, Steve.   III. Keynes, W. Milo.

ISBN 978-0-9546570-1-7

First published 2007 by the Galton Institute, 19 Northfields Prospect, Northfields, London SW18 1PE

Printed and bound in Great Britain by CM Print, 61 Station Road, Portslade, Brighton, BN41 1DF

Contents

Preface

In the production of this commemorative book, the Council of The Galton Institute wishes to record its gratitude to John Peel (1930-2006), who was its outstanding Treasurer from 1967 to 2006. He made this selection of twelve Galton Lectures, delivered between 1914 and 1982, from the complete list given at the end of this book.

The Galton Institute is a learned scientific society founded in 1907 as the Eugenics Education Society, changing its name to the Eugenics Society in 1926, and becoming the Galton Institute in 1989. Francis Galton, the subject of the first Galton Lecture given in 1914, defined eugenics as "the scientific study of the biological and social factors which improve or impair the inborn qualities of human beings and of future generations" in 1883. The annual Galton Lectures were first published in *The Eugenics Review*, which was the official publication of the Society from 1909 until 1968. Some of the selected lectures are interesting for their historical value in showing the out-dated views of the eugenics movement in the last century which were very much in tune with those then prevailing in some parts, and quite influential parts at that, of the Church of England and the legal profession. It was to demonstrate this wider context, and to show that eugenic ideas did not develop in isolation, that those lectures were chosen for this book.

The Galton Institute is committed to environmental and genetic studies with a membership drawn from a wide range of disciplines, including the biological and social sciences, economics, medicine and law. The Institute has long developed its interests in genetics and particularly the implications of this subject for society.

Introduction

Sir Francis Galton, FRS, was much honoured in his lifetime both by the State and by his academic contemporaries. Posterity has been no less generous in memorialising his life and work in a number of ways.

The most significant of these – a university department and associated chair – arose from initiatives Galton had taken in his own lifetime. In 1904 he made a grant of £500 per annum to found a Fellowship in Eugenics at University College London and in 1907 he persuaded that institution to establish the Francis Galton Laboratory for National Eugenics. At his death Galton left the whole of his considerable fortune (aside from two quite minor bequests) to UCL. This amounted to £47,000 (£3.3 millions at 2005 values) and enabled UCL to strengthen and consolidate the Galton Laboratory and to upgrade the Galton Fellowship to a chair with Karl Pearson as its first incumbent.

Today's Galton Institute was founded in 1907 as the Eugenics Education Society. Galton took no part in its formation but the Society's Council created for him the unique, but undemanding, office of Honorary President and following his death lost no time in establishing the annual Galton Lectures in permanent memory of the man who had inspired the Society and invented its name.

The named annual lecture is difficult to sustain in perpetuity. Endowments frequently prove inadequate; the enthusiasm of the founders may not be shared by their successors and the relevance of the work of the nominee will appear less significant with the passage of time. More generally, the freestanding lecture, a largely Victorian invention, has found it difficult to attract an audience with the advent of newer methods of communication, including radio and television. The combined resolve of the Galton Institute, the Royal Statistical Society and Pembroke College Cambridge has been scarcely sufficient to sustain the adequately funded Caradog-Jones Lecture in the face of dwindling attendances since the 1990s.

In these circumstances the virtually unbroken run of Galton Lectures from 1914 to 2006 (with only 3 omissions), all of them published and therefore retrievable, stands as an unusual achievement on the part of the Institute (see Appendix) and a valuable resource in the historiography of the eugenics movement. Collectively the lectures testify to the interdisciplinary nature of the Institute's concerns at various points in the social history of the twentieth century.   Individually they illustrate the eminence of those who were prepared to associate themselves with and to promote the interests of this science-based and uniquely apolitical social movement.   Socialists, Liberals, Conservatives and others united in a belief that biology and the social sciences could be applied to the task of human betterment.   Thus, though Thomas (Lord) Horder's views on socialised medicine were well known they found no expression in his activities and writings within the Institute.   And when J.D. Bernal, a long-time and influential member of the Council of The British Communist Party, gave the 1942 Galton Lecture he spoke not on Lysenko's contribution to the third Soviet five-year plan, but on the need for a social science research council, a need which went unmet for a further twenty years.

The earliest Galton Lectures were given on or near Galton's birthday and, under the title "Galton Day", the 1914 Annual Report states:

"On Monday, February 16th, took place the first celebration by the Society of the birth of Sir Francis Galton.   The celebration was inaugurated by a dinner at the Hotel Cecil, attended by 140 persons, members of the Society and their friends ... after the dinner the company repaired to the lecture room where a considerable audience had already assembled."

Introducing Sir Francis Darwin as lecturer the Society's President, Major Leonard Darwin, presciently hoped that "this may be the first of a long series of such anniversary meetings".

The practice of prefacing the Galton Lecture by a dinner was continued until the Second World War.   Attendances varied between 150 and 200; 1937 was a peak year with an attendance of 240.   The problems posed by the war are evident from the following paragraph from the *Eugenics Review* for 1940:

Galton Luncheon and Lecture - Owing to the war, the Galton Dinner arranged for February 16th was cancelled, and it was decided that a Luncheon on the 17th should take its place. The address at this luncheon, which was held at the St Ermins Restaurant and attended by fifty-eight members and their guests, was given by Lord Horder, who took as his subject the *Society's* activities in war time.

With Dr Blacker away in the forces (where he was to add a G.M. to the M.C. awarded him in the First World War) and the administrative staff directed to "essential" work the Society was virtually put on a care and maintenance basis. Two priorities, however, were established: the continuation of the Galton Lecture sequence and the uninterrupted production of the *Eugenics Review* in which those lectures were published.

The lectures selected for this volume reflect the changing concerns and interests of the Society's members and supporters during the twentieth century. It is readily evident how great was the change and how alien some of the attitudes prevalent in the 1920s and 1930s appear in the twenty-first century – indeed, they had no place in the Society and Institute of the second half of the twentieth century. But they reflected a concern with real social problems that troubled both the church and the judiciary – problems that trouble politicians to this day and to many of which no one has yet found a satisfactory solution.

The contrast with more recent lectures is striking. One can see how from the 1960s onwards the Society became focused on advances in the life sciences, particularly reproductive health and technology, and on contemporary concerns about population, the environment and genetic disease.

When interpreting the earlier lectures, it is important to recognise how the meaning of words changes over the years, sometimes subtly and sometimes significantly. For example, the word "race" as used in these lectures often refers to the human species as a whole, or even the human gene pool, rather than to a particular ethnic group.

There are some surprising absences. Havelock Ellis was asked on several occasions to give a Galton Lecture but refused even when Dr Blacker offered to send a car to fetch him from his West Country home. Marie Stopes, as the most visible and active of English eugenicists, might also have been invited but, ironically, it was birth control rather than eugenics which was a forbidden subject in the first half of the twentieth century – a reversal of today's taboos. No woman, in fact, gave a Galton Lecture in Marie Stopes' lifetime and only five appear in the whole series.

Despite these reservations these lectures do have a value in reflecting an important current of twentieth century concern. They are the way-marks in the intellectual debate revolving around the nature/nurture controversy in its various manifestations which W.H.G. Armytage explored in the series of articles "The Social Context of Eugenic Thought" published in the *Galton Institute Newsletter* between December 1994 and March 1999 (Issues 15-32).

Council is grateful to all those who have so generously and helpfully set these lectures in context and to Mrs Betty Nixon for assembling the final volume.

Notes on the Contributors

<u>The Galton Lecturers</u>

The Right Reverend E. W. Barnes, FRS (1877-1953) Mathematician, Trinity College, Cambridge, 1898-1915; Bishop of Birmingham, 1924-53

Sir William Beveridge, FBA (1879-1963) Director, London School of Economics, 1919-37; Master, University College, Oxford, 1937-44

Sir Cyril Burt, FBA (1883-1971) Psychologist to London County Council, 1913-32; Professor of Psychology, University College London, 1932-50

Alex Comfort (1920-2000) Physician and writer on ageing and sexual behaviour

Sir Francis Darwin, FRS (1848-1925) Botanist and biographer of Charles Darwin; Reader in Botany, University of Cambridge, 1888-1904; Fellow of Christ's College, Cambridge 1886-1925

Robert G. Edwards, FRS Professor of Human Reproduction, University of Cambridge; Fellow of Churchill College, Cambridge

Sir Julian Huxley, FRS (1887-1975) Zoologist, Oxford University; Professor of Zoology, King's College, London, 1925-27; Secretary, Zoological Society of London, 1935-42; First Director-General, Unesco, 1946-48; writer on science

Paul H Gebhard Anthropologist and sexologist; Director of the Kinsey Institute, 1956-82

John Maynard Keynes, FBA (1883-1946) Economist and international negotiator; Fellow of King's College, Cambridge, 1919-1946

Sir Henry McCardie (1869-1933) Judge of King's Bench Division, 1916-33

T. H. Marshall (1893-1981) Sociologist; Professor of Sociology, London School of Economics; Director, Social Sciences Department, Unesco, 1956-60

James E. Meade, FBA (1907-95) Economist; Nobel Prize in Economics, 1977; Professor of Economics, London School of Economics, 1947-57; Professor of Economics, University of Cambridge, 1957-67; Fellow of Christ's College, Cambridge, 1957-95; Treasurer, Eugenics Society, 1963-67

Other Contributors

Professor John A. Beardmore, Emeritus Professor of Genetics, University of Wales Swansea

Mr Peter R. Brinsden, Medical Director of Bourn Hall Clinic, Cambridge

Professor David Coleman, Professor of Demography, University of Oxford

Sheriff Douglas Cusine, the Sheriff of Grampian Highland and Islands, Aberdeen

Dr Lesley Hall, the Wellcome Library for the History and Understanding of Medicine

Geoffrey Hawthorn, Professor of International Politics, Department of Politics, University of Cambridge

Dr Milo Keynes, Fellow of The Galton Institute; Honorary Fellow of Darwin College, Cambridge

The Reverend Dr John Polkinghorne, KBE, FRS, Fellow (former President) Queens' College, Cambridge; Professor of Mathematical Physics, University of Cambridge, 1968-79

Professor David Vines, Professor of Economics, University of Oxford, and adjunct Professor of Economics at the Australian National University

Dr David Watt, Fellow of The Galton Institute; psychiatrist

Dr Kevan Wylie, Consultant in Sexual Medicine and Psychosexual Therapy, Porterbrook Clinic, Sheffield; Honorary Senior Lecturer, University of Sheffield

Mr Mazin Zecki, Fellow of The Galton Institute

Sir Francis Darwin, FRS

By permission of the Syndics of Cambridge
University Library, from the Charles Darwin
Papers.

Francis Galton, 1822-1911[1]

Sir Francis Darwin, F.R.S.

Introduction by Milo Keynes

The first Galton Lecture was delivered before the Eugenics Education Society on 16 February, Sir Francis Galton's birthday, in 1914 and published in the *Eugenics Review*[2]. In December 1906 Galton had written to a friend in London, Montague Crackanthorpe, asking whether "the time was not ripe for some association of capable men who are really interested in Eugenics."[3] The idea was put to the Moral Education League in November 1907, who decided however that the Eugenics Education Society should be formed independently: Sir James Crichton-Browne became the first President in 1908 and Crackanthorpe, the Secretary. Galton, by now aged eighty-six, at first had promised to help, but then withdrew until later in 1908 when Crackanthorpe (President 1909 -1911) persuaded him to become Honorary President and to give a paper, an address on eugenics[4], to the newly formed Society.

It was after Galton's death in 1911 that Leonard Darwin (1850-1943), fourth son of Charles Darwin (1809-1882), became, from 1911 to 1929, President of the Eugenics Education Society, renamed the Eugenics Society in 1926, and becoming the Galton Institute in 1989. The first Galton Lecture was necessarily biographical and was delivered by the botanist, Sir Francis Darwin

---

[1] Being the first Galton Lecture, delivered before the Eugenics Education Society, Feb. 16th, 1914. *The Eugenics Review*, **Vol. VI**, 1914

[2] Francis Darwin. 'Francis Galton, 1822-1911.' *Eugenics Review*, 1914; 6: 1-17.

[3] Karl Pearson. *The Life, Letters and Labours of Francis Galton.* 4 vols. Cambridge University Press, vol. I, 1914; vol. II, 1924; vols. IIIA and IIIB, 1930. Letter from F. Galton to M. Crackanthorpe in 1906. vol. IIIA, p. 339.

[4] Francis Galton. 'Address on eugenics.' *Westminster Gazette*, 26 June, 1908.

(1848-1925), Charles Darwin's third son and biographer, and who, like his brother Leonard, had known Galton all his life. *The Eugenics Review*, first published in 1909, was the official publication of the Society with an Editorial Board comprising members of the Council and the Editors members of the Council or paid employees of the Society. It ceased publication in 1968.

Francis (Frank) Galton, born in 1822, was a Victorian polymath with a compulsive scientific curiosity. Often pioneering and with his wayward personality the only connecting thread between them, his successful contributions to science were achieved despite an undistinguished academic record and never working in a research laboratory, and despite his lack of mathematical ability.[5] His originality depended on a lively intelligence, but he did not always show the necessary drive to reach the full, deserved conclusion from his important discoveries. John Maynard Keynes (1883-1946) once said of him:

> "It was not the business of his particular kind of brain to push anything far. … His original genius was superior to his intellect, but his intellect was always just sufficient to keep him just on the right side of eccentricity."[6]

Besides his 'ideas' which led him into so many strange, unexplored fields owing little to the researches of others, and where the discoverer unlike him was usually an expert in some more established field, Galton produced a succession of mechanical inventions and instruments over many years. He became a Fellow of the Royal Society in 1860 for his work on instruments used in geographical research, and it was the friendships and connections he made in this work that often led to his subsequent scientific evolution.

His maternal grandfather was Erasmus Darwin (1731-1802), doctor, inventor, thinker and poet – Charles Darwin's father Robert (1766-1848) was half-brother to Galton's mother Violetta (1783-1874) – and his paternal grandfather, Samuel Galton (1753-1832), who despite being a Quaker made a large fortune from the

---

[5] Michael Bulmer. *Francis Galton – pioneer of heredity and biometry.* Baltimore and London: Johns Hopkins University Press, 2003. Introduction, p. xvi.

[6] J. M. Keynes. Quotation in Milo Keynes. 'Sir Francis Galton – a man with a universal scientific curiosity' in Milo Keynes (ed.) *Sir Francis Galton, FRS – The Legacy of His Ideas*, London: Macmillan, 1993.

manufacture of muskets and started a bank in Birmingham. The bank was expanded by his son, Samuel Tertius (1783-1844), so that, when he died, his son Francis, then aged 22, inherited sufficient wealth to be financially independent for the rest of his life and could cease being a medical student. His half-first cousin, Charles Darwin, likewise was able to remain independent because of the financial help from his father Robert, who was both financier and doctor.

After Cambridge Galton spent a year in the Eastern Mediterranean, and lived as a country gentleman before travelling in Africa for two years and later completing his famous book, *The Art of Travel*[7] (1855). It was in Africa that he had begun thinking about the weather and on his return joined the committee of Kew Observatory. He collected weather data, defined the anticyclone in 1862, produced weather maps, published *Meteorographica*[8] in 1863, and was a member of the Meteorological Committee from 1865 to 1901. During his African trip he made a contribution to the science of animal behaviour, and later wrote a paper[9] on the domestication of wild animals (1864). He joined the Anthropological Institute in 1871 in developing an interest in what might now be called human biology, in which the quantitative variation in man involved him in the setting up of an anthropometric laboratory. He made a report[10] after obtaining measurements from 53,000 people in 1883, and his researches on the transmission of characters by descent included the use of photography. He systematically collected fingerprints and established their uniqueness, how to classify them, and their forensic importance, with his book *Finger Prints*[11] coming out in 1892.

On the publication of *On the Origin of Species* in 1859, Galton wondered whether the idea of evolution by natural selection could not be applied to man and particularly to human intelligence. After

---

[7] Francis Galton. *The Art of Travel*. London: Murray, 1855.

[8] Francis Galton. *Meteorographica*. London and Cambridge: Macmillan, 1863.

[9] Francis Galton. 'First steps towards the domestication of animals.' *British Association Report*, 1864; pp. 93-4.

[10] Francis Galton. 'Final Report of the Anthropometric Committee'. *British Association Report*, 1883; pp. 253-306.

[11] Francis Galton. *Finger Prints*. London: Macmillan, 1892.

1865 his main interests became centred around human heredity and psychology, leading to research into character inheritance, particularly hereditary talent.   Long before the recognition of Mendelism by William Bateson (1861-1926) in 1901[12] and the development of IQ tests, he employed pedigree analysis and twin studies, as well as anthropometry, in initiating the study of genetics, a scientific discipline only later given that name by Bateson in 1905. The investigations were mainly numerical or statistical in character: his research maxim was "whenever you can, count", and counting and figuring and the bringing of quantitative methods into biology with the invention of new statistical tools was the result.   He first used the term "Nature and Nurture" – it seems unlikely that this was derived from Prospero's description of Caliban in *The Tempest*, Act IV, scene 1 – in 1874 in a paper analysing the replies to a questionnaire sent to 180 selected Fellows of the Royal Society, including Charles Darwin.[13]

Hereditary Genius[14], where he later wished he had used the word talent in the title to imply high ability rather than genius, appeared in 1869 to be followed by further papers on human heredity in 1875, 1877 and 1885, *Natural Inheritance*[15] in 1889, and finally in 1897 *Theory of Ancestral Inheritance*[16].   In this Galton dealt with populations and continuously varying characters, and which was used later by the biometricians, Karl Pearson (1857-1936) and W. F. R. Weldon (1860-1906), to argue against William Bateson and the Mendelians, where Mendelism was based on discontinuous variation in individuals.   The differences were finally settled in a paper[17] by R. A. Fisher (1890-1962) in 1918 when he showed that continuous variation in groups was explicable in Mendelian terms.

---

[12] W. Bateson. 'Problems of heredity as a subject for horticultural investigation.' *J. R. Horticultural Soc.*, 1901; 25: 54-61.

[13] Francis Galton. 'On men of science, their Nature and Nurture.' *Proceedings of the Royal Institution*, 1874; 7: 227-36.

[14] Francis Galton. *Hereditary Genius*. London: Macmillan, 1869.

[15] Francis Galton. *Natural Inheritance*. London: Macmillan, 1889.

[16] Francis Galton. 'The average contribution of each several ancestors to the total heritage of the offspring.' *Proceedings of the Royal Society*, 1897; 61: 401-13; 'A new law of heredity.' *Nature*, 1897; 56: 235-7.

[17] R. A. Fisher. 'The correlation between relatives on the supposition of Mendelian inheritance.' *Trans. Roy. Soc. Edinburgh*, 1918; 52: 399-433.

The general idea of planned reproduction had already been around for centuries when Galton first used the term 'eugenics' in 1883. This was in *Inquiries into Human Faculty and its Development*[18] and which he later defined as "the scientific study of the biological and social factors which improve or impair the inborn qualities of human beings and of future generations."[19] He had derived the word from the Greek *eugenes* meaning good in stock and hereditarily endowed with noble qualities, qualities that he claimed were "equally applicable to men, brutes and plants".

The promotion of eugenics became a major preoccupation in his last ten years when he returned to it in 1901 in writing two papers[20,21] on the selective breeding of those perceived to be genetically superior. From his perception of a national decline, he felt "the augmentation of favoured stock" by deliberate breeding ought to be encouraged. Without the aid of Mendelism, he worked mainly from a social, and little from a biological, point of view when he thought that eugenic policies could be implemented by encouraging the fertility of families to which eminent men belonged, and without understanding that there is no class of human being that can be regarded as constituting an elite. He was far less interested in negative eugenics which he recognised as the prevention of those thought to be genetically inferior from reproducing.

He set up a Eugenics Record Office in 1904 which became the Galton Laboratory for National Eugenics in 1907 on its merger with the Anthropometric and Biometric Laboratories. From his bequest in 1911, the Galton Professorship of Eugenics was established at University College London, with Karl Pearson the first professor until he retired in 1933. It was then held by R. A. Fisher until 1943 when he was succeeded by Lionel Penrose (1898-1972), on whose retirement in 1965 the name Eugenics was dropped and changed to Genetics.

---

[18] Francis Galton. *Inquiries into Human Faculty and Its Development*. London: Macmillan, 1883.

[19] Francis Galton. *Essays in Eugenics*. London: Eugenics Education Society, 1909.

[20] Francis Galton. 'The possible improvement of the human breed under the existing conditions of law and sentiment.' *Nature*, 1901; 64: 659-65.

[21] Francis Galton. 'On the probability that the son of a highly-gifted father will be no less gifted.' *Nature*, 1901; 65: 79.

Galton was completely of his time in holding the views and prejudices of the affluent part of society to which he belonged. He could never have envisaged the more than 60,000 court-ordered sterilizations carried out in the United States and Sweden, or the 400,000 people sterilized on the recommendation of the German Genetic Health Courts for supposed genetic diseases such as alcoholism, feeblemindedness and schizophrenia, using the negative eugenic legislation of 1935 designed to "cleanse" the population of Nazi Germany of unwanted elements, that was made along with the encouragement of positive eugenics.

Few of Galton's books are available in modern reprints and his numerous papers are lost in nineteenth-century periodicals. In 1908 he wrote his autobiography *Memories of My Life*[22] which was much used by Sir Francis Darwin for his Galton Lecture[1] in 1914 before the beginning of World War I. The first volume of *The Life, Letters and Labours of Francis Galton*[2] by Karl Pearson also came out in 1914 though the biography was only completed in 1930. This massive work of 2000 pages in four volumes, but still with omissions, is reticent about Galton's personal affairs and is now quite unreadable. It was only in 1974 that the psychologist D. W. Forrest wrote the next biography[23] which brought Galton into much better focus but again in a somewhat disjointed study. In 1982 a memoir[24] by Dorothy Middleton was published by the Eugenics Society to celebrate the seventy-fifth anniversary of its founding, to be followed by a symposium on Galton organised by the Galton Institute in 1991, with its proceedings[25] published in 1993.

Forrest in his biography failed, in particular, in describing the conflict between the Mendelians and the biometricians. It is in the discussion of their quarrel, and how it affected the way that genetics developed, in which the admirably researched biography of Galton[26]

---

[22] Francis Galton. *Memories of My Life*. London: Methuen, 1908.

[23] D. W. Forrest. *Francis Galton –The Life and Work of a Victorian Genius*. London: Paul Elek,1974.

[24] Dorothy Middleton. *Sir Francis Galton 1822-1911*. London: Eugenics Society, 1982.

[25] Milo Keynes (ed.). *Sir Francis Galton, FRS – The Legacy of His Ideas*. London: Macmillan, 1993.

[26] N. W. Gillham. *A Life of Sir Francis Galton – From African Exploration to the Birth of Eugenics*. New York: Oxford University Press, 2001.

by the geneticist, Nicholas Gillham, in 2001 is strong. Gillham takes Galton seriously as a leading Victorian intellect and distances him from subsequent developments. He brings out the obsessiveness and pitiable lack of self-awareness of this strange man, but we do not come to know him as well as in Forrest. There is little insight into Galton's personality, for instance, about his nervous breakdowns – the psychiatrist Eliot Slater concluded that Galton's trouble was a liability to painful compulsive rumination – nor does Gillham comment on his incomprehension of the psychology of women whom he often ignored and whose virtues he disparaged.[27]

The biometrician Michael Bulmer starts in his book[4] of 2003 with the outlines of Galton's life and of the history of eugenics but does not establish that his work was shaped by his social opinions. It is a technical study of Galton's biometrical work and as a pioneer of the application of quantification to the study of variability in populations. He shows how the implications of his ideas had to be developed by others. The entry on Galton by Ruth Schwartz Cowan in the *Oxford Dictionary of National Biography*[28] is of interest unlike the book by Martin Brookes[29] in which it is difficult to judge whether he has done any research other than reading the other books that have been mentioned. Brookes's writing is flawed by its lack of historical sense, in not considering why Galton's contemporaries respected and honoured him, and in making him, most unhelpfully, look a buffoon.

The 1914 Galton Lecture: Francis Galton, 1822-1911

FRANCIS GALTON was born on February 16th, ninety-two years ago, and to-day we are met together to remember him – a word that seems to me more in tune with his nature than the more formal expression *commemorate*.

He disliked pomposity, but he seems to have loved little private ceremonials. For instance, when he opened the first notebook in preparation for his autobiographical *Memories,* he began page 1 with

[27] Eliot Slater. 'Galton's Heritage.' *Eugenics Review,* 1960; 52: 91-103.

[28] R. Schwartz Cowan. Entry on 'Francis Galton.' *Oxford Dictionary of National Biography,* 2004; vol. 21.

[29] M. Brookes. Extreme Measures – *The Dark Visions and Bright Ideas of Francis Galton.* London: Bloomsbury, 2004.

Falstaff's words: "Lord, Lord, how subject we old men are to this vice of lying." An inverted appeal to Truth which no man ever stood less in need of. And again at the foot of the very last page of his *Memories* is a drawing of *Galtonia candicans,* a little ceremony without words, a hieroglyphic glorification of the honour paid him in giving his name to this African plant.

Many persons, and even some reviewers, form their opinions of books by reading half-a-dozen passages at random. I have been more scientific in selecting the first and last pages, and from these I conclude that a simple and kindly commemoration is not out of harmony with the genius of this great and loveable man.

I should like to express my appreciation of the honour done me in asking me to give the first Galton lecture. In many ways I am a bad choice, since I have had no share in his science of eugenics, neither has my research-work been directly connected with evolution. I can only hope that in consideration of my delight in the fibre and flavour of Galton's mind, with its youth, its charm of humour, and its ever-springing originality and acuteness, I say that I hope these considerations may excuse me for having undertaken an office for which I am in so many ways unfitted.

One of his most obvious characteristics was his love of method; I do not mean methodicalness, but that he took delight in knowing how to do all manner of things in the very best way. He also liked to teach his methods to others. Those who never saw him, or even read his books, will exclaim "What a bore he must have been." You might as well call the lightening a bore for explaining that it was going to thunder, or complain of the match for boring the gunpowder as to the proper way of exploding. With Galton's explanations there was a flash of clear words, a delightful smile or gesture which seemed to say : " That's all – don't let me take up your time." Nobody was ever more decidedly the very antithesis of a bore than Francis Galton.

He first appeared on the literary and scientific stage as a traveller, geographer, and author of a book on South Africa (1853), and it was the experience there gained that enabled him to write two years later, in 1855, that wonderful book "The Art of Travel." There he teaches such vitally important things as how to find water, how to train oxen as pack animals, to pitch a tent, to build a fire, to cook, and a thousand other secrets.

He liked, of course, to be useful to weary and thirsty travellers, but he was as much, or more impelled by the love of method for its own sake. He was in fact an artist in method. The same thing is shown in a letter he wrote to "Nature" near the end of his life explaining how to cut a round cake on scientific principles so that it shall not become stale. This again was not so much a philanthropic desire that his fellow men should not have dry cake, as delight in method.

When I re-read "The Art of Travel" quite recently, I could not find his method of preventing a donkey braying. My recollection is that, observing a braying donkey with tail erect, he argued if the tail were forcibly kept down, as by tying a stone to it, that braying would not occur. I certainly believe myself to have read or heard that this most Galtonian plan succeeded. If anyone can tell me where to look for it I shall be grateful.

Later in life he tried to make his unique knowledge of use to his country. He writes[30] :–

"The outbreak of the Crimean War showed the helplessness of our soldiers in the most elementary matters of camp-life. Believing that something could be done by myself towards removing this extraordinary and culpable ignorance, I offered to give lectures on the subject, gratuitously, at the then newly-founded camp at Aldershot."

He received no answer from the War Office, but a personal application to Lord Palmerston led to his being installed. He speaks of a few officers attending his course, and adds that the "rude teachings of the Crimean War soon superseded" his own. The chief interest of the episode is the evidence it gives of great and elaborate pains spent in the teaching of methods.

---

[30] Memories, p. 163.

I must here be allowed to turn back to an earlier period of his life in relation to what I have been speaking of. In illustrating the different dispositions of his sisters, both of whom were dear to him, Galton writes[31] :—

"My eldest sister was just, my youngest merciful. When my bread was buttered for me as a child, the former picked out the butter that filled the big holes, the latter did not. Consequently I respected the former, and loved the latter."

Have we not here an early appreciation of method or must we merely class the memory with the scene in "Great Expectations," where the terrifying elder sister, Mrs. Joe, prepares bread and butter for her husband and for Pip (her little brother) in an eminently just and disagreeable manner. May I be allowed to add that a love of butter in the big holes is not hereditary in my branch of the family; I should have loved the sister who picked it out.

At a later stage in his boyhood, Galton transferred his study of method from his sisters to his schoolmasters. He describes what he suffered from the absurd limitations, which still exist, in the education of English boys, and "chafed" at the teaching he received. "Grammar." he says, "and the dry rudiments of Latin and Greek were abhorrent to me, for there seemed so little sense in them."[32] He suffered in fact like his cousin, Charles Darwin, who groaned over the classics at Shrewsbury School, and forgot what he learned, even to some of the Greek letters, by the time he was nineteen.

In 1838, when Galton was sixteen years of age, he became an indoor pupil at the Birmingham General Hospital. Here the education was practical enough to suit even his scientific mind, but to this coddled generation it seems a rough introduction to medicine. He had to prepare tinctures, extracts, decoctions, and learned to make pills by hand – a slow enough process. In later life, when he saw a pill-making machine at work, it must have been his boyish memories which inspired the characteristic calculation

---

[31] Memories, p. 14.

[32] Memories, p. 20.

that if a grandmotherly Government possessed forty-five of these engines, it could supply each inhabitant of the British Isles with one pill per diem.[33] But this is a digression.

It was in the surgery that he had most experience; he and the other indoor pupils were called up at all hours to dress burns, to patch broken heads, and reduce dislocations, with, as it seems, very little instruction. It was doubtless a fine bit of education in self-reliance, and he must have learned much that was of use in South African travels. Whether as a student of method he approved of his rough and ready education is not quite clear. His genius for experiment, or rather that priceless capacity for extracting unexpected conclusions from experience, comes out in his account of a case in the Birmingham Hospital.[34] An injured drayman was brought in dead drunk, and underwent amputation of the legs without any sign of feeling pain. This set Galton wondering whether patients might not with advantage be made drunk before operations – a query which was soon happily answered by the discovery of anæsthetics.

Another most characteristic event was his desire to learn the properties of all the drugs in the pharmacopœia by personal experience. He determined to dose himself alphabetically, but got no further than C., for the effects of croton oil put a stop to his thirst for first-hand knowledge.

We must pass over his time at King's College, London, where, as he sat at lecture, he could see the "sails of the lighters moving in sunshine on the Thames,"[35] a vision which stirred his blood with a longing for adventure, and which, as he characteristically noticed, always occurred when the weather-cock on the Horse Guards showed that the south-west wind was blowing.

We must, in like manner, skip his undergraduate days at Trinity, Cambridge. We thus arrive by a devious route at the period when he returned a traveller and geographer of recognized merit, and

[33] Memories, p. 28.

[34] Memories, p. 35

[35] Memories, p. 48

began the work with which he was practically connected for many years, as a member of the Meteorological Committee.[36] His best-known contribution in the science was in a paper read before the Royal Society in 1862, where his discovery of the anticyclone was first described; but he also had a good deal to do with the printing and publishing of the now familiar weather charts. Meteorology takes us from 1861 to 1863 that is nearly to 1865, when his first paper on Heredity appeared, which was at the same time his first paper on hereditary genius. This line of research was to form his chief claim to celebrity, and must be separately treated.

Meanwhile I wish to say something of his love of experiment which is a branch of his devotion to method. We only know of the more entertaining of his inquiries from his delightful book of *Memories,* but I cannot avoid the fear that he has left out many experiments even stranger than those he published. My father had a special affection for what in his own case he called "Fool's experiments." These are what, I am afraid, Galton may have omitted. Still there are records of some delightful lines of work.[37] He is probably the only man who ever attempted to solve by experiment the problem of free will and determinism. He limited his inquiry to the question whether there exists in human affairs such a thing as an "uncaused and creative action." The experiment, or rather self-observation was carried on (1879) for six weeks, almost continuously, and "off and on for many subsequent months." He found that with practice he could nearly always trace the "straightforward causation" of a given action, which at first seemed to have been performed "through a creative act, or by inspiration."[38]

Then there was his attempt to experience the feelings of the insane. "The method tried was to invest everything I met, whether human, animal, or inanimate, with the imaginary attributes of a spy."[39] The trial was only too successful; by the time he had

[36] Memories, p. 233.

[37] Memories, p. 295.

[38] Memories, p. 295.

[39] Memories, p. 276.

walked 1½ miles to the cabstand at the east end of the Green Park "every horse in the stand seemed watching" him, "either with pricked ears, or disguising its espionage."[40] He adds that hours passed before this uncanny sensation wore off.

On another occasion he managed to create in his mind the feelings of a savage for his idol, the idol in his own case being a picture of Mr. Punch.

These experiments seem to me very characteristic of the man in their originality, their humour, and their unexpected measure of success, for personally, I should have prophesied failure in all. They have a special bearing on Galton's belief that a quasi-religious enthusiasm for eugenics may be built up. I have sometimes wondered that he should believe this great change so feasible, but I understood how he came to think so when I read of his strange power of impressing beliefs on himself, with such force as to leave a trail of discomfort in the mind after the make-believe had ceased.

These and similar trials were, I think, made in relation to his desire to weigh and measure human faculty in a broad sense. I remember his telling me of his experiments on the mind of the British cabman. His method was to use alternately two different forms of the address to which he wished to go. Thus on Monday he would tell the man to drive him home to 42, Rutland Gate, on Tuesday he would say "Rutland Gate, 42," and so on. My recollection is that the cabmen understood quickest the familiar formula in which the number precedes the name of the street.

There was also a characteristic experiment or inquiry into the intensity of boredom in a lecture audience, by counting the number of fidgets per man per minute. In this case to avoid the open use of a watch, he estimated time by the number of his own breaths, "of which there are fifteen in a minute." I hope my brother will forgive my adding that he found the Royal Geographical Society meetings good hunting-ground for fidgets, for as Francis Galton remarks: "Even there, dull memoirs are occasionally read."[41]

---

[40] Memories, p. 276.

[41] Memories, p. 278.

Lastly, I must mention his plan of marking, by means of a hidden apparatus, the beauty of the women he met in the streets of different towns. He classified them as pretty, ugly and indifferent, and I am glad that in his beauty map, London came out top; Aberdeen, I regret to say was at the bottom.

But in speaking of measurement of human faculty we have got quite out of any reasonably chronological sequence, for the book bearing that title appeared in 1883. But the estimation of human characteristics especially in relation to heredity was in Galton's mind several years earlier, and in 1865 he wrote the two papers in *Macmillan's Magazine* which contain the germs of his later work on heredity and eugenics. It is unfortunate that the research on heredity, together with its practical application to human welfare in the new science of eugenics, should not have more space given to it in his autobiographical *Memories;* there are but thirty-seven pages – or 11 per cent of the whole book. The specific importance of the subjects here dealt with is so great that these thirty-seven pages outweigh, for this Society, all the rest of the book. We should like to have had a fuller account by the author of this remarkable work of 1865. He does, however, tell us – and it is a very striking statement – that the two articles "expressed then, as clearly as I can do now, the leading principles of Eugenics."[42] The chief point in which he came to differ from the Macmillan articles was that he was then "too much disposed to think of marriage under some regulation, and not enough of the effects of self-interest and of social and religious sentiment."[43]

I imagine that the pendulum has now swung the other way, and that one of the most hopeful and practical schemes is the prevention of marriage among habitual criminals and the feeble-minded.

Galton attributes his work in heredity in some measure to the publication of the *Origin of Species* which, he says, "made a marked

---

[42] Memories, p.312.

[43] Memories, p.310

epoch" in his "mental development as it did in that of human thought generally."[44]

That Galton personally felt no difficulty in assimilating the new doctrine, he characteristically ascribes to a "bent of mind that both its illustrious author" and himself had "inherited from" their "common grandfather, Dr. Erasmus Darwin."[45] But in our day the name of Galton is intimately connected in our minds with the science of heredity, and we forget that he, like lesser men, was as a mine fired by the *Origin*.

He was "encouraged," he says, by the new views to pursue many inquiries which had long interested" him "and which clustered round the central topics of heredity." This was the charge with which the mine had been loaded, – the *Origin* was the fuse.

When that book was published in 1859, nearly everyone here to-night must have been too young to know anything of the great change in the colour of human thought which was ushered in. There are more who may remember how twelve years later when the *Descent of Man* came out, there was still plenty of clerical and other forms of foolish bitterness. But a man needs to have been in the full swing of mental activity in 1859 to perceive the greatness of the change due to the *Origin of Species*.

His two papers in *Macmillan's Magazine,* 1865, pp. 157 and 318, seem to me very remarkable and, as I have said, they are passed over too lightly by the author in his *Memories* (p. 310). They contain a statistical proof of the inheritance of intellectual and moral qualities.[46] And those who would allow the truth of this statement must further agree that it is the first statistical demonstration of this important fact that the world has seen. And he insists that the whole spiritual nature of man is heritable, so that in his opinion there are no traces of that new element "specially fashioned in

---

[44] Memories, p. 287.

[45] Memories, p.288.

[46] In Memories, p. 310, he criticises the statistical methods of this work.

heaven"[47] which (he says) is commonly believed to be given to a baby at its birth.

The paper contains a very interesting discussion on the development of social virtues by natural selection. He gives, too, a characteristic explanation of that human attribute commonly known as original sin, the quality in fact which makes men yield to base desires against and in spite of their sense of what is right.

He says[48] that here "the development of our nature under Darwin's law of natural selection has not yet overtaken the development of our religious civilisation." It may be more briefly described as the conflict between the individual desires with the tribal instincts. It must be remembered that for all this discussion Galton had no *Descent of Man* to guide him.

I shall come back later to his clear and courageous statement of eugenics in 1865, meanwhile I must speak of heredity, a word, by the way, introduced by Galton and for which he seems to have been taken to task.

With regard to the machinery of reproduction the essay is remarkable for containing what is practically identical with Weismann's continuity of the germ-cell, and Galton's priority is acknowledged by that author. But in science the credit goes to the man who convinces the world, not to the man to whom the idea first occurs. Not the man who finds a grain of new and precious quality but to him who sows it, reaps it, grinds it and feeds the world on it. This is true of this very *Macmillan's Magazine* article. Who would know of these admirable views on Hereditary Genius and Eugenics, if this were Galton's only utterance? This is the grain which has increased and multiplied: and it is to-day familiar nutriment and is now assiduously cultivated by the Eugenics Education Society. But if *Natural Inheritance,* and *Hereditary Genius* had not been written; if the papers on eugenics had not appeared, and especially if he had not convinced the world of his seriousness by creating a eugenic foundation at University College, where his

[47] Memories, p. 316.

[48] Macmillan's Magazine, p. 327.

friend Professor Karl Pearson carries on the Galtonian traditions – why then the paper in *Macmillan* would have counted for very little. But it was not quite unnoticed. By my father it is referred to in the *Variation of Animals and Plants under Domestication.* Galton was encouraged and reassured by Darwin's appreciation of his work: his words in *Hereditary Genius*[49] are "I feel assured that, inasmuch as what I then wrote was sufficient to earn the acceptance of Mr. Darwin … the increased amount of evidence submitted in the present volume is not likely to be gainsaid." He was characteristically generous in owning his debt to the author of the *Origin of Species* and characteristically modest in the value he ascribed to my father's words of encouragement. The book on Hereditary Genius strikes me as most impressive. It seems as though the man whom the world had agreed to honour as an admirable and indeed a brilliant worker in geography and meteorology had suddenly grown big. He had shown himself to have the power of sustaining a weighty argument in strong and temperate phrase, speaking as a judge rather than an advocate, and to have definitely taken rank with Darwin, Lyell, Hooker and Huxley, men whose pens have dinted the world, leaving their ineffaceable mark on the road trodden by the march of science.

When I was working at the *Life and Letters of Charles Darwin,* I naturally asked Mr. Galton for leave to publish the letters he had received from my father. But he would not agree. Mr. Darwin, he said, had spoken far too kindly of his work and he preferred to keep the praise to himself. But later when he wrote his *Memories*,[50] he fortunately realised that it is wiser to think of the value to the world of such documents, than of private likes or dislikes. The letter my father wrote about *Hereditary Genius* which Galton says "made him most happy" begins :–

"I have only read about 50 pages of your book … , but I must exhale myself, else something will go wrong in my inside, I do

---

[49] Hereditary Genius, p. 2.

[50] He had already allowed Professor Seward and myself to publish them in *More Letters of Charles Darwin.*

not think I ever in all my life read anything more interesting and original."[51]

In reading this great book it is, I think, impossible to doubt about the strength of the work. The quiet relentless way in which his territory is pegged out, and the clear wisdom with which the very terms of the new science are defined are equally impressive. And for lighter enjoyment his illustrations are to be recommended. He has to settle precisely what he means by a man being *eminent* or *illustrious* before he can begin to ask are these qualities hereditary. An eminent man is one in four thousand, and to make clear what this implies, he writes, "On the most brilliant of starlight nights there are never so many as 4,000 stars visible to the naked eye at the same time; yet we feel it to be an extraordinary distinction to a star to be accounted as the brightest in the sky."[52] If we could imagine that each new night shows us a fresh set of stars, we might speculate as to how many nights we should watch the sky before we found one bright enough for Galton.

In the same way he tries to make us see a million, because in that number there is but one *illustrious* man. He worked it out in Bushey Park where he had gone to see the horse-chestnuts in flower, and came to the astonishing conclusion that taking one half only of the avenue and the flowers visible on the sunny side of that row, it would require to miles of avenue to give 1,000,000 spikes of blossom.

Later he defines *mediocrity* in a way not very flattering to those, who, like myself, live in the country. Mediocrity[53] then "defines the intellectual power found in most provincial gatherings, because the attractions of a more stirring life in the metropolis and elsewhere are apt to draw away the abler classes of men, and the silly and imbecile do not take a part in the gatherings." On this last point, by the way, I am not convinced. The research on the heredity of mental and moral characters leads naturally to eugenics, as in the

---

[51] Memories, p. 290.

[52] Hereditary Genius, p. 9.

[53] Hereditary Genius, p. 31.

Macmillan paper of 1865. But before dealing with this I must say a few words about what, in the opinion of some, is Galton's chief claim to eminence – the study of heredity as a whole. There is no doubt that he was the first to treat thoroughly and in a strict statistical method, the steps by which one generation passes into the next. He was pre-eminently a lover of statistics, he was indeed what Goschen called himself: "A passionate statistician."

He used Gauss's Law of Error, which Quetelet had already applied to human measurements. "The primary objects," he says,[54] "of the Gaussian Law of Error were exactly opposed, in one sense, to those to which I applied them. They were to get rid of, or to provide a just allowance for errors. But these errors or deviations were the very things I wanted to preserve and to know about."

This conception of variation impressed him deeply, so that he remembered the exact spot in the grounds of Naworth Castle where it first occurred to him "that the laws of heredity[55] were solely concerned with deviations expressed in statistical units."

What may be called the final result of Galton's work in heredity is, I imagine, his *ancestral law*, namely that "the average contribution of each parent" to its offspring is one quarter, or in other words that half of the qualities of the child can be accounted for when we know its father and mother. In the same way the four grandparents together contribute one quarter and so on. He illustrates this by calculating how much Norman blood a man has who descends from a Baron of William the Conqueror's. Assuming that the Baron weighed 14 stone, his descendant's share in him is represented by $1/50$ grain.[56]

This side of Galton's work is, in the judgment of many, his greatest claim to distinction as a master in the science of heredity. How far this is so I shall not attempt to pronounce. It is possibly still too soon to do so. Nevertheless it seems to me that Mendelism (the main facts of which are no longer in dispute) will

[54] Memories, p. 305.

[55] Memories, p. 300.

[56] Macmillan, p. 327.

compel the world (if it has not already done so) to look at variation in a very different way to that of Galton. The Mendelian does not and never will look at variation merely as a "deviation expressed in statistical units." Nor can he accept the ancestral law, because he has convinced himself that some ancestors contribute *nothing* in regard to certain characters.

The contrast between Galtonism and Mendelism may be illustrated by an example which if not a strict analogy has in it something illuminating, especially for those who do not know too much of the subject. Galton seems to me like a mediæval chemist while Mendel is a modern one. Galton can observe, or can follow the changes that occur when two compounds are mixed. But he knows nothing of the mechanism of what occurs. But the Mendelian is like a modern chemist who calls the chemical elements to his aid, and is able to express the result of the experiment in terms of these elements. This is an enormous advantage, and if my analogy is to be trusted it would seem as though a progressive study of heredity must necessarily be on Mendelian lines.

But it obviously does not follow that the laborious and skilful work of Galton and his school is wasted. Those who wish to have made plain to them how Biometrics may illuminate a problem which cannot as yet be solved in Mendelian fashion should read Dr. Schuster's most interesting book on eugenics. I am thinking especially of the question as to the heredity of tuberculosis and cancer. The relation between Galtonism and Mendelism is also well and temperately discussed in Mr. Lock's *Recent Progress in the Study of Variation,* 1906.

But it is time to speak of Galton as a eugenist – on which if we look to the distant future his fame will rest. For no one can doubt that the science of eugenics must become a great and beneficent force in the evolution of man.

We must be persistent in urging its value, but we must also be patient. We should remember how young is the subject. As recently as 1901 Galton was, in his Huxley Lecture, compelled to speak of eugenics in these terms[57] :–

"It has not hitherto been approached along the ways that recent knowledge has laid open, and it occupies in consequence a less dignified position in scientific estimation than it might. It is smiled at as most desirable in itself and possibly worthy of academic discussion, but absolutely out of the question as a practical problem." After explaining that the object of his discourse was to "show cause for a different opinion," he goes on with what, in his restrained style, is strong language: "I shall show that our knowledge is already sufficient to justify the pursuit of this perhaps the grandest of all objects."[58]

At the close of the lecture he speaks out as to the difficulties and the pre-eminent value of eugenics and once more of the oppressive "magnitude of the enquiry."

No one who reads this lecture of Sir Francis Galton's is likely to let eugenics go with a smile and a remark that it is not a practical problem. It is one of the functions of the Eugenics Education Society to spread the sanely scientific views here set forth by Galton, and as far as I am able to judge the Society has and is doing sound work in this direction.

In another essay,[59] Galton discusses the meaning of the "Eu" in eugenics in a characteristic way. He imagines an attempt among the animals in the Zoological Gardens to establish a code of absolute morality. With customary love of detail, he supposes the inquiry to be undertaken by some animal such as a sparrow or a rat which is intelligent and has easy access to all the cages, and is therefore able to collect opinions. There would be strongly pronounced differences between the carnivorous animals and those which form their natural prey. There would be a general agreement as to maternal affection, though fishes and the cuckoo would laugh at it. But all would agree on *some* eugenic principles: That it is

---

57 Essays in Eugenics, p. 1.

58 Essays in Eugenics, p. 1.

59 Essays in Eugenics, p. 35.

better to be healthy and vigorous than sickly and weak – well-fitted for their part in life rather than the reverse, in fact good specimens of their kind whatever that kind may be.

Sir Francis Galton goes on to give a list of qualities that "nearly every one except cranks would take into account in picking out the best specimens of his class." The list would include health, energy, ability, manliness and courteous disposition."[60] I wish he had thought of eugenic mothers and had translated manliness into the feminine equivalents of courage and endurance. When I first read this list it struck me at once how highly distinguished was Galton himself in all these qualities . As we dwell on the qualities one by one, they seem to call up echoes from the image we have of his character. "Ability, manliness, and courteous disposition," how strong these were in him! I cannot help feeling that he might have added one more quality from his own treasure-house, namely, a sense of humour, which is so priceless an antiseptic to sentimentality, and was strongly and individually present in his character.

In this same lecture,[61] Gallon sums up the stages in the development of eugenics (I.) "It must be made familiar as an academic question." (II.) As a practical subject worthy of serious consideration. (III.) It must be "introduced into the national conscience, like a new religion." He recapitulates in an eloquent phrase: "It has, indeed, strong claims to become an orthodox religious tenet of the future, for Eugenics co-operates with the workings of Nature by securing that humanity shall be represented by the fittest races. What Nature does blindly, slowly, and ruthlessly, man may do providently, quickly, and kindly."

Here we see the future of eugenics marked out for us, and the last sentence might well serve as a motto for this Society. How are we to work for the cause?

It is true that our opinions are formed by the daily papers, and our actions as a nation are determined by political parties which

---

[60] Essays in Eugenics, p. 37.

[61] Essays in Eugenics, p. 42.

come and go largely by chance. But, however our opinions originate, if they are strongly and persistently urged by a large majority of Englishmen, great changes in the manner of human life may be effected. Persistence is the great thing in all reforms, it is a case of my father's favourite quotation – "It's dogged as does it." Francis Galton has been temperately persistent in a marked degree. His caution and wisdom are illustrated by the dates of his writings on eugenics and heredity, which placed in order suggest a regiment at slow march, not a bunch of heroes rushing on a breach.

Two papers in Macmillan's Magazine 1865
Hereditary Genius 1869
Fraser's Magazine 1873
Human Faculty (word Eugenics first employed) 1884
Natural Inheritance 1889
Huxley Lecture..1901
Sociological Society Papers...1905
Memories 1908

The temperateness of his march is all the more striking when we remember the fiery impatience with which in *Hereditary Genius* he spoke of the harm done by the church by ordaining that the intellectuals, the literary, and the sensitive should be celibates, and of the wholesale slaughter by the Holy Inquisition of the courageous and clear minded who dared to think for themselves.

From the first he had the support of Charles Darwin who never wavered in his admiration of Galton's purpose, though he had doubts about the practicality of reform. His hesitation in regard to eugenic method is expressed with a wise proviso as to future possibilities : "I have lately been led," he says, "to reflect a little ... on the artificial checks, but doubt greatly whether such would he advantageous to the world at large at present, however it may be in the distant future."[62] In the first edition of the *Descent of Man*, 1874,[63] he distinctly gives his adherence to the eugenic idea by his assertion that man might by selection do something for the moral

---

[62] More Letters, II., p. 43 and 50.

[63] One Volume Edit. 1894, p. 617.

and physical qualities of the race. It is a great thing that this Society should have had Francis Galton for its Hon. President. It entitles us to feel assured that in following the line of action marked out for ourselves we are on the right track, and that in the difficult pioneer work of helping the English public to realise the deadly need of eugenic reform we are following in Galton's steps. We are also so fortunate as to have received the encouragement and help at the hands of some of the leaders in the science of heredity, Weismann, Yves Delage, Ray Lankester, the late Adam Sedgwick, Poulton, Bateson, Punnett, and others.

Galton says somewhere[64] that great men have long boy-hoods, this was certainly true of him, though I should rather describe as *youthful* the delightful qualities that never faded out of his nature. It is, I believe, the correct thing to speak of the "golden dreams of youth," and if by this hackneyed phrase we mean a keenly imaginative outlook, a hopefulness with a certain dash about it – a generous courage such as a hero of romance is credited with – then Francis Galton had undying youth. And this makes his seriously measured progress in eugenics all the more worthy of our admiration.

In one of the Macmillan articles (p. 324) he wrote: "Many plan for that which they can never live to see. At the hour of death they are still planning."

It was thus that Francis Galton died, and as year after year we meet together on February 16th, let us think of him and his plannings with affection and respect.

---

[64] Macmillan's Magazine, xii., p. 326.

The Rt Reverend E. W. Barnes

Courtesy of Birmingham Library Services

1926

Some Reflections On Eugenics And Religion[1]

The Right Rev. E. W. Barnes, ScD. Hon. D.D., F.R.S., Bishop of Birmingham.

Introduction by Revd Dr John Polkinghorne

Ernest William Barnes was elected an FRS for his researches in pure mathematics and in 1908 he was ordained a clergyman in the Church of England. After a spell as Master of the Temple, he returned to his native Birmingham in 1924 as its Bishop. As a theologian, Barnes was a prominent modernist, who gained a reputation for somewhat unsubtle calls for science to take a hand in the revision of traditional Christian belief. His Galton Lecture of 1926 reads today as a fascinating period piece.

The Bishop displays considerable confidence in making judgements of human worth. Race is an unproblematic concept, and the mixing of races is something to be discouraged, since 'the distrust of half-castes is not the outcome of mere prejudice' [30]. Religious belief is correlated with race and 'religious ideas are a very good criterion as to which strain in a mixed race has proved the stronger' [31], a comment followed by an unfavourable judgement on Roman Catholicism in Southern Italy. Much of the lecture is taken up with the problem of what to do about the 'feeble-minded', who are 'disastrously prolific, and their fecundity must be a grave concern to every religious man and woman' [34]. In consequence, 'very strong arguments can be brought forward for the sterilisation of mental defectives' [35]. Yet the Bishop is clearly somewhat uneasy and he has to acknowledge that 'Christianity affirms the rights and values of the individual simply as a human being' [35]. Of course these were the mid-1920s and the horrors of Nazi eugenics and the death camps still lay in the future, hidden from the eyes of well-

---

[1] The Galton Lecture delivered before the Eugenics Education Society at their meeting in London on Tuesday, February 16th, 1926 and published in *The Eugenics Review*, **Vol. XVIII,** 1926-27.

intentioned intellectuals. Yet there is a worrisome tone to the discourse when a Bishop can assert that 'The low-grade worshipper gives base metal for gold' [35] and say of religious work in the slums that it is 'practically hopeless' [37] – despite the fact that many Anglo-Catholic priests had had remarkable ministries in just such areas.

Also lying in the future for the 1926 Galton lecturer was the neo-Darwinian synthesis blending genetic mutation and natural selection, soon to be pioneered by R.A. Fisher, J.B.S. Haldane and Sewell Wright. Bishop Barnes expresses the wish that 'the experts could reach agreement as to how variations arise in what is apparently a fairly homogeneous stock' [32]. He toys a little with Lamarckian notions and, while disclaiming vitalism, speaks, in Bergsonian terms of the need 'to postulate some creative activity in the life-process' [32].

Bishop Barnes strongly affirms the belief that 'there is in the universe absolute values that transcend space and will outlast time' [33]. It does not seem likely that he would have been enthusiastic about E.O. Wilson's sociobiological approach to morality. Modern readers in our largely secular society will be surprised to be told that 'the absence of any kind of religious interest is evidence of mental abnormality' [37].

A final comment can pick up a theological point that is implicitly referred to by the Bishop when he hints at an insight that was to prove of particular significance for a great deal of Christian discussion in the second half of the twentieth century concerning a theology of nature. Barnes says that God 'allows a type of change which to our value judgements can be either good or bad. Within certain limits degeneration is as likely as progress' [32]. Behind this remark lies the idea that theologians call 'kenosis', the divine self-limitation that permits a letting-be of creation. The universe is not God's puppet theatre, with the Creator pulling every string, but it is given its own due degree of independence. This kenotic concept is as old as evolutionary thinking itself, for shortly after the publication of *The Origin of Species*, the English clergyman, Charles Kingsley, in welcoming Darwin's insights coined the phrase that is the key to appropriate theological response, saying that Darwin had shown us that instead of making a ready-made world, the Creator had done something cleverer than that in bringing into being a world in which creatures are 'allowed to make themselves'.

The 1926 Galton Lecture: Some Reflections On Eugenics And Religion

EUGENICS IS THE SCIENCE of human betterment. Its object is to discover how we may breed better human beings. The eugenist seeks to improve human racial stocks in the belief that he can thereby quicken the process of civilisation. He fixes attention primarily on the individual and not on his surroundings. He is concerned with nature rather than nurture, with the innate qualities which the individual inherits rather than with the environment in which those qualities have an opportunity of growth and expression. Eugenics and Sociology are thus complementary to one another. The extravagant eugenist says that the swine makes the stye. The extravagant sociologist says that the stye makes the swine. Neither statement expresses the full truth and even expert biologists differ widely as to the extent to which the balance of truth inclines one way or the other.

It cannot be disputed that the innate good qualities which a man inherits fail to develop in bad surroundings. Ignorance, dirt, vicious example and abject poverty degrade personality. They prevent the growth of that which is best in a child and stimulate its baser instincts. So strong in the life of a child are the influences of what the psychologists call *association* and *suggestion* that many think that environment is of more importance than heredity. It must be admitted that our knowledge as to what constitutes 'heredity' lacks precision. We are ignorant as to how far a child receives from its parents at conception a set of physical and psychical fundamentals which no environment will change. But statistical enquiries in general confirm the common saying that 'like begets like.' We have, moreover, to remember that civilisation is a racial product. The forces of association and suggestion which act on any individual within it, no less than most of his physical surroundings, are the creation of the race. If the racial stock be good such forces and physical conditions will gradually become more beneficial. If the stock be poor, both its physical environment and mental atmosphere will gradually degenerate. The ultimate creative power of a civilisation resides in the innate racial qualities of the people which make it, whatever be the process by which those qualities were initially produced.

No nation is homogeneous. Probably all races result from a blend of peoples of different types. A so-called pure race is one which has lived so long free from alien intrusion that a uniform type has been gradually evolved. In such a race the fundamentals due to heredity have been thoroughly mixed. Among its members there is therefore a naturally strong social cohesion. Individuals think, feel, and act in much the same way. In particular there will be uniformity of religious outlook. For a pure race what Disraeli called 'the religion of all sensible men' is a definite entity.

When a nation is mixed and, in particular, when one race imposes itself upon another there can be no such unity. At first the apparent civilisation will be that of the dominant race. Culture will be created by the ruling aristocracy: and the populace will accept organisation by which it benefits, though this be based on principles and ideas with which it has little sympathy or understanding.   This situation probably existed when Greek civilisation reached its zenith. Ultimately the ruling stocks died out, dissipated by war or luxury. Such of their descendants as survived were the offspring of mixed marriages, racially impure. Now when two races are thus mixed the individual seems to lack stability of organisation.   The characteristics derived from his parents are associated rather than blended. Probably it is only after a fairly large number of generations that a new type of harmony is created. In the early generations the physical characters of one or other of the parental types may be dominant: but the recessive strain cannot be ignored; and I believe that in the fundamentals of the mind there is disharmony. The distrust of half-castes is not the outcome of mere prejudice. They are often unstable in character.   In popular phrase 'you never know what they will do next'. It is impossible to foretell which side of their mental inheritance will be uppermost on any particular occasion.

After a sufficient number of generations a mixed race evolves a unity, a unity in diversity, of its own. Which of the two strands which go to make it is dominant? The answer seems to be that which is indigeneous to the soil. Black and white in England mate and white survives. Black and white in Jamaica mate and black survives.   There seems little doubt that in ancient Greece the original population gradually asserted itself.   Most certainly the great intellectual achievements of the Golden Age were gradually ignored; they were submerged by primitive folk-beliefs thrust up from the populace. Moreover where the physical characters of one of two mixed races prove the stronger, the mental qualities of that race are usually dominant; and vice versa. The half-caste in Jamaica not only becomes darker in successive generations but he also becomes more negroid in his habit of mind.   Language, as we know, is no criterion of racial origin.   But ideas and especially religious ideas are a very good criterion as to which strain in a mixed race has proved the stronger. The religious practices and beliefs of the black Republic of Hayti are not, according to good observers, vastly different from those of the African jungle.

I am suggesting that the fundamentals of the mind persist, from generation to generation, roughly to the same extent as distinctive physical characters of the body. Mental tendencies are, I believe, much more permanent than is commonly supposed. A higher culture or a new religion may be given to a race but, if left to itself, its old culture and its old religion will emerge but slightly camouflaged.   Take for instance Christianity in Southern Italy. Nominally the Iberian stock in Southern Italy has been Christian for some 15 centuries. Christianity is a form of ethical theism: but the actual faith of the Southern Italian is magical polytheism, camouflaged as sacramentalism and the prayers of the saints. It was essentially the worship which prevailed among the Mediterranean Iberians before the Christian era.   Invaders may sweep over the land: a new religion may be nominally established. But the old stock with the old faith effectively triumphs.

Such conclusions are disconcerting to enthusiasts; but this is mainly because enthusiasts are short-term optimists.   Can we rightly expect any great fundamental change in a well-established stock in a couple of thousand years? When we consider that the human race has been evolving for something like a million years must we not expect that progress will be slow, especially if conditions do not make for the survival of the fittest?

And here I come to the heart of my subject. How can we secure the survival of the fittest and therefore the survival and development of the fittest types of religious aspiration and understanding.

I wish that the experts could reach agreement as to how variations arise in what is apparently a fairly homogeneous stock. All admit that there is a tendency to fluctuation observable in successive generations. Is this tendency inherent in the life-process? Is it affected by use and disuse, so that acquired characteristics are ultimately inherited? Do small variations amid large mutations alike result from combinations of parental characteristics, latent or patent? Is the growth of the cell from which a new life takes its beginning merely dependent on the initial nature of the genes in the chromosomes? It seems to me that we must postulate some creative activity in the life-process, a constant 'more or less' flux. If we dislike any form of vitalism we may ascribe this to the activity of mind, of that unknown reality which in varying degrees is present in all living things. This carries us little further because we do not know what mind is, nor how it has seized upon certain chemical compounds of which carbon is the most important element. What I would insist upon is that a survey of the whole evolutionary process negatives the idea of a mere unpacking or reassortment of what was already present in primal organisms. New things have been created, new degrees of reality have emerged, in earth's life-history. We cannot, of course, separate the process by which life has become progressively more complex from the environment in which change has occurred. The environment may cause or direct the change. Most certainly the environment destroys individuals not adapted for survival within it.

We have, however, to recognise that the changes which occur owing, as I imagine, to creative activity within the life-process are not always what we should consider valuable. If I may use the language of religion, God has not made man, and is not perfecting human civilisation, by causing offspring to be always slightly better or slightly more highly organised than were the parents. He allows a type of change which to our value-judgments can be either good or bad. Within certain limits degeneration is as likely as progress.

And this is true whether the changes which we observe are large or small, inheritable or not. God's judgment on this random process of change is expressed by the subsequent action of the environment in which it occurs. By what is termed 'the ruthlessness of Nature' He weeds out the less valuable products of His plan.

The thought that God acts in this way is often disliked and ignored by those who wish to retain a belief in ethical Theism. They recoil from the idea that He permits degeneration as well as progress to take place. Their distress would be less acute if they remembered that environment is equally His creation. However perplexed we may be by the whole scheme, the fact remains that it has led to the successive emergence of more highly organised animal types culminating in man. And moreover in man there has been, owing to this process, a growth of moral excellence and spiritual understanding. By spiritual understanding I mean man's knowledge that the obligations of truth and goodness are imposed upon him from without by the very nature of things : that we ought to be loyal to absolute standards outside ourselves that there are in the universe absolute values which transcend space and will outlast time. Man by acquiring such understanding has begun to enter the Kingdom of the good, the beautiful and the true. The tree is known by its fruits and the character of the Creator must be judged by the final outcome of His plan - The existence of evil has always seemed to challenge the goodness of God : our knowledge of the evolutionary process does not really increase perplexity.

By whatever process new characteristics arise in man and lower forms of life it is certain that some are inheritable. It is certain moreover, that this is true alike of physical and mental characteristics. The structure of the mind is engendered with the body. Both are profoundly affected by the circumstances of life : yet some fundamentals are given at the start. And by the mind we mean the whole personality of a man. No dichotomy of human personality, such as St. Paul took from the philosophy of his time, is satisfactory. When we speak of the immortality of the soul, we mean the survival of human personality, or of such a development of that personality as gives it complete survival-value. I have said that the relation of mind to body is an unsolved enigma. We can only accept the fact that just as healthy well-formed parents normally have healthy well-formed children, so able parents usually have able children. Moreover there is no doubt that regard for religion and the ethical ideals with which it is associated is inherited. There are stocks in which spiritual aspiration shews itself, in various manifestations, generation after generation. Few religious leaders of fame and power lack ancestors, possibly in quite humble circumstances, who shewed religious enthusiasm. Equally of course parents of poor mental quality and vicious tendencies, unresponsive to the elevating influences with which they may gain contact, have like children. Such stocks are a burden and a source of weakness to the community.

But why do good stocks produce degenerate offspring? We all know cases when the parents, each apparently healthy and sound in mind, with a well-balanced nervous organisation, have a child which is semi-imbecile. Is feeble-mindedness a dysgenic mutation, the 'spontaneous' appearance of a new and bad variant? Is genius similarly a eugenic mutation? The probable answer is that each results from a chance combination of parental factors, a combination moreover which has some element of hereditary permanence. Statistical biology makes it certain that the man of genius, if he leaves descendants usually hands on to some among them more than average ability. And feeble-mindedness, once established, will crop out generation after generation.

We can leave genius to take care of itself, though we have to admit that it is curiously and distressingly unfertile. This lack of fertility manifests itself in men of religious genius, in a Wesley no less than in a Newton. But the feeble-minded are disastrously prolific, and their fecundity must be a grave concern to every religious man and woman. The problem constantly confronts religious teachers. A Bishop is asked what can be done as regards the confirmation of mentally-defective adolescents? They have no capacity of response to religious teaching and in the poorer quarters of our great cities the clergy are constantly met by border-line cases, children and adults, in whom it is impossible to arouse any spiritual aspiration. I do not ask you to be concerned with their non-acceptance of some particular form of religious faith. The trouble is that these people are at such a low mental level that they have no instinct for spiritual values.

What is to be done with them? The harsh conditions of our civilisation until a century ago weeded them out. There was a ruthlessness against which our humane instincts revolt. To-day social changes, consequent on the more Christian organisation of the State, enable them to survive.

Very strong arguments can be brought forward for the sterilisation of mental defectives. Such were advanced in a recent letter to *The Times* (Jan. 18th, 1926) signed by a number of eminent medical men. The signatories urged that sentiment and ignorance should not be allowed to prevent legislation. Though they did not explicitly say so, they must be well aware that Christian religious sentiment instinctively sets itself against their proposals. The opposition may not be permanent but its grounds are worth stating. Christianity seeks to create the Kingdom of God, the community of the elect. It tries to make what we may call a spiritually-eugenic society. It recognises that by no means all human beings are fit for this society. 'Many are called but few are chosen,' is a saying of its Founder, the truth of which continuous experience has verified. But, also, Christianity affirms the rights and value of the individual simply as a human being. And, together with this affirmation, the belief has been strong that all men are potentially sons of God, so made that, if they will, they can enter the Kingdom. 'No man is so vile, so degraded,' says the Protestant evangelist, 'that we can pronounce *a priori* that his conversion is hopeless.' 'Through the sacraments there is salvation for all,' says the Catholic. Yet an evangelical movement always ends by creating a spiritual aristocracy. And though group-suggestion through sacramental worship is powerful, suggestion is always a process of give and take. The low-grade worshipper gives base metal for gold. Thus insensibly the moral level of the group-consciousness becomes lowered. And in the end unethical sacramentalism becomes a drag on spiritual progress.

The facts are well known: yet belief in the possibility of the salvation of all men, of bringing all into the Kingdom, persists.

Such belief in the inherent value of the individual has great ethical importance. It is doubtful whether you will do unto others as you would that they should do unto you, if you think that they are not fundamentally of potentially equal value with yourself. The great bond of social unity is that we regard our fellow-citizens as sharing with ourselves the full heritage of humanity.

Now eugenists have made it clear that mental defectives not only lack some of the most valuable qualities of our human heritage, but also that they often transmit such lack to their off-spring. Yet a doubt remains as to whether there is no latent power of recovery. The question is asked: Among the children of parents both mentally defective is it not possible that normal human beings, or even genius, may be found? Until a negative answer can he given to this question Christian sentiment will be slow in giving approval to sterilisation proposals. The Christian community, though very conservative, is by no means devoid of common sense. If you could demonstrate that the feeble-minded were not only in themselves a social burden but also that there was nothing latent in them of value to the race you would rapidly win Christian sympathy and support. I doubt if you will ever be able to do this. But, if you shew, as it can be shewn, that the feeble-minded normally have so many defective descendants that their fecundity is a barrier to the extension of spiritual perception, you will gradually get Christians to approve action by which such fecundity is checked.

There seems to be no evidence which would warrant the belief that from bad stocks good can never be created. My friend Professor MacBride argues, from Tornier's work on the production of gold-fish, that mutations to be observed in domestic animals amid plants result from germ-weakening under artificial conditions. He consequently rejects the idea that such mutations can play a decisive part in the process of evolution. But does not the same line of argument suggest that mental deficiency may be due to germ-weakening under artificial conditions? I understand that if gold-fish were allowed to breed freely under natural conditions they would revert to the small grey carp from which they were derived. Domestic animals, when they run wild, tend to revert to natural types. Our sense of values is determined by human fancy and human appetite : and we therefore term such reversion a degeneration to the original type. But from the point of view of Nature the reversion is surely a reversal of the artificial disorder which man has produced. Has man not produced conditions which make for similar disorder in his own race? The industrial revolution has within half a dozen generations removed the greater part of our people from the healthy influence of unspoiled nature. Slum life, drugs, artificial pleasures and excitements may surely produce germ-weakening. But is it not possible that the simple life, to use a convenient phrase, would be sufficient to breed, even from the feeble-minded, a mentally healthy stock? I put the question diffidently in the search for information.

It is well known to all social workers that the part of our population which lacks ability, initiative, self-reliance and energy tends to remain in the central areas of our great cities. The clergy who work in these areas find that any individuals who shew exceptional enterprise soon move away. There is thus an automatic segregation of the unfit. But these unfit shew every possible degree of what I venture to call germ-weakening. Mental deficiency is not a definite abnormality to be sharply distinguished from the normal. It is the extreme illustration of a graduated process. The average level of mental life of a slum area in which segregation has taken place is exceptional, much lower than that of the community as a whole. Religious work in such an area is practically hopeless. Even among the children the response is slight : among adults it is negligible. The few who "have the religious sense" are those who sooner or later leave the area. Such facts, which are commonplaces to anyone engaged in religious administration, are worthy of the close attention of eugenists.

I suggest to you that absence of any kind of religious interest is evidence of mental abnormality. Man is a religious animal, though he is by no means always naturally Christian either in temper or thought. The saying 'the nearer the soil, the nearer to God' is of course an exaggeration. But those who are uprooted from the soil are a difficult religious problem. Some, as I have said, have no apparent capacity for religious response. Others, in more prosperous ranks of society, often turn to 'cranky' types of belief in which the student of comparative religion can recognise a close affinity to low-grade expressions of the religious sense which have previously arisen in human evolution. Those of us who are concerned to preserve the highest type of religion, which is a harmony in which the elation of the mystic is fused with reason and ethical principle, are greatly troubled by the present religious chaos. It is almost a commonplace that the religious fancies that run riot to-day bear a singular likeness to those which were widespread in classical civilisation during the second century of our era. Have they been produced by similar social conditions? Are they the result of urban life? Is it true that the development of the constituents of the chromosomes in the germ-cells is injuriously affected by the way in which infants are reared in crowded areas, by life under artificial light, by alcohol, by conditions which militate against a natural and healthy sexual life? The problem is immensely important. Religious decay is not merely a sign of social ill-health : its consequence is likely to be increased social degeneration. That such decay exists is undoubted. I receive an amazing number of letters, of manuscripts and printed disquisitions, which testify to its prevalence. And some experience of controversy has made me realise how weak is the regard for truth of certain types of religious zealots. The power of suggestion, emotional upset due to the war, imperfect education – all may be contributory factors to the prevailing religious degeneration: and we do not forget that the foolish are always with us. It may be that the type of our population is changing: that the Nordic strain is less resistant than the Iberian to hostile influences in our present manner of life. But it is hardly likely that such a change should have been so rapid. If the standpoint popularised by Professor Jennings in his *Prometheus* should pass the test of further research, we should be tempted to conclude that the artificial conditions of modern urban life are injurious to the development of the genes which the individual receives from his parents We should then deduce that a return to the simple life would be the best way of furthering religious progress. Most certainly observation of the Quakers confirms this conclusion. They are our spiritual aristocrats and by the simplicity of their manner of life they stand apart from the great mass of the community. I would add that the simple life need be neither barren nor falsely ascetic : marriage and children should normally have a place within it

A group of representative citizens, including some leading surgeons, has recently urged the value of the simple life as a protection against ill-health. In my belief that the physical and psychical characteristics of humanity are in much the same fashion products of heredity and environment, I welcome their plea. It seems to me that such knowledge as we have indicates that a more natural way of living would create mental no less than physical health and, in particular, that it would be of direct religious value.

Darwin's philosophy has been well summarized by Professor D'Arcy Thompson in the words: 'Fit and unfit arise alike but what is fit to survive does survive and what is unfit perishes.' Whatever be the detailed mechanism of evolution, the broad principle thus enunciated admits of no dispute. It has destroyed the old narrow teleology. It has made us see that we must assign as much importance to the environment which God has created as to the capacity for variation which He has given to living organisms. But, if we take this wider standpoint, there is nothing in this philosophy inconsistent with the Christian outlook. God's progressive action, His creative activity leading to spiritual understanding in man, remains. God, by allowing fit and unfit to arise alike and by using environment to destroy the unfit, has produced in humanity spiritual understanding. But He has also made man to a small yet increasing degree master of his own fate. We can do something, much more than we have yet done, to make human environment favourable to the survival of those qualities in humanity which we rightly value and of human beings in whom those qualities occur. But we must not create an environment in which the feeble-minded, the criminal, and the insane can multiply rapidly. Though such persons may have some descendants of social value, it is statistically demonstrable that the average of their descendants will be below the normal.   When they breed freely they are an impediment to the creation of what the Christian terms the Kingdom of God on earth. The humane man, as a consequence of his religious instinct, desires a good environment for all who may be born into the world. He is learning that he cannot get his desire unless his social organisation is such that degenerates leave no offspring. When religious people realise that, in thus preventing the survival of the socially unfit, they are working in accordance with the plan by which God has brought humanity so far on its road their objections to repressive action will vanish.

The Honourable Mr Justice McCardie

Photograph supplied by TopFoto.

1933

My Outlook on Eugenics[1]

The Honourable Mr. Justice McCardie

Introduction by Douglas J Cusine

Looking back at Mr Justice McCardie's comments, we can see immediately that some of what he aired is still discussed today, but also that we have progressed so much. His main themes were sterilisation of the medically unfit, divorce reform, the law on abortion, and birth control.

In 1933, divorce was not easy to obtain, except perhaps for the landed classes. There cannot be much doubt that there must have been many unhappy unions, with some spouses resorting to adultery, or prostitution. Some found ingenious ways of getting round the strictures of the divorce law, as can be seen from *Holy Deadlock* by A.P. Herbert published in 1934. Nowadays, divorce is available if the marriage has broken down irretrievably and the minimum period for the duration of marriage before proceedings can commence is constantly being debated. We have moved on from having to establish one of the grounds for divorce, e.g. adultery, desertion, cruelty to the recognition that these are manifestations of a marriage in trouble. Whether the relaxation of the divorce law has in turn resulted in people taking a more relaxed view of marriage vows is for debate elsewhere.

Although abortion was illegal in 1933, and remained so until 1967, many humane doctors would have provided abortions to those whom they thought would benefit and they would include the type of person identified by McCardie. It must be remembered that not only were these doctors humane, but they also risked prosecution as can be seen from the case of R v. Bourne (1938) in which the mother's mental and physical health was an issue. It was not until David Steel's Private Members' Bill became law in 1967 that doctors were allowed to perform such operations in the circumstances defined. The Act also meant that procedures which hitherto might have been

---

[1] Delivered on Thursday, February 16th, 1933 and published in *The Eugenics Review*, Vol. XXV 1933-34.

carried out by the untrained in some back street establishment were to be a thing of the past. There are some who feel that abortions are too freely available, but anyone who for good reason does not wish to participate in abortions is free not to be involved. Legislation needs to take account of these views, but also the ills caused by the absence of legislation, or the existence of very restrictive legislation.

Birth control has, of course, been practised for centuries, but it was not until the advent of the contraceptive pill and the morning-after pill that women, for the first time, were solely in charge of their own reproductive timetables. Most of the debate today centres on the side-effects or the long terms effects of these forms of contraception, e.g DVT risks, rather than on whether or not they should be available, except perhaps where the proposed recipient is under 16. In such a case, a girl will be counselled e.g. about involving her parent(s), but, if in the end, she is mature and understands, she will be provided with contraception, without her parents' knowledge.

McCardie's main theme was that of sterilisation of the medically unfit. Our immediate reaction might be to ask how anyone could even consider raising this, because we could not conceive of it being aired today, even in the form of a Government White Paper. However, in 1933, McCardie was not raising the unthinkable. The topic was being discussed in Germany in the 1930s. In 1927, in the United States, Mr Justice Oliver Wendell Holmes said in a case (Buck v. Bell) that a Virginia statute was not violation of substantive due process and hence sterilization of state institutionalized mentally defectives or insane residents was within the state's powers. That was against the background of similar legislation in a number of American States. In the UK, there have been several cases such as the House of Lords case of F. v. West Berkshire Health Authority (1989), it which it was held that a mentally-retarded person could be sterilised where she was sexually active and contraception was not appropriate. Other decisions have been made in favour of sterilisation for those under 16 in appropriate cases. Cases such as these will continue to come before the courts and it may be that governments are content to leave decisions in individual cases to the courts, without formulating any policy which, in the light of the experiences of Nazi Germany, Stalinist Russia and Iraq under Saddam Hussein would be unthinkable.

What of the future? In McCardie's day, many things which took place may have been "justified" on the basis of "clinical judgment." That, for example, may have been the justification for some abortions carried out prior to 1967. Given the advances in new reproductive techniques, such as in vitro fertilisation and all that has followed, we now have bodies such as the Human Fertilisation and Embryology Authority which seek to balance the legitimate interest and duty of the researcher to expand the fund of human knowledge with the legitimate concern that the public has in ensuring that research meets with the broad approval of the populace. The future will see a great deal of emphasis on things such as stem cell research and that may eliminate disorders which have plagued people in the past. That elimination and other developments will not take place as a result of government dictat, but should be as a result of reasoned debate. Not everyone will agree with the outcomes, but that process is infinitely better than leaving matters to particular governments or solely to the judgment of clinicians.

The 1933 Galton Lecture: My Outlook on Eugenics

I HAVE been asked to speak to-night on my " Outlook on Eugenics." I chose that title because I am addressing you not as a lawyer or biologist, but as a British citizen with a deep and abiding interest in the welfare of the nation.

No one can speak at a gathering such as this without paying a tribute to the late Sir Francis Galton. It was he who first gave impulse to the eugenic movement and brought home to the minds of thinking people the vital significance of the hereditary factor in each individual life. It was he also who exposed the dangerous fallacy that good environment could of itself restore health and strength to the nation. He loved the truth and he had the courage to proclaim it. His name will live in the social history of this country as a great pioneer in the work of racial improvement.

If Sir Francis Galton could be here to-night he would find that his work and inspiration had produced a rich harvest of results. It is just over sixty years since he published his famous book on *Hereditary Genius*. It is fifty years since he created the great word 'Eugenics.' What magnificent progress has been made since then. It stirs my heart to know that with every decade, aye, with every year, the rate of advance is accelerated and that men and women in all ranks are now demanding that the truth shall no longer be concealed, that the facts of life shall be faced with unswerving courage, and that ignorance and prejudice shall no longer be allowed to menace the happiness and the advance of our race.

You have already captured many outposts, and you will, I hope, soon overcome the citadel of opposition – with the strong weapons of argument, of fact, and of unconquerable truth. For truth is greater than false modesty, and knowledge is a nobler thing than ignorance. The certainties of modern science are more than the baseless theories of former centuries. I hope that before long we shall find that mere tradition has ceased to be an excuse for the continued existence of preventable human misery.

The Basis of Eugenics

I speak on matters which have long occupied my attention, on which I have collected information and statistics from many quarters, on which I have read widely, and thought much. But to-night I must speak in broad outline only. You know the foundations laid by Mendel, the experiments of Bateson, the brilliant work of Morgan and his colleagues, and the distinguished labours of De Vries, of Gates, of Punnett, of Castle and of many others. Biology and bio-chemistry are contributing in full measure to our knowledge. *Eugenics* is *now a science.* It rests on the rock of established fact. An excellent summary of the results achieved is given in the recent volume by Dr. Hurst entitled *The Mechanism of Creative Evolution.*

To-night is not an occasion for technical detail, but rather for general review and broad outlook. There are some things, I suppose, which are clear to all of us:

First : That many of the habits and traditions of the nation are still profoundly anti-eugenic and that we are suffering gravely from centuries of false ideas.

Secondly : That eugenics is in fact the most momentous issue before the nation to-day. It transcends all mere political controversy. The problem of tariffs, for example, is from the racial point of view a transitory one only. The problem of taxation is also a passing one from the like point of view. It can he dealt with by a few Acts of Parliament. But the sound life of our nation, not for a decade only, but for the long range of years ahead, depends on the views which the people of this country adopt on the great matter of eugenics.

What path shall we choose? National strength or national decay? National fitness or national inefficiency? Nature cares nothing for the catchwords of politicians. She will always enforce her penalties in the end.

In my view *eugenics and national welfare must stand or fall together.*

For a long time past not only have we produced the unfit to an appalling extent, but we have preserved them with all the ingenious and kindly resources that the modern humanitarian instinct can command. We have already created a burden under which the nation begins to stagger. Let us face the far-reaching truth that the more we procreate and then preserve those who are unfit in mind or body, the lower the nation must ultimately sink. The strength of a people depends, in the final result, on the physical and mental quality of its citizens. A nation cannot thrive if the basis of its physical life becomes increasingly wrong.

The Burden of The Unfit

As I speak to-night I do not trouble with minor variations of statistical result. The actually insane may be 150,000 instead of 200,000. Those who are actually mentally defective may be 300,000 instead of 400,000. But there is still one grave and predominant fact which no honest investigator can doubt. It is this : *One-tenth of those who make up the nation are physically or mentally unfitted to be citizens.* It is this terrible aggregate of defective stock which is sapping our life as a people, and which exists and grows like a cancer in our midst.

It is significant indeed that about *one in every ten of our people is either too dull or too weakly to earn a living unaided.*

Let us remember that we can never separate the economic and financial life of the nation from its eugenic life. The two are interlinked and they react in the closest fashion. The public of this country will soon, I hope, begin to realize the position as it is to-day. May we not hope that statesmen and politicians will in due

course give their thought and their public utterances to the gravest
evils and problems of all?

Let us glance for a moment round the world. Mark the position
of Great Britain. She is ringed round with powerful, with
splendidly equipped and merciless competitors in every branch of
world trade and industrial activity. She stands at bay. She is
struggling not for mere prosperity but for the very standards of life.
She has a vast population on a very small island. She must fight for
her needed share in world trade. She must fight for her
commercial existence. By the issue of that struggle we shall stand
or fall in the great contest which is taking place before our eyes.

How can the British maintain their place amongst the nations if
they are *cumbered* and *weighed* down by an *ever growing mass of the
physically and mentally unfit?*

The back of the nation is bending beneath the burden. I abstain
from statistical detail. It can only emphasize the weight of the load
we already carry. A nation can only survive in the world struggle if
the units of national life are healthy and strong.

I venture to emphasize that eugenics – the science and the duty
of racial improvement – is the paramount issue at the present time.
He who can awaken a eugenic conscience amongst our people will
in very truth be the saviour of the race.

The Present and The Future

We have reached a critical period in our history. The march of
science is bringing freedom to men and women. The future of
Britain depends on our response to the new knowledge and the
new principles, and on the resolve of *all* classes to achieve a higher
standard of mental and physical efficiency.

We must all be forced to realize the grim facts of heredity. And
so I feel that every member of the *Society* should be a *crusader*. He
represents a great cause. He must not flinch from opposition. He
can ask for the support of all who place the welfare of the people
above the appeal of obsolete tradition and ill-founded dogma.

There are some broad truths which I wish we could drive home
at once to every member of the public.

First : that the *physically unfit* usually beget the physically unfit.

Secondly : that the *mentally unfit* usually beget the mentally unfit.

Thirdly : that *mental defectives,* whether low grade or high grade, usually beget mental defectives.

Fourthly : that we shall never improve the *general standard* of life in this country until we greatly lessen the proportion of the mentally and physically unfit to the general population.

The Democracy of Eugenics

Eugenics is not a science which exists to help the well-to-do. It is a science which will give its best and noblest results when applied by the poor, the suffering, and the afflicted. It is, in my view, the greatest single instrument which thought could devise or theology suggest for raising the masses of England to a higher level of life.

I wish that each one of the general public would realize that the *birth of each single defective child helps to thrust down the standard of living throughout the whole of the country.*

Divorce Reform

I have spoken of the broader aspects of eugenics. If I am asked to name the first practical proposal that I make, my answer is that I would at once reform the divorce law of this country. I think that such a reform is desirable for psychological as well as practical reasons. Until we achieve an improvement in the present system of divorce we shall find it the more difficult to make rapid progress in the general adoption of eugenic principles.

In my view the existing divorce law of this country represents in striking degree that narrow vision and erroneous prejudice which hinder so greatly the march of social progress. We can never separate eugenics from the question of marriage and we can never separate the question of marriage itself from the question of the dissolution of the marriage tie. Marriage is an institution, a great institution, which touches most closely the main objects of eugenic reformers. The vast majority of the physically and mentally deficient are born within and not outside the marriage bond. We cannot divide the social and family life of the people into separate compartments, any more than we can divide that social and family life from the grave economic problems of to-day.

I need not dwell on the significance, from a eugenic point of view, of the vast number of separation orders made throughout the country by Courts of Summary Jurisdiction. By judicial decree the husband and wife live apart, but the marriage tie remains. The widespread evils are known to every social reformer.

But there is something graver still when we look with unbiased eyes at the law which must be administered by Act of Parliament in the Divorce Division of the High Court. For over twenty years the report of Lord Gorrell's Commission has been, to a large extent, *ignored.*

I can feel no doubt that those who live in Great Britain thirty years hence will look upon our existing divorce law as unworthy of the civilization we claim to possess. It will seem as incredible to them as it is to me that divorce should he granted for a single act of adultery, whilst it should be denied where the whole purpose of marriage has been utterly frustrated by deliberate and permanent desertion.

Equally strange will it seem that the law should insist on the lifelong continuance of the marriage tie although one of the spouses should become incurably insane; and perhaps it will seem even stranger that divorce should be denied to a wife who has suffered the most brutal and repeated physical violence from her husband.

These are only a few of the illustrations. There are others just as cogent. I do not wonder at the indignation expressed by the late Lord Birkenhead in his great speech on divorce reform in the House of Lords on March 4th, 1920. It seems to me that when once the principle of dissolution was established by the famous Act of 1857, it should have been applied long before this in accordance with the rules of obvious justice and good sense.

A future generation will also think it remarkable that in the year 1933 the law still was that if only one of the spouses has committed adultery a divorce would be granted, whereas if both spouses had committed adultery (even in pursuance of a permanent attachment on each side to a third person) a divorce would often be refused. I abstain from technical detail. It is enough to state things broadly. I trust the time is not far distant when the repulsive duties of the King's Proctor will be swept away and when the unhappy doctrine of collusion as it at present exists will be reduced to a narrower and more reasonable compass. The doctrine of collusion is a relic of a deplorable past, and it is the ugly concomitant of a code which is entirely out of date.

The restricted nature of our existing divorce law is, in my view, opposed to the eugenic interests of this country. I do not forget that the children of a marriage must be considered. But, in my view, it is never in the true interests of the children that a repugnant or worthless marriage tie should be permanently maintained.

I should like to point out that never before has there been so large a body of those who criticize our existing marriage institution. The dissatisfaction grows day by day. It is gripping the minds of many of the ablest amongst the younger writers and speakers. The area of resentment is ever widening owing to the harshness of our present law of divorce and its disdain of the realities of life. The fabric of marriage can only be preserved in good order by the repair and reform which are long overdue. I have long held the opinion that those who oppose the reform of the divorce law are in fact the worst enemies of the great institution of marriage. *They are undermining the fabric itself.*

The Need for Sterilization

The eugenist is bound to face the question of the sterilization of the mentally defective and of certain types of the physically unfit.

You are familiar, I know, with the literature and statistics on the matter both as to Britain and other countries. The task that lies before you is to make the nation realize the need of measures for sterilization. We may take it that there are about 350,000 at least of mental defectives scattered throughout Great Britain. Of these only a small percentage are under institutional treatment; and a certain number are under supervision, which may or may not be effective. But a vast number of mental defectives are to be found throughout the country who are not only free to beget children outside the marriage tie, but are also free to marry at their own will and to beget offspring as often as they wish.

Now heredity is, by far, the largest single cause of mental deficiency. The hideous taint is transmitted on and on and on, and many thousands of innocent children are thereby brought into the world with the doom of misery and degradation about them. I need scarcely pause to give illustrations. You will find them not only in official reports, but in any source of information you care to consult. They are appalling. Again and again I have myself come upon cases where a mentally defective mother has produced seven or eight mentally defective children. I recall one case where a mentally defective woman, who was unmarried, had produced eight mentally defective children, and where several of those mentally defective children had in their turn produced mentally defective offspring.

This stream of tainted children is still flowing throughout the country. It may be said that about one in every 110 of the population is a mental defective. Do the public realize what that means?

The cost of institutional treatment for all mental defectives would be gigantic. The country cannot afford the burden. Hospitals, institutions, schools, organizations of every sort already sap our resources.

Unless something be done on this and on allied eugenic matters we may almost take the view that the democracy of this country is slowly committing suicide. The physically and mentally unfit, together with this great army of mental defectives, is indeed one of the greatest problems of to-day. Mere political phrases afford no help. Politicians prefer to blame the slums for the inefficient (whether certifiable or not) rather than the inefficient for much of the degradation of the slums.

What *is* to be done?

We are not concerned with political tactics. The truth and the remedy alone are our concern. Can anyone doubt that sterilization is essential in many cases? What else of a practical nature can be suggested as a first barrier against the terrible output of the tainted?

I do not over-estimate the immediate effects of any legislation that may be passed permitting sterilization. I know the points in dispute and the difficulties that have to be faced. But if we can only secure legislation which will permit, under proper safeguards, the voluntary sterilization of those who are either mentally defective or who rightly fear to transmit hereditary taints to their children we shall have made a great advance.

It is necessary to go step by step in the great work of creating a eugenic conscience in the nation at large. I cannot myself see any good reason which can be urged against sterilization in suitable cases, and under adequate safeguards. I believe also that there are many thousands throughout the country who would welcome, not only in the public interest but for themselves, a system of voluntary sterilization which would prevent the transmission of hereditary taints.

Abortion and The Law

I should like (before I speak briefly on Birth Control) to say a few words on the disputable subject of abortion.

I do not hesitate to repeat to-night what I have said before, that in my view the existing law of abortion requires amendment. I know that this subject gives rise to acute differences of view. But those who press for amendment have just as deep a belief in righteousness and the moral welfare of the nation as those who oppose the suggestion of revision.

I do not propose to deal with the general subject of abortion. It is a wide and serious matter. But in my own view there are clearly some circumstances in which abortion, now forbidden, should under proper safeguards be allowed.

May I take some of the illustrations given by me publicly some time ago.

Too often a mentally defective woman or girl is pregnant either by a normal man or by one who is himself a mental defective.

Should the child be born with the horrible taint upon it and with all that the taint implies?

Sometimes a young girl is pregnant by her own father or brother : incest is not uncommon. If a child be actually born, what will be its future, particularly if the girl herself he mentally defective? I speak of cases which you and I know only too well.

Not infrequently a man, released from a mental hospital, after a long term of treatment, will return home to make his wife pregnant against her wish. For she knows or suspects that the taint of insanity is still latent within him. What of the child – and what of the wife?

But take two illustrations more – quite apart from the well-known medical aspects of abortion. I remember well the case where a beautiful and delicate girl of fourteen, the daughter of a country gentleman, was raped by a drunken tramp. She became pregnant. What of the future of the child born to her? What of the untold misery of the girl, her parents, and of the child itself?

I remember also the case where a young and respectable married woman with a baby five months old, was raped in brutal fashion by an epileptic. She became pregnant. What was the future, after the child was born, for the woman, her husband, and the offspring of the rape?

May I remind you that from time to time all over the country there have been and are cases where girls of 15, 14, or even 13 years of age have become pregnant either by grown men or by those who are little more than boys? What is the future of the offspring when once born? In my view the law of abortion calls for consideration and amendment.

Birth Control and Population

May I be allowed to occupy a few minutes only on the subject of birth control?

In my view the question of birth control must affect in large measure the future of this country. It is now over fifty years since the movement started. In spite of opposition from those who should have supported it, it has slowly but surely gained ground.

The common sense of many of the nation has been steadily asserting itself. The instinct of the people is turning in the right direction. I am glad to recognize the great work that has been done in past years by so many devoted women and men. The birth control movement is now seen to be one of international importance.

The future will call on the nations to face the problems created by the rapid and perilous increase of populations. When I look to the East I see, in certain regions, a growth of population so great that it may burst the barriers of normal territory and involve the outbreak of long and terrible war. Everyone of international vision will appreciate what I say. When I look at Europe I see again, in certain regions a growth of population so serious as to presage an outpouring which may lead to appalling conflict. If the nations cannot control their populations they will not be able to control the outbreak of war. Birth control will, I hope, become in due course one of the greatest agencies for the furtherance of international peace, through international co-operation.

But I must limit myself to-night to the subject of birth control in Great Britain. I have long held the view that this country is heavily, and indeed dangerously, over populated. The question of birth control is not only a matter of health and efficiency. It is interwoven in vital fashion with the serious economic problems that confront us. As a nation we are at the cross-roads and we must face the question of population with resolute minds. The vast extent of unemployment is more than a transitory thing.

The Machine Age

Let us be under no illusion. The incredible growth in the productive power of mechanical apparatus is one of the most significant factors in the unemployment problem. The application of science and mechanics to industry and agriculture will not cease. It will become more intense and more widespread. Every year will show that less and less manual labour is required for many purposes. What is to become of those who are not needed for the tasks of production? And, above all, what are we to do with the four or five millions of the nation, the submerged tenth, who are physically and mentally inefficient?

Emigration will not help. The Dominions will never take our inefficients.

Let us grasp the full significance of the fact that at the present time a large proportion of the nation represents *not assets but heavy liabilities*.

If birth control had been widely practised by the poor and inefficient during the last thirty years, the national difficulties of to-day would be infinitely less and the general standards of life would be considerably higher. It is a matter of regret that birth control started at the wrong end.

It has developed amongst those who represented the best of our racial stock, including the strongest sections of well-organized labour. If it had started at and spread upward from below we should have been saved from the menacing fact that there is now a larger rate of growth amongst the physically or mentally inferior than amongst the mentally and physically fit.

To get a strong and healthy nation it is essential that we breed from the right stocks. There is no other way. The time has surely come when statesmen should face the grim realities of the present position and when it should become the duty of the State to spread amongst the poor and inefficient a knowledge of birth control methods which will begin to rectify the present deplorable situation.

Every year will show more acutely the terrible results that flow from the random output of unrestricted breeding. Those results are with us to-day largely because the knowledge of birth control methods has been so harshly and unwisely withheld from those who needed it *most*.

A knowledge of birth control methods should not remain as a privilege of the well-to-do. It should become the right, yes, the right, of the millions of poor and struggling women who seek for a fuller measure of well-being and for the opportunity so to limit their families as to permit of health and strength not only for their children but also for themselves.

The Ethics of Birth Control

Let those who are unfit for maternity have the opportunity of saving the nation and themselves from the tragedy of unfit offspring. Let those who are fit for maternity have the opportunity of restricting and spacing the birth of their children in order that health may be where misery now exists. As Lord Buckmaster so well said. " To regulate and control birth is not to degrade but to elevate human nature."

Everyone of us is deeply concerned with the repulsive conditions which prevail in the slums of London and of all the great cities. It is, I think, beyond dispute that there are innumerable women who, through ignorance of birth-control methods, are bearing unwanted children under conditions which make for misery and degradation.

Children in The Slums

The absence of proper *birth spacing* is responsible for infinite suffering and injury to women and children throughout the country. Every social reformer knows the facts. Throughout every slum and in all depressed areas women already exhausted with child-begetting, already over-burdened with many children born in successive years, are faced with yet another unwanted child to add to the existing wretchedness. Can we wonder that self-abortion is prevalent to an extent not realized by the general public, and that the demand amongst the poor for assisted abortion is so incessant and so widespread?

A woman, however poor she be, should be taught to realize that she is a *responsible citizen of the State* and *not the mere instrument for the reckless begetting of offspring.* In my view, it is the duty of every suitable Local Authority throughout the country to provide for married women the birth-control knowledge they may ask for.

The unwanted child who is born to neglect and wretchedness is one of the great causes of the misery in our midst. It is far better that the nation should have a smaller number of healthy children than a large multitude of neglected and useless weaklings.

Statesmen, I am told, have wept in public when they have mentioned the slums. I respect their emotion. I share it. But I profoundly wish that some amongst them would have the courage to announce to the public generally the *great ameliorating power* of birth-control methods.

The present state of things cannot go on. The instinct of the people is, I believe, awakening to the truth of the present situation. I hope, I deeply hope, that the instinct already stirring will soon be translated into a widespread demand for action.

I believe that those who now oppose so strongly the spread of birth-control knowledge amongst the miserable and the distressed will be condemned emphatically by a future and more enlightened generation. In my view they are hostile to social progress, and enemies to the true interests of the poor.

The birth-control movement is, I think, the greatest hope yet offered to the multitude of women in this country who live not only in the dark places of poverty, but also under the grim shadow of unwanted pregnancies. Birth control is one of the sure foundations of social progress and happy motherhood, and it is the absolute pre-requisite to national eugenic advance.

Conclusions

I have dealt in broad outlines to-night with several subjects. I have abstained, through pressure of time, from detailed arguments and elaborate statistics. I have used no technical phrases. I have merely touched on vital matters. I do not forget that the world is a place of conflict and that the pathway of reform is a pathway of effort. But let us remember that truth will make its advance in spite of all obstacles and that it gains its victory in the end.

I rejoice to think that this *Society* represents the ideals of which the future will approve. I believe with all my heart that in the coming years the great principles of eugenics will be adopted and applied by the vast majority in this realm as the only true guides to national health and national happiness.

J. M. Keynes

Photograph courtesy of Milo Keynes

1937

Some Economic Consequences of a Declining Population[1]

By J. M. Keynes

Introduction by David Coleman

For demographers, and for members of the Galton Institute, John Maynard Keynes (1883-1946), Baron Keynes of Tilton, may be most remembered for having turned his astonishing talents to address the issue of population in his famous Galton Lecture of 1937, which is reprinted below. Before considering that essay, however, we should step back to consider Keynes the academic economist, the civil servant, the international negotiator, the college bursar, the patron of art. In early life he oscillated between civil service life in the India Office (1906–08), and lecturing in economics at Cambridge (1908–13), where he began his editorship of the *Economic Journal* up to 1945. He returned to the civil service in 1915, joined the Royal Commission on Indian Finance and Currency 1913–1914 and acted as the principal representative of HM Treasury at the Versailles Peace Conference in 1919. There, his farsighted belief that the Versailles proposals on changing European borders, and on German reparations, were destructive and counter-productive provoked his resignation in 1919. His objections were set out in 'The Economic Consequences of the Peace' (1919), the first and one of the most famous of a number of books which set out strong opinions in compelling, lucid and elegant prose seldom if ever approached by latter-day economists and demographers. A short example may suffice, from the 'General Theory' (Ch. 24):

"The ideas of economists and political philosophers, both when they are right and when they are wrong, are more powerful than is commonly understood. Indeed, the world is ruled by little else. Practical men, who believe themselves to be quite exempt from any intellectual influences, are usually the slaves of some defunct

---

[1] The Galton Lecture, delivered before the Eugenics Society on February 16th, 1937, and *Eugenics Review*, Vol.XXIX, pp.13-17, 1937.

economist. Madmen in authority, who hear voices in the air, are distilling their frenzy from some academic scribbler of a few years back. Now 'in the long run' this [way of summarizing the quantity theory of money] is probably true … But this 'long run' is a misleading guide to current affairs. In the long run we are all dead. Economists set themselves too easy, too useless a task if in tempestuous seasons they can only tell us that when the storm is long past the ocean is flat again'.

His chief work was in his influential books and pamphlets attacking laissez-faire economics and the return to the gold standard, advocating instead a radically new approach to economic management that was widely adopted, and widely misunderstood, post-war. Other innovative ideas related to interest rates and short-term equilibrium. He returned to the Treasury in 1940 and in 1944 played a leading part in the Bretton Woods Conference. He was the first British governor on the International Monetary Fund and the International Bank, but these institutions owed more to US Treasury orthodoxy than to Keynes's ideas. He was responsible for the negotiations with the United States on Lend-Lease 1944–45 and for a crucial post-war loan, helping to save Britain from the 'economic Dunkirk' that faced us after paying for global war for six years.

Keynes was from an academic family (his father was an economist and logician at Cambridge) and moved in elite cultural and intellectual circles, being a member of the 'Apostles' at Cambridge and the Bloomsbury Group in London. He had wide interests. Marriage to the Russian ballerina Lydia Lopokova (1925) developed his taste for ballet. He built and financed the Arts Theatre, Cambridge (1935) and helped to found the Arts Council, being its first chairman. His brilliant writing style not only elucidated economic problems but covered wider areas. For example his 'Essays in Biography' (1933), still highly readable, included an essay on Malthus, although he concentrated on Malthus the economist, with whose views he had much sympathy, rather the Malthus the pioneer 'demographer'. I put that word in quotes because of course it was not used in Malthus' time. Malthus' demographic writings were essentially those of an economist; indeed it was Malthus' pessimistic outlook that gained for economics the epithet of 'the dismal science'. Putting his abilities to practical use Keynes also amassed a large fortune for himself and for King's College Cambridge, of which he was Bursar from 1919-46.

Apart from his condemnation of the Versailles arrangements his best-known works are the Treatise on Money (1930) and the

'General Theory of Employment, Interest and Money' (1936), the most influential single work on economics of its age. This showed how aggregate demand, and therefore unemployment, was determined. Keynes believed that economic systems at equilibrium had no necessary tendency to full employment and that such systems were in many ways inherently unstable and had to be managed. In a depression, even the lowest wages could not eliminate unemployment. Individual consumer spending was often inadequate to create sufficient demand; a fear he shared with Malthus. Instead unemployment could be cured by state demand management through public works, through subsidies or the stimulus of private investment, funded by budget deficit. In these theories, the notion of the income/expenditure multiplier held a central place. All this was strongly opposed to Treasury orthodoxy and to the views of other economists such as von Hayek.

Post-war governments adopted 'Keynesian' policies and committed themselves to full employment. His followers, however, were often more 'Keynesian' than was Keynes himself. A new era has moved on from demand management; a position challenged by the revival of monetarist and supply-side thinking. His concern with the problems of 'oversaving', the failure of demand, and the need for public works echoed similar concerns first voiced by Malthus in 1820. In today's world this combination of 'lowest-low' fertility, and oversaving leading to the failure of domestic demand and economic stagnation, is most acutely obvious in Japan, where population decline is imminent.

Keynes devoted no major work to population issues, only short pieces, although some major works make strong demographic assumptions. For example, a 'neo-Malthusian' view is prominent in his 'Economic Consequences of the Peace'. There he noted that Europe's dense population had enjoyed pre-war a high standard of living although no longer self-sufficient in agriculture or raw materials, relying instead on manufactured exports. He feared that such large populations, especially those of Germany (then 68 million) and Russia (then 150 million), could no longer be sustained following the destruction of industry and in the absence of opportunities for mass emigration.

Keynes was thus initially concerned with the 'Malthusian devil O of Overpopulation'. This devil, chained up when conditions were favourable and productivity rising, would be released when the temporarily advantageous conditions which had provoked population growth came to an end. Keynes campaigned against the then current 'pronatalist' opinion, which he feared would tend to reduce the standard of living. He felt that the falling birth rate of the early post-war years reflected favourable social developments, although he feared, as did many other intellectuals of his day, the adverse eugenic consequences of the more prudent nations, and classes, who were reducing their fertility before others did. These views were summarised in his 1912 lecture on 'Population', which has only recently been made generally available (in a recent review of Keynes' on population (Toye, 2000) where a much more detailed analysis may be found).

However, Keynes changed his mind somewhat radically during the later 1920s, coming to reject his earlier economic pessimism and with it some of his Malthusian views on the perils of over-population. Instead he became more concerned with the risk of inadequate demand, giving in his 1933 biographical essay on Malthus much more prominence to Malthus the economist (worried, like Keynes, about failure of demand) than to Malthus the demographer (worried, as Keynes had been, about overpopulation). In his Galton Lecture of 1937, his most balanced view of population issues, Keynes points to the opposite threat that population decline, for the first time in centuries a real possibility by the 1930s, might unchain the other 'Malthusian devil U of Underemployed resources', through excessive savings and underconsumption. In a stationary population, he argued that the two 'Malthusian devils' could only be kept in balance by increased consumption, more equal incomes and low interest rates. He ended up promoting family allowances and other pronatalist policies to avert population decline, which he had earlier condemned, while recognising that overpopulation could exist elsewhere. Keynes cannot be blamed too much for changing his mind. He defended such flexibility in one of the numerous epigrams attributed to him, asking unanswerably 'when I find that I have made a mistake, I change my mind. What do you do?'

Despite his skills as an economist, his inconstant efforts on population, little supported by data or technical understanding, did not show him at his best. It will be noted in the essay printed below that very little statistical evidence is presented either on demographic or on economic trends or on the relationship between the two. Instead everything is based on first principles. These days Keynes' twin worries are still with us, but separated in space. Population growth does continue in the poorest countries of the world at a high rate, although the global rate, and even the annual absolute increment, has been declining for some time. In the richer countries, however, only the United States has a current birth rate able to maintain its population in the long run. Family allowances or other, more subtle welfare measures are now part of most western countries' basic social policies. Ostensibly these have been developed for family welfare purposes and to enhance the flexibility of the labour force. Dictatorships of left and right have given overt pronatalism a bad name. But as population momentum runs out of steam, and as the population decline envisaged in Keynes' time finally starts to become a reality in some European countries, the demographic as well as the welfare importance of enabling women to have the number of children that they say they want is gaining ground in public debate in a number of Western countries, as well as in Japan, and is most recently articulated in the EU Commission's Green Paper. Other prominent concerns of today, the inevitability of population ageing and the rise of mass migration, were not really considered in Keynes' work, even though the former at least should have been seen as the writing on the wall by technical demographers in the 1930s as an inevitable consequence of lower birth rates.

Keynes was probably the most influential economist of the 20th century and often regarded as the 'father of' modern macroeconomics'. He suffered a major heart attack in 1937, and worn out by his exertions to secure a post-war economic settlement, died in 1946. He had no children.

Bibliography

The Economic Consequences of the Peace (1919). London, Macmillan

A Treatise on Money (1930) (2 volumes). London, Macmillan

Essays in Biography (1933). London, Macmillan

The General Theory of Employment, Interest and Money. (1936) London, Macmillan.

Some Economic Consequences of a Declining Population (1937), *The Eugenics Review XXIX*, 13 - 17.

Biographical and critical works

Blaug, M. (1990). *John Maynard Keynes*. London: Macmillan with the Institute of Economic Affairs.

Blaug, M. (Ed.). (1991). *John Maynard Keynes*. Aldershot: Edward Elgar (2 Volumes)

Chick, V. (1983). *Macroeconomics after Keynes: a reconsideration of the General Theory*. Oxford: Philip Allan.

Eltis, W., & Sinclair, P. (Eds.). (1988). *Keynes and Economic Policy: the relevance of the General Theory after fifty years*. Basingstoke: Macmillan with the National Economic Development Office.

Hicks, J. (1974) *The Crisis in Keynesian Economics*. Oxford, Basil Blackwell

Hutchison, T. W. (1977). *Keynes versus the 'Keynesians' … ?. : an essay in the thinking of J. M. Keynes and the accuracy of its interpretation by his followers*. London: Institute of Economic Affairs.

Keynes, Milo (1975) *Essays on John Maynard Keynes*. Cambridge, Cambridge University Press

Toye, J. (2000). *Keynes on Population*. Oxford: Oxford University Press.

Wickham Legg, L.G. and E.T. Williams (1959). *The Dictionary of National Biography 1941 - 1950*. Oxford: Oxford University Press pp 452 - 457.

The 1937 Galton Lecture: Some Economic Consequences of a Declining Population

I

THE future never resembles the past – as we well know. But, generally speaking, our imagination and our knowledge are too weak to tell us what particular changes to expect. We do not know what the future holds. Nevertheless, as living and moving beings, we are forced to act. Peace and comfort of mind require that we should hide from ourselves how little we foresee. Yet we must be guided by some hypothesis. We tend, therefore, to substitute for the knowledge which is unattainable certain conventions, the chief of which is to assume, contrary to all likelihood, that the future will resemble the past. This is how we act in practice. Though it was, I think, an ingredient in the complacency of the nineteenth century that, in their philosophical reflections on human behaviour, they accepted an extraordinary contraption of the Benthamite School, by which all possible consequences of alternative courses of action were supposed to have attached to them, first a number expressing their comparative advantage, and secondly another number expressing the probability of their following from the course of action in question; so that multiplying together the numbers attached to all the possible consequences of a given action and adding the results, we could discover what to do. In this way a mythical system of probable knowledge was employed to reduce the future to the same calculable status as the present. No one has ever acted on this theory. But even to-day I believe that our thought is sometimes influenced by some such pseudo-rationalistic notions.

Now I emphasize to-night the importance of this convention by which we assume the future to be much more like the past than is reasonable – a convention of behaviour which none of us could possibly do without – because, as I think, it continues to influence our minds even in those cases where we do have good reason to expect a definite change.   And, perhaps, the most outstanding example of a case where we in fact have a considerable power of seeing into the future is the prospective trend of population.   We know much more securely than we know almost any other social or economic factor relating to the future that, in the place of the steady and indeed steeply rising level of population which we have experienced for a great number of decades, we shall be faced in a very short time with a stationary or a declining level.   The rate of decline is doubtful, but it is virtually certain that the changeover, compared with what we have been used to, will be substantial.   We have this unusual degree of knowledge concerning the future because of the long but definite time-lag in the effects of vital statistics.   Nevertheless the idea of the future being different from the present is so repugnant to our conventional modes of thought and behaviour that we, most of us, offer a great resistance to acting on it in practice.   There are, indeed, several important social consequences already predictable as a result of a rise in population being changed into a decline.   But my object this evening is to deal, in particular, with one outstanding economic consequence of this impending change; if, that is to say, I can, for a moment, persuade you sufficiently to depart from the established conventions of your mind as to accept the idea that the future will differ from the past.

II

An increasing population has a very important influence on the demand for capital.   Not only does the demand for capital – apart from technical changes and an improved standard of life – increase more or less in proportion to population.   But, business expectations being based much more on present than on prospective demand, an era of increasing population tends to promote optimism, since demand will in general tend to exceed, rather than fall short of, what was hoped for. Moreover a mistake, resulting in a particular type of capital being in temporary over-supply, is in such conditions rapidly corrected. But in an era of declining population the opposite is true. Demand tends to be below what was expected, and a state of over-supply is less easily corrected. Thus a pessimistic atmosphere may ensue; and, although at long last pessimism may tend to correct itself through its effect on supply, the first result to prosperity of a change-over from an increasing to a declining population may be very disastrous.

In assessing the causes of the enormous increase in capital during the nineteenth century and since, too little importance, I think, has been given to the influence of an increasing population as distinct from other influences. The demand for capital depends, of course, on three factors: on population, on the standard of life, and on capital technique. By capital technique I mean the relative importance of long processes as an efficient method of procuring what is currently consumed, the factor I have in mind being conveniently described as the period of production, which is, roughly speaking, a weighted average of the interval which elapses between the work done and the consumption of the product. In other words the demand for capital depends on the number of consumers, the average level of consumption, and the average period of production.

Now it is necessarily the case that an increase in population increases proportionately the demand for capital; and the progress of invention may be relied on to raise the standard of life. But the effect of invention on the period of production depends on the type of invention which is characteristic of the age. It may have been true of the nineteenth century that improvements in transport, standards of housing and public services were of such a character that they did tend somewhat to increase the period of consumption. It is well known that highly durable objects were characteristic of the Victorian civilization. But it is not equally clear that the same thing is true to-day. Many modern inventions are directed towards finding ways of reducing the amount of capital investment necessary to produce a given result; and partly as the result of our experience as to the rapidity of change in tastes and technique, our preference is decidedly directed towards those types of capital goods which are not too durable. I do not believe, therefore, that we can rely on current changes of technique being of the kind which tend of themselves to increase materially the average period of production. It may even be the case that, apart from the effect of possible changes in the rate of interest, the average period may be tending to diminish.   Moreover an improving average level of consumption may conceivably have, in itself, the effect of diminishing the average period of production. For as we get richer, our consumption tends to be directed towards those articles of consumption, particularly the services of other people, which have a relatively short average period of production.

Now, if the number of consumers is falling off and we cannot rely on any significant technical lengthening of the period of production, the demand for a net increase of capital goods is thrown back into being wholly dependent on an improvement in the average level of consumption or on a fall in the rate of interest. I will attempt to give a few very rough figures to illustrate the order of magnitude of the different factors involved.

Let us consider the period of just over fifty years from 1860 to 1913. I find no evidence of any important change in the length of the technical period of production. Statistics of quantity of real capital present special difficulties. But those which we have do not suggest that there have been large changes in the amount of capital employed to produce a unit of output. Two of the most highly capitalized services, those of housing and of agriculture, are old-established.   Agriculture has diminished in relative importance. Only if people were to spend a decidedly increased proportion of their incomes on housing, as to which there is indeed a certain amount of evidence for the post-war period, should I expect a significant lengthening of the technical period of production. For the fifty years before the war, during which the long-period average of the rate of interest was fairly constant, I feel some confidence that the period was not lengthened by much more than 10 per cent., if as much.

Now during the same period the British population increased by about 50 per cent., and the population which British industry and investment was serving by a much higher figure. And I suppose that the standard of life must have risen by some where about 60 per cent. Thus the increased demand for capital was primarily attributable to the increasing population and to the rising standard of life, and only in a minor degree to technical changes of a kind which called for an increasing capitalization per unit of consumption. To sum up, the population figures, which are reliable, indicate that about half the increase in capital was required to serve the increasing population. Perhaps the figures were about as follows, though I would emphasize that these conclusions are very rough and to be regarded only as broad pointers to what was going on:

	1860	1913
Real capital ...	100	270
Population ...	100	150
Standard of life ...	100	160
Period of Production	100	110

It follows that a stationary population with the same improvement in the standard of life and the same lengthening of the period of production would have required an increase in the stock of capital of only a little more than half of the increase which actually occurred. Moreover, whilst nearly half of the home investment was required by the increase in population, probably a substantially higher proportion of the foreign investment of that period was attributable to this cause.

On the other hand it is possible that the increase in average incomes, the decline in the size of families, and a number of other institutional and social influences may have raised the proportion of the national income which tends to be saved in conditions of full employment. I do not feel confident about this, since there are other factors, notably the taxation of the very rich, which tend in the opposite direction. But I think we can safely say – and this is sufficient for my argument – that the proportion of the national income which would be saved to-day in conditions of full employment lies some where between 8 per cent. and 15 per cent. of the income of each year. What annual percentage increase in the stock of capital would this rate of saving involve? To answer this we have to estimate how many years of our national income the existing stock of capital represents. This is not a figure which we know accurately, but it is possible to indicate an order of magnitude. You will probably find when I tell you the answer that it differs a good deal from what you expect. The existing national stock of capital is equal to about four times a year's national income.   That is to say, if our annual income is in the neighbourhood of £4,000 millions, our stock of capital is perhaps £15,000 millions.   (I am not here including foreign investment, which would raise the figure to, say, four and a half times.)   It follows that new investment at a rate of somewhere between 8 per cent and 15 per cent. of a year's income means a cumulative increment in the stock of capital of some where between 2 per cent. and 4 per cent. per annum.

Let me recapitulate the argument. Please take note that I have been making so far two tacit assumptions – namely that there is no drastic change in the distribution of wealth or in any other factor affecting the proportion of income that is saved; and further, that there is no large change in the rate of interest sufficient to modify substantially the length of the average period of production. To the removal of these two assumptions we shall return later. On these assumptions, however, with our existing organization, and in conditions of prosperity and full employment, we shall have to discover a demand for net additions to our stock of capital amounting to somewhere between 2 per cent. and 4 per cent. annually. And this will have to continue year after year indefinitely. Let us in what follows take the lower estimate – namely *2* per cent. – since if this is too low the argument will be *a fortiori*.

Hitherto the demand for new capital has come from two sources, each of about equal strength: a little less than half of it to meet the demands of a growing population; a little more than half of it to meet the demands of inventions and improvements which increase output per head and permit a higher standard of life.

Now past experience shows that a greater cumulative increment than 1 per cent. per annum in the standard of life has seldom proved practicable. Even if the fertility of invention would permit more, we cannot easily adjust ourselves to a greater rate of change than this involves. There may have been one or two decades in this country during the past hundred years when improvement has proceeded at the rate of 1 per cent. per annum. But generally speaking the rate of improvement seems to have been somewhat less than 1 per cent. per annum cumulative.

I am here distinguishing, you will see, between those inventions which enable a unit of capital to yield a unit of product with the aid of less labour than before, and those which lead to a change in the amount of capital employed *more* than in proportion to the resulting output. I am assuming that the former class of improvements will proceed in the future as in the recent past, and am ready to take as my assumption that they will proceed in the near future up to the best standard we have ever experienced in any previous decade; and I calculate that inventions failing under this head are not likely to absorb much more than half of our savings, assuming conditions of full employment and a stationary population. But in the second category some inventions cut some way and some the other, and it is not clear – assuming a constant rate of interest – that the net result of invention changes demand for capital per unit of output one way or the other.

It follows, therefore, that to ensure equilibrium conditions of prosperity over a period of years it will be essential, *either* that we alter our institutions and the distribution of wealth in a way which causes a smaller proportion of income to be saved, *or* that we reduce the rate of interest sufficiently to make profitable very large changes in technique or in the direction of consumption which involve a much larger use of capital in proportion to output. Or, of course, as would be wisest, we could pursue both policies to a certain extent.

III

What relation do these views bear to the older Malthusian theory that more capital resources per head (chiefly envisaged by the older writers in the shape of Land) must be of immense benefit to the standard of life, and that the growth of population was disastrous to human standards by retarding this increase? It may seem at first sight that I am contesting this old theory and am arguing, on the contrary, that a phase of declining population will make it immensely more difficult than before to maintain prosperity.

In a sense this is a true interpretation of what I am saying. But if there are any old Malthusians here present let them not suppose that I am rejecting their essential argument. Unquestionably a stationary population does facilitate a rising standard of life; but on one condition only – namely that the increase in resources or in consumption, as the case may be, which the stationariness of population makes possible, does actually take place. For we have now learned that we have another devil at our elbow at least as fierce as the Malthusian – namely the devil of unemployment escaping through the breakdown of effective demand. Perhaps we could call this devil too a Malthusian devil, since it was Malthus himself who first told us about him. For just as the young Malthus was disturbed by the facts of population as he saw them round him and sought to rationalize that problem, so the older Malthus was no less disturbed by the facts of unemployment as he saw them round him and sought – far less successfully so far as his influence on the rest of the world was concerned – to rationalize that problem too. Now when Malthusian devil P. is chained up, Malthusian devil U. is liable to break loose. When devil P. of Population is chained up, we are free of one menace; but we are more exposed to the other devil U. of Unemployed Resources than we were before.

With a stationary population we shall, I argue, be absolutely dependent for the maintenance of prosperity and civil peace on policies of increasing consumption by a more equal distribution of incomes and of forcing down the rate of interest so as to make profitable a substantial change in the length of the period of production. If we do not, of set and determined purpose, pursue these policies, then without question we shall be cheated of the benefits which we stand to gain by the chaining up of one devil, and shall suffer from the perhaps more intolerable depredations of the other.

Yet there will be many social and political forces to oppose the necessary change. It is probable that we cannot make the changes wisely unless we make them gradually. We must foresee what is before us and move to meet it half-way. If capitalist society rejects a more equal distribution of incomes and the forces of banking and finance succeed in maintaining the rate of interest somewhere near the figure which ruled on the average during the nineteenth century (which was, by the way, a little *lower* than the rate of interest which rules to-day), then a chronic tendency towards the under-employment of resources must in the end sap and destroy that form of society. But if, on the other hand, persuaded and guided by the spirit of the age and such enlightenment as there is, it permits – as I believe it may – a gradual evolution in our attitude towards accumulation, so that it shall be appropriate to the circumstances of a stationary or declining population, we shall be able, perhaps, to get the best of both worlds – to maintain the liberties and independence of our present system, whilst its more signal faults gradually suffer euthanasia as the diminishing importance of capital accumulation and the rewards attaching to it fall into their proper position in the social scheme.

A too rapidly declining population would obviously involve many severe problems, and there are strong reasons lying outside the scope of this evening's discussion why in that event, or in the threat of that event, measures ought to be taken to prevent it. But a stationary or slowly declining population may, if we exercise the necessary strength and wisdom, enable us to raise the standard of life to what it should be, whilst retaining those parts of our traditional scheme of life which we value the more now that we see what happens to those who lose them.

In the final summing up, therefore, I do not depart from the old Malthusian conclusion. I only wish to warn you that the chaining up of the one devil may, if we are careless, only serve to loose another still fiercer and more intractable.

Sir William Beveridge

Photograph courtesy of National Portrait Gallery, London

1943

Eugenic Aspects of Children's Allowances[1]

Sir William Beveridge, K.C.B., F.B.A.

Introduction by Mazin Zeki

William Beveridge, OM (1879-1963) was one the most illustrious members of the Galton Institute. After presenting his seminal report to Parliament in 1943 he hurried to the Mansion House to deliver the Galton Lecture. Unusually he answered searching questions about the child welfare provisions of his Bill. As a eugenicist he wanted state support for childhood, a theme which he first explored in a paper given to a members' meeting of the Institute in the early 1920s and which has proved to be of continuing, and increasing, relevance.

Beveridge uniquely embodied the contradictory and complementary features of the social forces and value systems which helped to shape and arguably were eventually undermined by, the welfare state. He was born in Bengal the eldest son of a judge in the Indian civil service, and was educated at Charterhouse and Balliol. Thus he combined what Carey has called the imperialist ethic of duty and self-sacrifice with a "to-the-manor-born" old school *noblesse oblige*. Like his European counterparts he was a patrician and over the course of a long life this grand old man of social reform was actively connected to the East end settlements, the non-conformist tradition, the Fabian-social democratic search for order, LSE (its longest-serving Director), the aristocratic impulse, utopian collectivism and utilitarianism. A political Liberal he abandoned his laissez-faire inclinations to embrace some of the collectivist solutions offered by large-scale state intervention a number of which had already been adopted on the continent and in Russia.

The Beveridge Plan, elaborated in two separate reports published in 1942 and 1944, proposed that all persons of working age should

---

[1] Delivered on 16 February 1943 and published in *The Eugenics Review*, **Vol. XXXIV**, 1942-43.

pay a weekly contribution to government from which benefits would be paid to the sick, unemployed and retired providing a minimum standard "below which no one should be allowed to fall". If Beveridge was naïve in thinking that such a scheme could be self-financing it is worth remembering that Aneurin Bevan was concurrently arguing that his National Health Service would require *decreasing* finance from government as the population's health improved.

The Plan suffered from the law of unintended consequences. As Jose Harris points out, the history of the welfare state poses a number of recurring questions none of which have altogether conclusive answers. Beveridge, like many observers, would have been horrified at surveying the ruins of everything he ever believed in.

What would Beveridge make of voluntary worklessness and its clearly dysgenic effects? Or the fiction of looking for jobs which do not exist without offering training for future jobs? Or the failure of the state to train its workers for essential tasks which are being outsourced through globalisation? Lifelong welfare dependency, aided and abetted by the wholesale changes in social housing which have helped to create a rootless underclass in welfare ghettos, would have been utterly repellent to him.

Single parenthood has become normalised with millions now living in workless households even at a time of serious labour shortages. The 'cycle of deprivation' is a concept which is being accepted even by those who until recently denounced it. As Peter Henessey makes clear, in *Never Again,* a generation which had experienced the depression and the solidaristic and rapid social mixing of the war, was determined to reorder society. Perhaps most important of all has been the imperceptible abandonment of the non-conformist ethos which had helped to shape it.

The welfare state was created as a living instrument of entitlements based on the principle of contributory universal insurance. While the principle of social insurance has been eroded the welfare and tax systems have not been integrated. Entitlement is now based not on contributions but on residence and current needs. Snapshots in time on an individual basis have replaced collective reality.

Has the welfare state created stronger bonds or accelerated the fragmentation and individualisation of society? The 'golden age' of the welfare state lasted only until 1974 before it came under serious ideological assault, together with cuts which undermined the principle of universal welfare while at the same time ensuring that more people were wholly dependent on it. Consequently total welfare expenditure rose relentlessly.

Future historians may well date the beginning of the end as 1966 when the Social Security Act came into force. The 'poor law' of the National Assistance Board was replaced by the Supplementary Benefits regime and an allegedly more dignified system with officer discretion.

These changes were made under the first Wilson government and Harold Wilson's own involvement at this critical point in the history of the Welfare State is both crucial and equivocal. Wilson was a brilliant politician and could clearly see the unsustainability of existing arrangements. Moreover, he had the moral authority to seek to intervene. In April 1951 he had resigned cabinet office in protest at budget proposals to impose prescription charges on the NHS. Aneurin Bevan, then Minister of Labour, also resigned as did a number of junior government members who together formed the Bevanite Movement. No one had greater moral credentials to speak out on this problem. On the other hand, Wilson had a genuine political commitment to welfare economics. He had, after all, been a research assistant to Beveridge at Oxford in the 1930s, an experience he writes amusingly about in his autobiography, *Memoirs 1916-1964* (London: 1986). The result was a political compromise, a fudge which in the long term achieved little. Wilson was himself faced with resignations when he increased prescription charges. As more benefits became rights they became the focus of formalised demands and ultimately organised official resistance and overlaid by the dominant need for relentless cost cutting.

The welfare state, strangled by bureaucracy and extremely detailed and complicated rules, itself became a producer interest antagonistically opposed to its consumers.

The greatest failure may be that its beneficiaries are totally unaware of its origins except as a vehicle for claims. Stakeholders existed without being aware of the fact. It may be that the Beveridge model is unsustainable in a post-industrial state without a strong set of citizenship bonds which have been steadily undermined by supporters on the left as well as by ideological opponents.

The welfare state also included unwritten contracts which have been repudiated (as in the Community Care Act which governs old age care and creates the false distinction between health and social care) without explanation. The pensions issue beset by actuarial and demographic factors is only the most obvious. On the other hand, such realities may necessitate strengthening the welfare state with such initiatives as a citizen's income (which itself has Social Credit and distributist origins). But the model has also created a number of absurdities, injustices and intrusions into privacy which erode its legitimacy.

Now the welfare state is being renegotiated and to some extent recast in its very birthplace, the London School of Economics. The model is now buttressed by an emphasis on child poverty and child bonds, which may cost billions without achieving their objectives.

To a certain (if sometimes overstated) extent the welfare state is not nearly as universal as it should be as a result of growing wealth. However while welfare (as in other EU countries) has been redistributative it has not significantly altered patterns of social inheritance in terms of education and life chances. Has it entrenched poverty as a by-product of the attempt at eradicating it?

The greatest expansion of property ownership occurred in the 1950s and subsequent social wealth has not displaced but redefined poverty. Arguably, patterns of wealth have not changed significantly over the past hundred years. The fatal flaw is that a welfare state must also meet the needs of a non-marginalised majority. It can only be sustained by a large coalition at a time of growing social and income inequality.

Full employment has a totally different current meaning. Retraining, now necessary more than ever before, is becoming marginalised.

Pre-war poverty has been replaced by growing home ownership and total wealth is also illusory with record amounts of debt balanced against paper assets of the majority. All this amidst novel, contradictory, growing (as measured by recent IMD figures) and startling forms and definitions of inequality. Poverty is now measured not by starvation but by postcoded denial of access to credit, insurance and home ownership, and lack of access to universal forms of technology.

Opponents of the welfare state are not restricted to the ideological right. They are now joined by the liberals unhappy with the high cost and unintended consequences. Perhaps nothing exemplifies this better than the career of Frank Field MP the former CPAG director who became a fierce critic of the welfare state.

Above all it is the present and future pensions crisis which may create a new contract based not on state provision but on better stakeholder control of unaccountable pension funds whose wealth exceed state funds and national insurance. Such funds, a latter version of benevolent societies, may be the bulwark of a different welfare state.

A Beveridge plan would not get off the ground today. But elements strangely persist. On the eve of the 1906 centenary, itself the high point of Edwardian domestic labour, amidst growing wealth and concentrated poverty there is now more actual domestic labour than ever before whatever the terminology. Now the demands are for more oblique tax help for domestic labour, nursery and childcare including the informal employment of relatives. A contradictory disguised welfare state may be taking shape as universal child trust funds /bonds over-optimistically promise to eradicate child poverty.

The 1943 Galton Lecture: Eugenic Aspects of Children's Allowances

I do not mind telling you that I have spent most of to-day in the gallery of the House of Commons listening to the opening debate on the Beveridge Report. During the latter part of it – in fact just before I came here – Sir John Anderson was speaking amid considerable protest from the other side because he was reading his speech, and a discussion arose as to whether or not he was entitled to read a speech in the House of Commons. I am in rather the opposite difficulty, in that I am supposed to be reading you a lecture, but I have nothing written which I can read. I shall have to "speak" a lecture, for I have not had time to give to the preparation of what I have to say to you to-day anything like the care that my subject deserves.

Nevertheless, just because the subject is so enormously important, I felt bound to accept your invitation, and, having accepted it, to fulfil my promise. I ought perhaps to add that there was a secondary reason which led me to accept your invitation, namely that I did not answer it for some time, and when that is the case I find it harder to send a refusal than an acceptance. But I am glad to be here, and I want to make it plain that my title is, not the eugenic aspects of social insurance, but the eugenic aspects of children's allowances. That is really what I am going to talk about, and I hope none of you will he very much disappointed by that limitation.

The economic aspect

In this question of giving allowances for children – that is to say, adjusting the income of the family according to the size of the family and to the number of the children – there are both economic and biological aspects. My approach to this question of children's allowances hitherto has been wholly economic. In the Report which the House of Commons is debating at this moment I have proposed children's allowances as a means of preventing want and putting an end to lack of physical necessities for the nurturing of children already in existence.

Any of you who may have read my Report, or Part I of it, will note that it starts by pointing out that there are two causes of want in this country. One of these is the interruption of earnings by unemployment, accident, disease, and so on, and the other is the non-adjustment of the family income to the size of the family. The latter factor leads to a very sinister concentration of poverty upon the children. If one takes the various surveys made by sociological experts, like Mr. Rowntree, of want or poverty in the period between the two wars, one finds everywhere that of the people who have not enough to keep them physically healthy not far short of one-half are children under 14. The proportion varies generally from 40 to 50 per cent.

I want to emphasize this fact because it has a bearing on what I am going to say later about the working of our financial or economic system upon family life and the prospects of people who belong to different sizes of families. Before the war more than 40 per cent of the want in this country was experienced by children under 14. Another way of putting it, by Mr. Rowntree, is that at least half the population pass through two periods of physical want in their lives, even in relatively prosperous Britain as it was in 1936. One of these is the period when they are children, the other is the period when they are old; poverty in this later period has been diminished a good deal since the social surveys were made by the grant of better old-age pensions. There is a third period of want which occurs very frequently, namely, among young married people with dependent families.

That is the problem with which I was faced and for which I have recommended a system of children's allowances. I may remind you that my actual proposal is that there should be an allowance for each child after the first at the average rate of 8s. per week, in addition to the existing provision in the way of school meals and so on, which is taken as of the value of 1s. a week, giving 9s. as the assumed cost, on the average, of children from 0 to 14. Of course, the cost is much less for the younger and more for the older ones. This cash allowance of 8s., plus 1s. by way of what is given already, should be provided by taxation.

I may say that about the last thing I heard in the House of Commons just before I came away was Sir John Anderson's announcement that the Government proposed to give children's allowances, beginning with the second child, but that they thought that the services now provided might be regarded as equivalent in money value to 2s. 6d. a head as against the 1s. assumed by me, and that the rate of children's allowances should be fixed at 5s. for the second and other children instead of the 8s. recommended by me. That makes only 7s. 6d. as compared with 9s., but it is a forward step of great importance in dealing with this problem. That is what Sir John Anderson has announced, and one may assume that children's allowances in one form or other will become part of our social and economic structure, and will do so essentially on economic grounds, as a means of dealing with want.

Effects on numbers and quality of population

That makes it all the more important to consider what is likely to be the biological effect of such a change in our economic and social structure. What will be its effect on the number of the population and on the quality of the breeding?

On the first point, as to the number of the population, I have very little to say here to-day. It is not essentially an eugenic question. I will only say, as I have said in my Report, that I do not imagine that there will be much direct effect from children's allowances on the number of children born. Nobody is going to have children in these days as a profit-making business, if he or she does not want them otherwise; in any case 8s. a week is not a profit, it merely neutralizes the extra cost of the child. But I do think that children's allowances will have some effect on the number of the population. There are certainly some parents who have already one or two children and would like to have more, but have been deterred hitherto by fear of damaging the prospects of their children already born. Children's allowances will make it easier for such parents to have additional children. But making a large change in the birth rate will depend not on children's allowances but on the formation of public opinion.

What I am concerned with to-day is the eugenic question, the effect of family allowances on the quality of the population. The thought of that makes me very much alarmed indeed to come among you, partly because I come wholly unprepared, and partly because, at one time at any rate, your *Society* condemned in rather strong terms just exactly what I have proposed to the Government.

Professor Fisher had the kindness to send me a paper which he read to this *Society* in 1932, in which he said that a proposal to give 5s. for each child through the post office, whether the parent was employed or unemployed, could be received with little enthusiasm on eugenic grounds. In another paper I think he referred to a statement of eugenic policy which this *Society* got out in 1928 or 1929, saying that the *Society* was strongly opposed to redistribution of income by means of taxation or to allowances being made a charge on the State. Well, children's allowances such as I have proposed, and such as to some extent the Government has accepted, are a charge on the State and a means of redistributing income by means of taxation, as between those with family responsibility and those without it.

What I am here to find out, among other things, is whether people who are interested in eugenics would take the same rather critical view of the actual proposal which I put forward and which has been accepted by the Government to-day, of something like a flat subsistence allowance for children, as expressed in those statements which I have read. I rather hope they will not take a critical view, and I am fortified in that hope by something else I read by Professor Fisher, in which he discussed the possible eugenic effects of a system of family allowances, as a means of correcting the main dysgenic factor in our society to-day, namely, the inverted birth rate.

Economic versus *biological success*

As you all know – as everybody really knows although they do not always realize how much it means – there is in Britain to-day an inverted birth rate, in the sense that the poorer and less successful sections of the community, generally speaking, are more prolific than the more prosperous and successful sections of the community. That, of course, is not confined to Britain. I think Professor Fisher points out that it is found in every civilized country wherever the data have been examined, and it is not, of course, confined to the contrast between the wealthy and the poor. The inversion of the birth rate extends right through the social scale. The data derived from our census of 1911 show that bricklayers' labourers, for example, have more children than bricklayers; that agricultural labourers have more children than agricultural foremen. All the way up the scale you get fewer and fewer children. If you group together – I think Professor Fisher gives this figure – all the people of a social status equal or superior to a railway booking clerk you will find that they have a birth rate just about half that of the population as a whole, which means that they are replacing themselves to the extent of only 40 per cent, while the population as a whole is replacing itself to the extent of 80 per cent. One need not use many words to suggest that that is an unsatisfactory state of affairs. It is summed up again by Professor Fisher when he says that it means that economic success implies biological failure, that in the struggle for existence, which is essentially dependent upon the birth rate, the man most likely to be selected as the ancestor of future generations is he who has been least successful in getting either admiration or rewards in this generation. Biological and economic tendencies are in conflict. The position is a bad one and not one to be contemplated with contentment. But if one is asked how it is to be remedied, the first and most sensible thing is to find out what is the cause of this state of affairs. There is an interesting division of opinion as to the reason why in Great Britain and other civilized societies economic success means biological failure, or, if it may be put the other way, biological failure means economic success. The phenomenon has two sides, and raises, therefore, the question as to which of the two sides is cause and which is consequence. Does success lead to infertility? Do people tend to have relatively fewer children because they are rich, or is it the other way round, that infertility is the cause of economic success?

The common-sense view, of course, is the former ; that wealth itself, or being successful in life, or being well-educated, taking a university degree, and so on, causes people to have less children, either because they do not want them or because there is some connection between intellectual ability and infertility. Most of you who have read Professor Fisher's work know that he takes the exactly contrary view, that it is the biological failure which leads to economic success, because to belong to a small family – that is, to belong to an infertile stock – gives one the best chance of social promotion to a position above that to which one was born. It is quite obvious that that does happen. Consider the case of the labourer with six children and the labourer, with the same income, with one child. The one child has a far better chance of being allowed to stay at school and take higher education than any of the children in the six-children family, because the first of those six children will have to go out and earn at the earliest possible moment and the others will be in want at some time or other during their childhood.

That is the argument of Professor Fisher, which, of course, he deduces from the founder of this *Society,* Francis Galton. Biological failure is the cause of social promotion, and not the other way round. People just because they come of small families rise in the social scale along with those who rise through their ability and service, and as people tend to marry in their own social class, infertility tends to breed ability out of the race.

The classical illustration of that is found in Galton's study in which he pointed out how the able men who rose to eminence – judges, statesmen, soldiers, and others – having founded peerages, all thought they must marry a heiress, or have their sons to marry a heiress in order to maintain the peerage, and the heiress – not necessarily but more often than not – came of an infertile stock. Galton speaks of the "destroying influence of heiress blood." He even went so far as to say that the rate at which peerages became extinct varied according to the higher or lower scale in the peerage; that dukedoms were more deeply infested with heiress blood than earldoms, and earldoms more than baronies. With each step in the peerage a fresh heiress was brought in; she brought money, but she destroyed the race.

The inverted birth rate is an established fact. The theory to explain it has, of course, two sides. It has a positive side, that the fact that infertility causes social promotion must inevitably mean that the higher social classes are less fertile. The other, the negative side, is that there is no other cause of this lower fertility of the higher social classes.

I have some doubts myself as to the negative side. I do not feel that the evidence which Professor Fisher gives for that view is as decisive as the rest of his evidence, and it is not easy to believe that there has been enough time for selection, working by itself, to produce those enormous differences between the relative fertility of different classes. After all, natural selection is a relatively slow process. When the chance of secondary education is accorded to the poorest class, the boy with the best chance of secondary education is the boy from the small family; but secondary education is a modern development, and there have not been enough generations for selection to produce the result which you see. Therefore I am inclined to think that probably there is also a reverse action; that economic or social success, rising in life, for one reason or another has also a direct effect in causing people to have fewer children than otherwise they would have. Not only is infertility the cause of social promotion, but social promotion in turn causes infertility.

Social promotion of the infertile

But whether I am right or wrong in doubting the negative side of the theory, I do not myself see that one can reject the positive side, namely, that so long as a premium is placed upon belonging to a small family, so long as in every class the child of the small family has an economic advantage over the child of a large family, forces are set in motion which bring about the social promotion of the infertile. At the same time rendering special service also leads to social promotion, putting people up into a higher place on account of ability. Ability and infertility rise together and infertility tends to kill ability out of the race. As a layman in these matters, I am inclined to accept that argument as a positive explanation, not necessarily of the whole but of a substantial part of the inverted birth rate.

I want to refer at this point to the figures which I gave you at the beginning, of the severity of the pressure from poverty on children: that about half the population passed through actual physical want at some time in their lives, and that 40 per cent of all want is that of children. This means that the difference between life in a small and life in a large family in the lower economic groups of the community is very great indeed. It means that the child of the small family may never have been in want throughout his life, while of the children of large families in this country only a very small proportion can have avoided being in actual physical want during their childhood, or can have avoided the necessity of going out to earn money at the earliest possible moment. A very large proportion of all the children in this country come from the large families, and therefore have passed through this period of want.

The social promotion of the unfertile, therefore, tends to breed out ability from the race. Professor Fisher introduces the biological argument for children's allowances by pointing out the fact that if you give subsistence allowances for children you equalize the conditions as between large and small families and therefore remove the present premium on infertility. The child of the poor man who has six children has in that event just as good a chance of living as the single child of the poor man. The premium on infertility is removed.

Eugenic consequences and limitations of proposed allowances

Accepting that, as one is entitled to do from Professor Fisher's argument, I would suggest that the proposal I put forward in my

Report so far as it goes is good and not bad eugenically. I think it is good eugenically for the reason that it will diminish the premium on infertility and so diminish the social promotion of infertility and for a second reason, that in so far as it adds to the number of births at all, it can only do so by influencing parents who take some thought over the begetting of their children. You cannot influence people, whether by money or anything else, who take no thought at all. People who have no thought for the size of their families will not be affected by children's allowances. The people who will be affected are the parents who have certain social virtues, who want children and will take care in bringing them up. For that reason also children's allowances, so far as they go, should have a eugenic effect.

But the children's allowances on this basis which I proposed – 8s. a week, in addition to what is given in kind, for each child – do not go far enough from the eugenic point of view. They will equalize the conditions between the large and the small family in the very poorest families, but only in the very poorest families. They will not do so for any family which is above the subsistence level. Of course, it is pretty certain that the actual expenditure on each child rises with the income of the parent. It does not rise strictly in proportion; but there is no doubt that the parent with an income of £500 a year is apt to find each child a larger expense than the parent with an income of £100 a year. The cost of children rises with the family income. What people think they should spend, and in fact do spend, on each child rises with the earnings. Thus, wherever you have a child according to the common standard costing more than subsistence, a child's allowance based on subsistence does not equalize, conditions between the large and the small family, does not remove the premium on infertility, and does not check the social promotion of the infertile.

Supplements to Government scheme

That leads to the suggestion that a system of subsistence allowances for children such as I propose in order to abolish want, needs, from the eugenic point of view, to be supplemented in two ways. First I should like to see it supplemented by occupational schemes of allowances in the various occupations which are open to ability and which have an entrance test of ability. Such occupations include teaching of all kinds, in universities and schools, the civil service, local government service, law, medicine, accountancy, and others.

One general thing which I would say about an educational scheme of children's allowances is that the cost would not have to be borne by general taxation – for you cannot tax the general taxpayer for the benefit of members of a particular profession. Every profession would have to deal with the children's allowances for its own members. At the London School of Economics, with the very important help of the late Lord Stamp, I did introduce a system of children's allowances on a very much larger scale, namely, £30 a year for every child up to the age of 8, and £60 a year for every child from 8 to 21, for as long as the child was being educated; that was paid by the School as an addition to the standard salary. The exact nature of these occupational schemes would depend upon the occupation. There is a good deal to be said for applying to children's allowances the principle of the superannuation scheme in the case of university staffs, in which deductions are made proportionately to income from everybody's salary and something is added by the employer. I do not see why that should be limited to providing for old age and should not be accepted as providing for posterity. Such a scheme would have the advantage of adjusting the allowance to the salary. Most occupational schemes probably should give allowances to some extent graded to income.

The second direction in which subsistence children's allowances should be supplemented is by the system of income-tax rebates. Many people have suggested that if you give subsistence children's allowances as I propose them, and as the Government say they are going to introduce them, you ought to abolish income-tax rebate. To me that proposal is both wrong and reactionary. The method by which you tax has nothing to do with children's allowances at all. On the contrary, I would like to see income-tax rebates for children maintained and even extended. They have one great advantage. The chances are that income-tax will fall upon a larger proportion of the total community after the war than in the past, and that means that if you get income-tax rebates for children you can get a scheme of children's allowances right down the social scale into groups of people like the skilled wage earners, where it is very important indeed to have them. I suspect that the greatest store of unused intellectual ability in the country is among the skilled wage earners. So many of these have been kept where they are by their relatively high fertility. The more easy you make it for them to rise now into the frigid unfertile atmosphere of the social classes above them, the more you are going to breed out that ability. I do not want people to rise out of that class by infertility. Instead of a policy of diminution of income-tax rebates for children, I should like to see the maintenance or even extension of them.

I am sure you will not think that I have any impression that intellectual ability is now confined to a small section of the community. It is not. Of course, you find more of it in occupations which have been selected for it; but you find people of above the average intellectual ability in all sections of the community, and quite a substantial number of them. That is because they have not been socially promoted. But we are now busily engaged in looking for ability and sending it up the educational ladder. If you are continually looking for ability and sending it up the educational ladder and, on the other hand, by your salary and wage system are putting a premium on infertility and sending that up also to mate with ability, you are strengthening the tendency to the inverted birth rate, and helping infertility to kill out the ability. Everything we can do to give greater equality of opportunity as between different classes of the community emphasizes the importance of giving greater equality of opportunity as between the large and the small family.

I have confessed my own doubt as to the negative side of Professor Fisher's argument. If, contrary to what he said, the lower fertility of the wealthy class is due, to some extent, not to selection, but to the fact that they are wealthy or are educated, that still more strengthens the argument for what I may call super-allowances for children, for allowances above the subsistence level in these higher grades so as to remove as completely as possible the premium on infertility in these higher grades.

Criticisms of the proposals

I have already talked as long as I should. I want to conclude by looking at certain difficulties which will be put forward by the general public against my proposal that the community should concern itself with the future of its breed. First, I suggest that it is not in the least undemocratic to consider children's allowances as a means of neutralizing the premium on infertility and improving the quality of the race. The differential birth rate is not a difference simply between the rich and the poor. It extends throughout the social scale, and what I suggest as a reason for children's allowances is from many aspects extremely democratic. It is the acceptance of the democratic idea of equality of opportunity. You do not get equality of opportunity as between children of large and of small families so long as you have the cost of children wholly borne by the parents. You get instead inevitable inequality of opportunity according to the size of the family. Like most scientific arguments, this argument cuts across the ordinary political differences. In one sense it looks undemocratic to say that people are unequal and therefore you must favour those who have greater ability. On the other hand, it is democratic because it favours equality of opportunity for children whether they belong to large families or small. My argument is "left-wing" also in the sense that it is an argument against inheritance of wealth concentrated by infertility on heirs and heiresses.

A second objection certain to be taken is that any interference with human breeding is dictatorial and against the liberty of the subject. What I am proposing here is not that at all. It involves no interference with the liberty of individuals in choosing their mates or in rearing their children. All that I am suggesting is that one should use children's allowances to bring economic and biological tendencies into line with one another.

Finally, if one advocates children's allowances as a means of improving the breed, people will say: "But what will it do in this generation? "Well, it will not do anything in this generation, and probably not much in the next. It is not a question of to-day, but of 200 years hence. One of the things which we in this country like to do is to look back with pride upon our ancestors. As a nation we look back with pride on our ancestors of 200 or 300 years ago, and some can look back individually to ancestors of distinction. If we look back, I do not see why as a community we should not look forward 200 or 300 years and see that we ensure the best possible posterity. That depends on breeding not from the worse stocks, but from the better. That is worth doing and ought not to be regarded as anything fantastic or unreasonable. We ought to take thought not of to-day, nor perhaps of to-morrow, but of 100 or 200 years ahead. We have need to look forward as well as to look back.

I hope that what I have said will lead you to agree with my appeal that the biological argument should be regarded as reinforcing the economic argument for children's allowances. The actual proposal which I have made, with some modifications, seems likely to be accepted for a children's subsistence allowance for every family. That is good so far as it goes, but the next step, and an essential one on eugenic grounds, is to be sure that those allowances are supplemented in the two ways I have suggested, through income-tax rebates and through the development of schemes of occupational allowances, including occupations of all kinds – whether manual or intellectual – in which there is a test of ability.

Professor T. H. Marshall
Photograph courtesy of Mrs N Marshall

1953

Social Selection in the Welfare State[1]

T. H. Marshall, C.M.G., MA.[2]

Introduction by Professor Geoffrey Hawthorn

In 1944, the National Government promoted an Education Act to provide every child in England and Wales with a free secondary education according to its 'aptitude and ability'. T. H. Marshall was one of a number of British sociologists who were interested in the consequences of this. Aptitude and ability were assessed by what were thought of as 'intelligence tests' at the age of 10 or 11. On the basis of their performance in these, children were selected for an education of a more academic kind in grammar schools, or of a more technical kind in technical schools, or of a more general kind in 'modern' schools; in the event, few technical schools were provided, and selection was made for one or other of the remaining two. Most of the sociologists who were interested in the change were unequivocally committed to what came widely to be thought of as 'equality of opportunity'. They were discovering, to their dismay, that although a number of working-class children were indeed being selected for grammar school, this was not proportional to their number in the population; children from the middle class were doing disproportionately better.

Marshall, who was a progessive liberal, had years of experience in what was called 'adult education', and welcomed reform, shared both the commitment and the concern. He differed only in seeing more sharply than many that what purported to be selection by natural ability was in fact allocation by administrative convenience, and in his arguably more complex sensitivity to the paradoxes of equality itself. As he explained in this lecture, it was striking that the kinds of 'intelligence' the new tests purported to measure coincided

---

[1] The Galton Lecture delivered at a meeting of the Eugenics Society on February 18th, 1953. *The Eugenics Review*, **Vol. XVL**, 1953-54.

[2] Professor of Social Institutions in the University of London

with the kinds of school that the Act provided for. Selection was better seen as allocation. As he also explained, the other sociologists were discovering that although there had been a small degree of change since the Act came into force, the new allocations were correlating more with class than with any plausible distribution of ability, and that a surprisingly large number of middle- and working-class parents accepted that this should be so. Only in the middle of the class structure was there any marked quickening of ambition.

Moreover, in so far as there was any increase in equality through education, it was an increase in opportunities for individuals. But the 'welfare state' (Marshall did not altogether welcome the name, but it had come to stay) was intended also to strengthen community. The segregation of children at 11 into different schools would do nothing for this, and the old distinctions and divisions of the class structure would remain unchanged. It would be foolish, Marshall argued, to suppose that one could approach the matter from the other direction, assume that all children had the same aptitudes and abilities, and give them all the same education. (It would also be foolish, although he did not raise the question, to suppose that anything very fundamental would be changed by increasing the proportion of grammar school places, which continued to remain unequal between local authorities throughout the 1940s, 1950s and early 1960s.) But not all was hopeless. Children's achievements would continue to differ. That was unavoidable, and for what the country and the labour market demanded, which were not always the same thing, probably not desirable. But there was no good reason, as he put it, to accept 'rigid class divisions and … anything which favours the preservation or formation of sharply distinguished culture patterns at different social levels'.

In 1953, Marshall did not say how these might be overcome. One answer, which was already being canvassed by a few educationists, would be to refuse to select (or allocate) altogether and offer just one kind of secondary school for those who could not pay. This was the answer that a Labour government eventually arrived at. In 1965, local authorities were directed to replace grammar and 'modern' schools with those that were 'comprehensive'. It did not solve everything. In the more academic subjects, children were allocated within the new schools according to their perceived aptitudes and abilities, and disproprtionately more working-class childen continued to leave school altogether as soon as they could. These persisting difficulties were later compounded by the arrival of new cultures. The old discriminations and divisions of class remained, and were to be complicated by others. Later governments continued to strive to overcome them. They have tried to improve education in basic skills before 11, and have adjusted the qualifications that can be used to select young people for education after 15 and again after 18. They have also greatly extended the provision of tertiary education. If Marshall would have been the first to point out that the division between secondary and tertiary might become the new social divider, he would also have agreed many of the differences in pay and working conditions and so on that made the class structure itself what it was have been reducing, and that many distinctions of status have been fading. Yet it is still true, more than fifty years after his lecture, that the best single predictor of children's achievements in education and of their social destination is their parents' postcode. It may indeed be 'fortunate', as he said at the end of the lecture, 'that human affairs cannot be handled with perfect mechanical precision'. But aware as he was, much more so than most of his more unequivocally enthusiastic contemporaries, of the paradoxes and perversities of reform, he would certainly have agreed that there is always more to do.

The 1953 Galton Lecture: Social Selection in the Welfare State

IT is a great honour, which I highly appreciate, to be invited by the *Eugenics Society* to deliver the Galton Lecture, and it is an honour which may, I think, appropriately be bestowed upon a sociologist. But for a sociologist who, like myself, is ignorant of biology and genetics and unskilled in those statistical techniques, now so widely and expertly used in social surveys and psychological investigations, it is also an embarrassment. What subject should I choose? I pondered over this for some time before I felt sure I could accept the invitation. Social selection seemed to be the most promising general field, but I knew it was one in which I should have to walk warily. For I should find in it signposts pointing in directions in which I must on no account allow myself to travel – signposts bearing such words as "Nature and Nurture," "Fertility and Intelligence," or perhaps the mystic letters "g, F and k" pointing the way to certain shady paths in and around the garden commonly known as "I.Q."

So I devised a title, a rather elaborate one, which would keep me out of danger and also make it fairly clear what I intended to talk about. But it had two disadvantages. It was too long to get on to the cards and notices of the lecture, and it might have committed me in advance to a task which I should later find it impossible to execute. So I decided to seek refuge in brevity and obscurity, with the result that you have before you: "Social Selection in the Welfare State." This title gave me no pleasure, partly because "Welfare State" is a term for which I have developed a strong dislike, and partly because the subject indicated was obviously far too big for a lecture. But when I began to consider it more carefully, I found it was better than I had expected. I think it really does mean something, which is a great relief. But I shall have to spend a little time explaining what it is that I think it means.

There need be little ambiguity about "social selection." I take it to refer to the processes by which individuals are sifted, sorted and distributed into the various positions in the social system which can be distinguished one from another by their function, status, or place in the social hierarchy. I shall be considering, in this lecture, social selection through the educational system.

The Principles of the Welfare State

The Welfare State is a tougher proposition, because it would be difficult to find any definition acceptable both to its friends and to its enemies – or even to all its friends. Fortunately I needn't try to define it ; I have only to explain what are the characteristics of the Welfare State which seem to me to provide a distinctive setting to the problem of social selection. I take the most relevant aspects of the Welfare State, in this context, to be the following.

First, its intense individualism. The claim of the individual to welfare is sacred and irrefutable and partakes of the character of a natural right. It would, no doubt, figure in the new Declaration of the Rights of Man if the supporters of the Welfare State were minded to issue anything so pithily dramatic. It would replace property in those early French and American testaments which speak of life, liberty and property; this trinity now becomes life, liberty and welfare. It is to be found among the Four Freedoms in the guise of "Freedom from Want" – but that is too negative a version. The welfare of the Welfare State is more positive and has more substance.   It was lurking in the Declaration of Independence, which listed the inalienable rights of man as "Life, Liberty and the Pursuit of Happiness." Happiness is a positive concept closely related to welfare, but the citizen of the Welfare State does not merely have the right to pursue welfare ; he has the right to receive it, even if the pursuit has not been particularly hot. And so we promise to each child an education suited to its individual qualities, we try to make the punishment (or treatment) fit the individual criminal rather than the crime, we hold that in all but the simplest of the social services individual case study and family case work should precede and accompany the giving of advice or assistance, and we uphold the principle of equal opportunity, which is perhaps the most completely individualistic of all.

But if we put individualism first, we must put collectivism second.   The Welfare State is the responsible promoter and guardian of the welfare of the whole community; which is something more complex than the sum total of the welfare of all its individual members arrived at by simple addition.   The claims of the individual must always be defined and limited so as to fit into the complex and balanced pattern of the welfare of the community, and that is why the right to welfare can never have the full stature of a natural right.   The harmonizing of individual rights with the common good is a problem which faces all human societies.

In trying to solve it, the Welfare State must choose means which are in harmony with its principles.   It believes in planning – not of everything but over a wide area.   It must therefore clearly formulate its objectives and carefully select its methods with a full sense of its power and its responsibility.   It believes in equality, and its plans must therefore start from the assumption that every person is potentially a candidate for every position in society.   This complicates matters; it is easier to cope with things if society is divided into a number of non-competing social classes.   It believes in personal liberty because, as I choose to define it, it is a democratic form of society.   So although, of course, like all States, it uses some compulsion, it must rely on individual choice and motivation for the fulfilment of its purposes in all their details.

How do these principles apply to selection through the educational system? The general social good, in this context, requires a balanced supply of persons with different skills and aptitudes who have been so trained as to maximize the contribution they can make to the common welfare. We have, in recent years, seen the Welfare State estimating the need for natural scientists, social scientists and technicians, for doctors, teachers and nurses, and then trying to stimulate the educational system to produce what is required. It must also be careful to see that the national resources are used economically and to the best advantage, that there is no waste of individual capacities, by denying them the chance of development and use, and no waste of money and effort, by giving education and training to those who cannot get enough out of them to justify the cost.

On the other side, the side of individualism, is the right of each child to receive an education suited to its character and abilities. It is peculiar, in that the child cannot exercise the right for itself, because it is not expected to know what its character and abilities are. Nor can its parents wholly represent its interests, because they cannot be certain of knowing either. But they have a rather ambiguous right at least to have their wishes considered, and in some circumstances to have them granted. The status of parental rights in the English educational system is somewhat obscure at the moment. There is no reason to assume that the independent operation of the two principles, of individual rights and general social needs, would lead to the same results. The State has the responsibility of harmonizing the one with the other.

So far I have merely been trying to explain the general meaning which I have discovered in the title of this lecture. As I have already said, I shall first limit this broad field by concentrating on selection through the educational system. I shall then limit it further to the two following aspects of the problem. I shall look first at the selection of children for secondary education and try to see what is involved in bringing it into harmony with the principles of the Welfare State. I choose this particular point in the selection process partly because of its intrinsic and often decisive importance, and partly because so much has recently been written about it. I shall look in the second place rather at the social structure and consider how far it is possible to achieve the aims of the Welfare State in this field – particularly the aim of equal opportunity – in a society in which there still exists considerable inequality of wealth and social status. In doing this I shall be able to draw on some of the still unpublished results of researches carried out at the London School of Economics over the past four years, chiefly with the aid of a generous grant from the Nuffield Foundation.

Selection for Secondary Schools

We are all, I expect, aware that for some time past educationists (both teachers and administrators), and psychologists and statisticians (I sometimes find it hard to distinguish the one from the other) have been hurling themselves at the problem of selection for secondary schools with a determination and a ferocity of purpose which are positively terrifying. A good general survey of the campaign can, I think, be extracted from four sources. There is first the Report of the Scottish Council for Research in Education on *Selection for Secondary Education,* presented by William McClelland in 1942. This is an impressive document which might be described as a bold and challenging advance by the forces of pure science and exact measurement. It was met and held in check by a counter attack delivered by the National Union of Teachers in its Report on *Transfer from Primary to Secondary Schools,* published in 1949. Meanwhile there had opened, in June 1947, a friendly contest conducted under strict tournament rules in the *British Journal of Educational Psychology,* in the form of the "Symposium on the Selection of Pupils for Different Types of Secondary Schools," which continued until February 1950. It was richly informative, and contained a little bit of everything. Finally we have the two Interim Reports of the Committee of the National Foundation of Educational Research on *The Allocation of Primary School Leavers to Courses of Secondary Education,* published in 1950 and 1952. It is too soon to say exactly what position this new detachment will take up on the battlefield, but the wording of its title is highly significant when compared with that of the Symposium. "Selection" has been replaced by "allocation" and "types of secondary school" by "courses of secondary education."

The first point to note is that, in this matter of selection for secondary education, the State is in full command of the whole situation. It provides the primary schools which prepare children for the examination, it designs the secondary school system for which they are being selected, and therefore determines the categories into which they are to be sorted, and it invents and administers the tests. Such power is dangerous. It is easy in these circumstances to make sure that one will find what one is looking for, and it is, no doubt, gratifying to discover that one's artistic masterpiece has been faithfully copied by Nature. I find it unfortunate that, just as there are three main types of secondary school, so there are three types of ability with which educational psychologists juggle – g or general, F or technical and k or spatial. I am afraid people may come to regard this as evidence of collusion, when in fact, of course, the two trinities do not correspond.

The second point to note is that the principles of the 1944 Act, which I take to be the principles of the Welfare State, have not yet been put into effect. The Act, according to the N.U.T. Report, "has given the problem of transference from the primary to the secondary school an entirely new form," which necessitates a thorough reassessment of our old methods of selection (p. 16). The profound change referred to is that from competitive selection of a few for higher things to allocation of all to suitable schools, or, as Kenneth Lindsay phrased it nearly twenty years before the Act, from "selection by elimination" to "selection by differentiation."[3] When allocation is working fully, says the NUT., "the situation ought not to arise in which it is impossible to send a child to the school most suited to his needs because there is no place available for him in a school of this kind" (p. 20). We are still a long way from this, and for the time being the sole certain indication for a

---

[3] *Social Progress and Educational Waste*, p. 28.

modern school is unsuitability for a grammar or technical school" (p. 18).

I see danger lurking here too. If too long a time passes during which an ideal cannot be realized, it may become unrealizable – a myth, as it were, which has lost contact with the world of experience, and which has never been through the testing which must lie between the blueprint and the finished machine. There is a danger, too, that we may imagine we are preparing the instruments for use in the new operation when in fact we are only perfecting those which are suited for use in the old. In the first interim Report of the National Foundation there occurs the sentence: "It is the procedure of competitive entry to grammar schools that has been responsible for the undue importance which has been attached to objective tests and to external examinations" (p. 62). Note "external examinations," for there is some thing pretty fundamental there.

But the principle of allocation is not a new idea. It was implicit in the Act of 1918 which stated that sufficient provision must he made to ensure that no children are "debarred from receiving the benefits of any form of education by which they are capable of profiting through inability to pay fees," and it has been steadily developing since that date. And the importance attached to objective tests and external examinations is not an old phenomenon which happens to have survived into the new age. It has grown side by side with the growth of the idea of allocation, and continued to grow after the passing of the 1944 Act.

The movement in the field of ideas towards allocation instead of selection, and the movement in time field of practice towards uniform general standardized testing have been contemporaneous. I think, too, that any reader of the Symposium must he struck by the intense interest shown in the possibility of devising objective tests accurate enough to be used for allocation on the basis of special aptitudes, as well as for selection on the basis of general ability. There are, of course, signs of movement in other directions among education authorities, such as the greater use made of cumulative school records and so on; and, as regards the Symposium, it must not he overlooked that Sir Cyril Burt opened boldly with the statement that the problem was administrative rather than psychological."[4] This sounded very much like the old-fashioned rebuking the new-fangled, and no doubt some psychologists thought that he was letting the side down.

In all this I seem to see evidence of a clash between what I earlier referred to as the collectivist and individualist elements in the Welfare State. Allocation, interpreted along N.U.T. lines, represents unqualified individualism. The right of each child to receive the education best suited to its unique individual needs should not be inhibited by reference to the cost of providing the necessary schools and teachers nor to the demand in society at large for particular numbers of persons educated and trained in particular ways. But to the collectivist principle these limiting factors arise from rights of the community as a whole, which the Welfare State cannot ignore. And they may favour a provision of grammar school places which is less than the provision needed to accommodate all who could benefit from a grammar school education. As long as this happens, competitive selection will remain with us. How long that will be, I do not propose to guess. But, when selection is competitive, the authorities must reach a decision somehow, using the best means at their disposal. And they must be able to enforce the decision negatively (that is to say, the decision not to admit) against the wishes of the parent. When faced with the necessity of filling the last five places in a grammar school from twenty applicants, all backed by ambitious and determined parents, you may feel that the best means of selection are either to follow the mark order or to toss up. The public may prefer you to follow the marks, even though you know that in this border zone the verdict of the marks has no real validity. So the use of imperfect selection methods can be justified by the inadequacy of the educational system, as judged by the ideal of allocation.

But in my view, if allocation replaced selection, then no amount of improvement would make the tests sufficiently exact to carry the weight of decisions enforceable against parental wishes. For the

---

[4] Loc. cit., June 1947, p. 57.

question to be answered in each case would not be : "Is this child better suited to a grammar school than the other applicants? If so, we must tell the others we are full up." But : "What, as judged by absolute standards and without reference to competing claims, is the education best suited to this child's needs?" I feel convinced that, in the majority of cases, questions in this form will remain unanswerable by tests and examinations – unanswerable, that is, with the degree of assurance necessary before the answer can be made the basis of administrative action. So we should find, I think, that instead of allocation in the sense of the definitive assignment of each child to an appropriate school or course, we should have something more like an advisory service which left the responsibility of decision to the parents. And that, I understand, is what happens now in so far as the principle of allocation already enters into our system. And in support of the view that it *should* be so, I can quote, from the Symposium, Mr. Dempster of Southampton, who writes: "The wishes of the parents are possibly the best guide at present available to selectors in deciding between grammar and technical school education."[5]

This sounds in many ways a very attractive prospect, though we ought to know a little more about how parental wishes work before we acclaim it, and I shall have something to say on that later. But I fancy it conflicts with another aspect of the collectivist element in the Welfare State. The principle I have in mind is the one which says that all should be judged by the same procedure, as impartially and impersonally as possible, that favouritism and privilege must be eradicated, and also the effects of differing social environments on the critical turning-points in life. So far so good. The principle must be allowed to have full weight. There is one obvious point at which it favours objective tests. Because children come to their examination at 11+ from schools and neighbourhoods of very different quality, they cannot be judged by their attainments only; an attempt must be made to discover natural abilities which may have been frustrated by circumstances but may still be able to come to fruition if given a fair chance. But latent capacities are

---

[5] *Loc. cit.*, November 1948, p. 130.

concealed, and something more scientific than a teacher's judgment or a school record is needed to reveal them.

But the collectivist principle goes farther, and sometimes assumes shapes which are more open to question. The doctrine of fair shares and equal opportunity sounds admirable, but it may become so distorted as to merit the cynical comment that fair shares means "if we can't all have it, nobody shall," and that equal opportunity means "we must all have an equal chance of showing that we are all equally clever." And the present situation may encourage this type of distortion, if it leads us to regard competitive selection as a necessary evil. If the Welfare State is to bring its two principles into harmony, it must conceive of the basic equality of all as human beings and fellow-citizens in a way which leaves room for the recognition that all are not equally gifted nor capable of rendering equally valuable services to the community, that equal opportunity means an equal chance to reveal differences some of which are superiorities, and that these differences need for their development different types of education, some of which may legitimately be regarded as higher than others. The notion, therefore, that selection, even competitive selection, can be eliminated from our educational system seems to me to be a pipe-dream and not even a Utopian one.

Obstacles to Equal Opportunity

I will defer making any general comment until I have considered my second question, to which I now turn. This relates to another dilemma or antithesis inherent in the principles and structure of the Welfare State. It is the problem of establishing equal opportunity without abolishing social and economic inequality. I say this is inherent in the nature of the Welfare State because it is my opinion – which I do not propose to argue here – that the Welfare State, as we know it, must necessarily preserve a measure of economic inequality. This problem, therefore, is a permanent and not a transitory one.

One of the most striking passages in Kenneth Lindsay's well-known and far sighted study of this question in the inter-war period is the quotation from Lord Birkenhead which runs: "There is now a complete ladder from the elementary school to the university, and the number of scholarships from the elementary to the secondary school is not limited, awards being made to all children who show capacity to profit."[6] This fantastic illusion was blown sky-high by Lindsay's book, and later studies showed that equality of educational opportunity was still a distant ideal at the outbreak of World War II. The research carried out at L.S.E. during the past four years, to which I have already referred, has drawn in more firmly the outlines of the picture and added some details. We can see pretty clearly what the situation was when the Welfare State took over and what were the obstacles it had to overcome.

This research included a 10,000 sample survey of persons aged 18 and over in Great Britain in 1949. Mobility was examined on the basis of the seven-point scale of occupational status, widely known as the Hall Jones scale, which had been prepared for this study. Groups 1 and 2 include the professional and managerial occupations, and groups 3 and 4 the supervisory and clerical – to give a rough idea of their character. Together they comprised about 30 per cent. of the sample which can be called the middle-class section (the upper class is too small to appear in a sample of this size). Group 5, including routine non-manual and skilled manual jobs, was a very large one comprising 40 per cent, while groups 6 and 7, semi-skilled and unskilled manual, provided approximately another 30 per cent. Of the general picture I will say little; I would rather wait for the papers to be published with full statistical tables. But one or two points may be noted. We find that the social forces holding a son to the occupational group of his father are significantly strongest in groups 1 and 2 and weakest in group 5. We can summarize crudely by saying that money and influence count for most at the top, and life's chances lie most widely open, for good or ill, in the melting-pot in the middle of the scale. This is interesting, because it is at this middle point in the scale that we might expect to find many families ambitious for their children's future and ready to forgo their earnings while they get

---

[6] *Op. Cit.*, p. 9

secondary and further education, but not in a position to pay fees. It is precisely among such families that the building of an educational ladder is likely to have the greatest effect.

The second point of relevance in the general picture is that the returns show what to many may be a surprising amount of downward movement. There is a common saying, which in the United States has had the force of a political dogma, that "there is plenty of room at the top." And one remembers benevolent members of the upper layers of society who have strongly advocated the building of a social and educational ladder under the impression, apparently, that it could carry one-way traffic only, and that the ascent of the deserving from below would not have to be accompanied by a descent on the part of any of their own children to make room for the newcomers. But, if we take all the male subjects in time sample, we find that 35.2 per cent had the same occupational status as their father, 29.3 per cent had risen and 35.5 per cent had fallen. These figures probably exaggerate the falls because they include the young men in the sample who had not yet reached their final occupational level, and, of course, they tell us nothing of the distance risen or fallen, which is an important factor. The believers in one-way traffic thought that upper- and middle-class jobs were increasing faster than jobs in general, while upper- and middle-class families were producing fewer children than families in general. But it seems clear, and the 1951 census sample confirms this, that this was true, as regards middle-class jobs in general, only of women's employment. The proportion of occupied men in such jobs showed no significant increase from 1911 to 1951, while the proportion of occupied women in such jobs rose approximately from 24.5 per cent to 45.5 per cent. There was some increase in clerical jobs for men, but even here the spectacular advance was in the employment of women. In 1947, to quote one illustrative case, of those leaving secondary grammar schools at the age of 16 to go straight into jobs, just about 43 per cent of the boys went into the "clerical and professional" category and of the girls 68 per cent, or, if nursing is included, nearly 77 per cent. Since there was an expansion of grammar schools during this period, and since grammar schools were largely an avenue to middle-class jobs, these facts are interesting. There may have been many boys who hitched their wagon to a white collar without realizing that their most serious competitors were their own sisters.

The educational data in the survey confirm and extend the picture presented in 1926 by Kenneth Lindsay. The most interesting general lesson to be drawn is that it is harder than one might suppose to ensure that the new opportunities created go to the people for whom they are intended, provided the fundamental principles of a free democracy are preserved. The survey covered the period of the introduction and expansion of the Free Place system in secondary schools, and its successor, the Special Place system, and it is possible to compare the experience of the first wave of entrants following the Act of 1902 (those born from 1890 to 1899) with the last prewar wave (those born from 1920 to 1929). In the period covered by this comparison the percentage of boys in families belonging to the top three occupational groups who went to grammar schools rose from 38.4 to 45.7, and the corresponding figures for group 5 (the skilled manual and routine non-manual workers) are 4.1 and 10.7. The percentage increase for the working-class group is much greater than for time middle-class group, but the inequality that remains is enormous. And it is still greater if one includes boarding schools. The reason for this was not only that the total provision was insufficient, but also that a considerable part of the benefit went to the middle classes. It is true that the proportion of children in grammar schools who are occupying free places increases as you go down the social scale. But the proportion of the whole company of children of an occupational group who hold free places in grammar schools is highest at the top, 13.2 per cent in status groups 1 and 2 (upper middle class) and per cent in group 5 (upper working class). I have picked these pieces of information from the analysis which Mrs. Floud has made of this part of the survey and which contains many more points of equal interest.

My point is this. It may look at first sight as if the bourgeoisie had, as usual, filched what should have gone to the workers. But, in the circumstances, that was bound to happen in a free democracy and is bound to go on happening in the Welfare State.

For the Welfare State is not the dictatorship of the proletariat and is not pledged to liquidate the bourgeoisie. Of course more and more middle-class families made use of the public elementary schools as the quality of these improved, and of course more and more of them competed for admission to secondary schools through free and special places. And since the children were backed by a better educational tradition and stronger parental support, because more of their families could afford to forgo the earnings of the children, because they came from more comfortable homes, where it was easier to work, and from smaller families, they were certain to be more successful And when it came to deciding as to remission of fees for Special Places, many of the middle-class families had a genuine claim. Today, with the 100 per cent free place system in maintained schools, there can be no question of discriminating against middle-class families and the competitive advantages of social and economic status can operate without check. Other inquiries conducted at the L.S.E., either within or in close relation to the main project, have begun to throw some light on the nature and extent of these competitive advantages.[7]

That there is a greater preponderance of working-class children in the modern schools today and of middle-class children in the grammar schools is a fact which no one is likely to dispute. In an article in the March 1953 issue of the *British Journal of Sociology*, Messrs. Halsey and Gardner produce evidence to show that, in the London areas they studied, this uneven distribution could not be attributed solely to the intelligence of the children, but must be in large part the result of social forces. When, for instance, comparison was made of two groups with the same mean I.Q., one of which had been assigned to a grammar school and the other to a modern school, it was found that the middle classes were heavily over-represented and the working classes, especially the unskilled families, heavily under-represented in the grammar school group.

---

[7] The work has been done by Dr. Himmelweit, Mr. Martin and their associates. Since the information has been collected in intensive local studies it cannot be used for generalization of any kind as yet.

It is also interesting that of working-class children in grammar schools in the areas studied 63 per cent came from small families with one or two children and 37 per cent from larger families with three or more. Among working-class children in modern schools the proportions were almost exactly the reverse, and among middle-class children there was no significant relation between type of school and size of family. No known correlation between fertility and intelligence could possibly explain this, and it is clear that powerful social influences are at work. And they show themselves in other ways. A similar, though less marked, correlation with size of family appears when we ask how much thought parents give to their children's school career, how much interest they show in their work and progress, and how ambitious they feel about their future. Here, then, is a social factor causing what might be called "unfairness" in social selection about which the Welfare State can do very little. Positive action, by improving the physical conditions in poorer families and by stimulating greater interest and ambition among apathetic parents, can only be a very slow process. Family differences will continue to have their influence as long as the family is the basic cell in the social structure.

Social Ambition and Educational Achievement

The interest of parents may be shown by their giving thought to the matter of secondary schooling for their children. In one county area parents of children about to sit for the examination for secondary schools were asked whether they had thought a lot, a little, or not at all about the matter. The proportion claiming to have thought a lot declined steadily as one moved down the social scale and was little over a third among the unskilled workers. But the preference for a grammar school education, though it showed the same trend, did not fall so low. The lowest proportion preferring the grammar school was 43.4 per cent and the highest preferring the modern school 23.9 per cent – these figures being those for unskilled workers. But over two-thirds of the unskilled worker parents preferring the grammar school did not want their child to stay there after the age of 16. Their ambitions were limited. And about half the professional and a quarter of the clerical families said that if their child did not get a grammar school place they would not send it to a modern school.

The picture is slightly distressing. It suggests that those who care about education, and some who do not care much, almost automatically aspire to a grammar school for their children but the aspiration may vary from the desire of a steady job, with good prospects, to be entered at sixteen, to the hope of admission to a university and a professional career. There cannot be much homogeneity of purpose in a grammar school population. And, looking at the other side of the picture, we find a low opinion of the modern school which to many appears as a catastrophe and a disgrace. Talk of "parity of esteem" is a little premature.

Now these likes and dislikes owe something, no doubt, to real or supposed differences in the quality of education received in the different types of school. But I doubt whether most parents are following the advice of the N.U.T. to concentrate on the present educational needs of the child and not to think too much "what these needs may be at some later stage in his development."[8] They are thinking of what the school may lead to in the way of employment or further education, and perhaps of what it stands for in terms of social prestige. This last point is one on which it is extremely hard to get reliable information, since much of the mental process involved may be only semi-conscious. If social status is not offered by the questioner as a possible reason for aiming at a particular school or job, it is not likely to be put down spontaneously ; if it is offered, it may score a fair number of votes, but less than such job attributes as good prospects, security, and interesting work. Another cause of difficulty is the lack of uniformity in the use of class names. People differ widely in the way they classify themselves or typical occupations as middle or working class, and it is clear that the term lower middle class is becoming abhorrent. But, in spite of this, there is fairly close agreement as to the order in which jobs should be ranked, even though there is disagreement as to the social class to which they should he assigned.

---

[8] *Op. Cit.*, p. 20

The material dealing with job ambitions is too complicated to be briefly surveyed in an intelligible form. So I shall confine myself to two points. In a sample of adults in two urban areas who were asked what occupation they would like their son to enter, more than a fifth of the working-class subjects chose a profession and less than 8 per cent a clerical job; the commonest choice (about 36 per cent) was for a skilled trade. The figures are not complete, as a good many said their son must choose for himself. In the middle-class section of the sample, clerical jobs were even less popular, and the total vote for independent business was practically negligible. A similar dislike of the sound of clerical and office jobs was found by Dr. Jahoda among school leavers in Lancashire – that is to say, among the boys. The girls put office work at the top of the list. When boys were asked what jobs they most definitely rejected, office work was the one most often chosen, but half of those who named it did so because they did not think they were qualified for it.[9] It would be very rash to jump to conclusions from such fragmentary evidence, but it does seem possible that office work is losing its charm. It is often described as dull and monotonous, and perhaps the rise in wages for manual work and familiarity with conditions of full employment are robbing it of some of its other former attractions.

The second point of interest is the clear evidence, at present confined to one area, that working-class boys who get into grammar schools have very high expectations that they will rise in the world, while middle-class boys in modern schools are inclined to expect to fall below the position of their parents. No less than 63 per cent of the boys of lower working-class origin in grammar schools expected to rise at least two steps on a five-point status scale above their fathers; only 12 per cent of their comrades in the modern schools were equally ambitious. But, if we measure the rise by the boys' own estimate of it and not by objective standards, the percentage falls from 63 to 21. This inquiry was reported in Dr. Himmelweit's article in the *British Journal of Sociology*, June 1952. It suggests that the boys themselves feel that selection for

---

[9] *Occupational Psychology*, **26**, pp. 132-4.

secondary schooling has a decisive effect on future careers, and that boys from the humbler working-class families who get into grammar schools may overrate their chances without fully realizing how ambitious their success has made them. So long as this is the case, parity of esteem is hardly possible.

Effects of Social Distance

My last point relates to the possible effects of social distance on life in a grammar school. Grammar schools, one might say, have a tradition, an educational atmosphere, and contacts with the world outside which have for some time past belonged to the way of life of the middle classes. And the middle classes are over-represented in the school population, even though the skilled working-class families may supply the largest absolute numbers. If, then, we introduce boys and girls from outside this circle, can they fit in? Can they become sufficiently assimilated to enter into the life of the school and get out of it what it has to give, and yet retain enough of their identity to break down, in time course of time, any class barriers which exist, and thus make the way easier for their successors, and for the Welfare State? Much study is needed before this question can be fully answered. We have evidence to show that middle-class boys in grammar schools (in the area studied) do better on average in class examinations in pretty well all subjects than working-class boys, and that, when teachers are asked to rank the boys in their class in terms of such things as industry, responsibility, interest in school affairs, good behaviour, and popularity, the middle-class boys do definitely better than the rest. And working-class boys are inclined to care less about their marks and to take less part in general school activities, and yet, as we have seen, they expect great results from their grammar school status when the time comes for them to get a job. On the other hand may not a school have an assimilating influence and mould its members into a more homogeneous group than they were to start with, thus producing in reality the category of children which until then existed only in time imagination of the selectors? That is a question which points the way to a fascinating piece of research which has hardly yet been begun.

The Americans have similar problems today, and there is much evidence of status-consciousness in the high schools of the United States.   The book *Who Shall Be Educated?* by Lloyd Warner, Havighurst and Loeb (1946) is a revelation on this point. We hear a junior high-school principal say: "You generally find the children from the best families do the best work. The children from the lower class seem to be not as capable as the others," and on this the authors comment that "this correlation holds true. There is a strong relationship between social status and rank in school." A teacher then says that there is a lot of class feeling in the school, "Sections [i.e. streams] are supposed to be made up just on the basis of records in school but it isn't [*sic*] and every body knows it isn't. I know right in my own A section I have children who ought to be in B section, but they are little socialites and so they stay in A," and there is much more in the same strain (p. 73). But the problem there is allocation between streams or courses, rather than between schools.

It was on this general question that Sir Cyril Burt made one of his most challenging remarks. "A realistic policy," he wrote, must take frankly into consideration the fact that a child coming from this or that type of home may as a result he quite unsuited for a type of education, occupation or profession, which lies at an excessive social distance "from those of his parents and friends."[10] Whereupon Dr. Alexander descended on him like a ton of bricks, saying that no Authority could act on the view that "the present social circumstances of a child should be a criterion limiting his future opportunity."[11] Undoubtedly he is right. No Authority can act on the principle that social circumstances must limit educational opportunity, but in fact they do, and the accepted methods of educational selection cannot wholly prevent this. The remedy lies in the reduction of "social distance."

---

[10] *Loc. cit.*, June 1947, p.67.

[11] *Ibid.*, November 1947, p. 123

Conclusions

I must now try to sum up. The Welfare State, as I see it, is in danger of tying itself in knots in an attempt to do things which are self-contradictory. One example, I submit, is the proposal to assign children to different schools, largely on the basis of general ability, and then to pretend that the schools are all of equal status. If this means that we shall take equal trouble to make all schools as good as possible, treat all the children with equal respect and try to make them all equally happy, I heartily endorse the idea. But the notion of parity of esteem does not always stop there; and I feel it really is necessary to assert that some children are more able than others, that some forms of education are higher than others, and that some occupations demand qualities that are rarer than others and need longer and more skilled training to come to full maturity, and that they will therefore probably continue to enjoy higher social prestige.

I conclude that competitive selection through the educational system must remain with us to a considerable extent. The Welfare State is bound to pick the children of high ability for higher education and for higher jobs, and to do this with the interests of the community as well as the rights of the children in mind. But the more use it can at the same time make of allocation to courses suited to special tastes and abilities the better. It further seems to me that, for the purpose of selection on grounds of general ability, the objective tests are already accurate enough to do all that we should ever ask them to do, while, so far as "allocation" is concerned, they will never be able to give a decisive verdict in more than a minority of cases, although they can be of great value in helping to decide what advice to give.

So I agree with Sir Cyril Burt that the problem which now faces us is more administrative than psychological. There is less to be gained by trying to perfect the tests and examinations than by thinking how to shape the structure of our educational and employment systems. It is better to minimize the effects of our decisions in doubtful cases than to imagine that, if we only try hard enough, we can ensure that all our decisions in such cases are correct. The word "correct" has no meaning in this context; it is a bureaucratic fiction borrowed from the office where there is a correct file for every document.

By "minimize the effects of our decisions" I mean refrain from adding unnecessary and artificial consequences to acts whose real meaning and necessary consequences I have been urging that we should frankly recognize. A system of direction into distinct "types of secondary school" rather than "courses of secondary education" (to use the titles I quoted earlier) must, I think, intensify rather than minimize the consequences.   I am aware of the educational arguments on the other side, but do not intend to enter into a controversy for which I have no equipment.   The other point at which artificial consequences may be added is the point of passage from education to employment.   The snobbery of the educational label, certificate or degree when, as often, the prestige of the title bears little or no relation to the value of the content, is a pernicious thing against which I should like to wage a major war.

There is another matter on which the Welfare State can easily try to follow contradictory principles.   It relates to occupational prestige, social class and the distribution of power in society.   All I can do is to throw one or two raw ideas at your heads as a parting gift.

Although the Welfare State must, I believe, recognize some measure of economic inequality as legitimate and acceptable, its principles are opposed to rigid class divisions, and to anything which favours the preservation or formation of sharply distinguished culture patterns at different social levels.   The segregation when at school of those destined for different social levels is bound to have some effect of this kind and is acceptable only if there are irrefutable arguments on the other side.   Further a system which sorts children by general ability and then passes them through appropriate schools to appropriate grades of employment will intensify the homogeneity within each occupational status group and the differences between groups.   And, in so far as intelligence is hereditary and as educational chances are influenced by family background (and I have produced evidence to show that they are), the correlation between social class and type of school will become closer among the children.

Finally, the Welfare State, more than most forms of democracy, cannot tolerate a governing class. Leadership and power are exercised from many stations in life, by politicians, judges, ecclesiastics, businessmen, trade unionists, intellectuals and others. If these were all selected in childhood and groomed in the same stable, we should have what Raymond Aron calls the characteristic feature of a totalitarian society – a unified élite.[12] These leaders must really belong to and represent in a distinctive way the circles in and through which their power is exercised. We need politicians from all classes and occupational levels, and it is good that some captains of industry should have started life at the bench, and that trade unions should be led by genuine members, men of outstanding general ability who have climbed a ladder other than the educational one. It is important to preserve these other ladders, and it is fortunate that the selection net has some pretty big holes in it. It is fortunate too, perhaps, that human affairs cannot be handled with perfect mechanical precision, even in the Welfare State.

---

[12] *British Journal of Sociology*, March 1950, p. 10.

Sir Cyril Burt

Photograph courtesy of National Portrait Gallery, London

1955

The Meaning and Assessment of Intelligence[1]

Professor Sir Cyril Burt, D.Lit., Ll.D., D.Sc., F.B.A.

Introduction by David C. Watt

Cyril Burt (1883-1971) is among the most distinguished British psychologists. He came from a settled and caring family who supported him in gaining a place in Christ's Hospital school where he had a first class classical education (1895-1902) and won a scholarship to Jesus College, Oxford. His father was a doctor who moved with his family from London to live and become a country general practitioner in Snitterfield, a small village near Stratford-on-Avon. Among Dr Burt's patients was Francis Galton and his family at Claverton, close to Snitterfield, who became a friend and adviser of Cyril on whom he exercised a strong influence particularly in psychology and eugenics.

When Burt became a student at Oxford at the beginning of the twentieth century he was obliged to continue classical studies because it was for this purpose that he had won the scholarship to Christ's Hospital. The second year of this course allowed him to study philosophy, which included mental philosophy, the latter only on a strictly non-experimental basis. This was a continuation of the accepted scholarly branch of study of mental abilities in the philosophy curriculum. In Germany, however, about twenty years previously in Leipzig a faculty of Psychology and a psychology laboratory were instituted and a Professor appointed. There was at that time no opportunity for Burt to study experimental psychology, which was introduced to him particularly by Francis Galton, but later William McDougall – an enthusiast for experimental psychology, who borrowed a physiology laboratory for the purpose, collected a small group of students to work with him including Burt, for whom it brought to fruition the seed Galton had planted. In 1908 Burt was

---

[1] The Galton Lecture delivered on May 4th, 1955 and published in *The Eugenics Review*, Vol. XLVII, 1955-56.

awarded a John Locke scholarship which he used to travel to Germany and spend several months visiting the universities of Wurzburg, Frankfurt and Heidelberg which with Leipzig formed a centre of experimental psychological renown.

At the beginning of the twentieth century two ideas struggled to birth and then had a momentous influence comparable to that of Harvey's revealing discovery of blood circulation in the seventeenth century. The first was Darwin's demonstration from animals and plants of "the survival of the fittest" in the physical kingdom which was later applied to development of humans by Galton and as a social force by Herbert Spencer. The second was Mendelism which did not gain wide attention to its effect on the accepted rules of heredity until its rediscovery when it rapidly challenged the reigning precept of "like breeds like".

In 1908 Burt was appointed as an assistant lecturer in Physiology and Experimental Psychology in the Faculty of Science of Liverpool in Professor Sherrington's department for teaching educational and medical students. He later worked in a section of particular interest to him in a comprehensive survey of the population of Great Britain under the supervision of J. MacDougall. Publication of the results of this work appeared in 1911-12, the first showing correlations between tests on logic and apperception in school children which gave the highest correlation with general intelligence and the second measured difference in intelligence between the sexes which was found to be much smaller than was generally supposed.

In 1913 Burt took up the post of Psychologist for the London County Council Education Department for which he was very warmly commended by Professor Spearman of University College London and Professor Sherrington of Liverpool University. His work was a new venture in education but he had had considerable experience of testing children in schools in the course of his research in Liverpool. His responsibility to the L.C.C. however covered all the children in L.C.C. schools, particularly identifying mental defectives which 'assisted the detention of mental defectives enabled by the passing of the Mental Defective Deficiency Act 1915 which required specific evidence for certification to take place. Burt's appointment was half-time but in 16 months he was able to report the results of examining over 2000 children of whom about 600 were of subnormal intelligence and in 1917 he published 'The Distribution and Relation of Educational Abilities', hailed by the Chief Education Officer of London as the first of its kind in Europe or elsewhere'. In 1922 Burt took a half-time appointment with the

National Institute of Industrial Psychology as a senior investigator of vocational research for which he published with others the results of vocational research in 1926. This led to a year's more continuous studies in subsequent subjects with Burt retaining an advisory capacity. In 1924 he became a part-time Professor in Educational Psychology at the London Day Training College and in 1932 this was followed, in succession to Spearman, to the full-time Chair of Psychology at University College London in 1932, from which he retired in 1950 at the age of 67 years.

Along with his steady progress, increase in responsibility and authority in his subject of principal interest, general intelligence and other specific cognitive factors, Burt maintained a powerful interest in other cognate subjects; juvenile delinquency, eugenics, genetics, typology and evolution received concentrated interest issuing in research and influential publications. He was also at this time recognised as a leading figure in educational psychology in Britain with significant interests in other applications of psychology, as he had in the Eugenics Society in which he held influential office.

The 1955 Galton Lecture: The Meaning and Assessment of Intelligence

Current Criticisms

DURING the last two or three decades the use of intelligence tests has spread with a rapidity that would have seemed incredible fifty years ago. It is therefore not surprising that many people have begun to ask how far the evidence really justifies these widespread applications. Some of the more vigorous criticisms have come from psychologists themselves. Unfortunately, however, neither critics nor supporters seem to have a very clear notion of what intelligence implies or what are the limitations to which the tests in current use are subject.

Most of them apparently suppose that there is a distinct mental quality which every man of the world can recognize and identify as intelligence, but that no one can say precisely in what that quality consists. Dr. Blackburn, for example, declares (and probably many teachers and doctors would agree with him) that "we all have some idea of what we mean by 'intelligence'; it is when one comes to define it that the difficulties arise." Others, however, flatly deny that there is any such thing : the concept of "general intelligence," they say, was invented by a small group of statistical psychologists (Dr. Kirman mentions Pearson, Spearman and myself), who derived the idea from a mathematical analysis of test-data by a fallacious method of deduction that has since been exploded. Dr. Heim, in her recent book on *The Appraisal of Intelligence,* seeks to combine both these views. "The supporters of factor analysis," she writes, "treating their technique as an end in itself," have "taken a popular and relatively unambiguous word, and tried to restrict its meaning": they equate it with an abstract "factor".

When pressed to say in what this factor consists, every psychologist gives a different reply. And, she adds, during the last few years the statistical proofs on which the factorist has relied have been "publicly discussed and discredited".[2]

The Meaning of Intelligence

Now all these criticisms rest on a mass of confusions, and entirely overlook the true history of the subject. A mere glance at the relevant literature will quickly show that intelligence is not a conception "introduced by a small group of statistical psychologists." Nor is the term itself "a word of popular speech" whose meaning has recently been restricted and distorted by psychological specialists. It is, and always has been, a technical term introduced to designate a technical concept. And the concept itself has been reached and clarified by inquirers working along half a dozen different lines. Observational psychology, introspective psychology, experimental psychology, the speculations of the biologist, the theories of the neurologist, and finally the objective study of individual differences, each has contributed valuable

---

[2] J. Blackburn, *Psychology and the Social Pattern*, 1945, chap. V, "Intelligence and Ability"; B. Kirman, *This Matter of Mind*, 1952, pp. 67 f.; Dr. Heim, like many other critics, quoted the American symposium in which fourteen psychologists were asked to explain "what I conceive intelligence to be" (not, be it noted, to *define* the word), and gave "fourteen different replies" (*J. Educ. Psychol.*, 1921, **12**, pp. 123-147, 195-216). But this was a quarter of a century ago, when (owing largely to the war) very little research had been attempted.

evidence. The application of statistical methods has come only at the very end; their function has mainly been to decide between alternative explanations of certain observable facts, and so to clinch and confirm what had been provisionally inferred on far more concrete grounds.

May I therefore begin by briefly tracing the history of the concept?

1.   Observation and Introspection

The basic notion goes back to the days when the human mind first became the subject of philosophic curiosity. Plato, a shrewd observer of individuals, was, as Galton has so often reminded us, the first to recognize the social implications of mental heredity and to advocate something very like a eugenic policy.[3] His psychological disquisitions are incidental and sporadic; but they had a profound influence on later thought.

He draws a clear contrast between "nature' and "nurture" (φνσις and τροφή) ; and he then goes on to distinguish three "parts" of the soul – the "rational or intellectual (τὸ λογιστικὸν) having its seat in the brain, and appetite (ἐπιθνμία) and "spirit" (θνμός) located respectively in the belly and chest. This threefold distinction has often been compared with the modern distinction between "cognition," "affection," and "conation" – the intellectual, emotional, and moral elements in human behaviour. But none of these modern terms accurately expresses what Plato was trying to convey. In a famous passage *(Phaedrus*, 253D) he uses an analogy which gives a better notion of the difference: the first element he compares to the charioteer who holds the reins, and the others to a pair of horses who draw it : the former guides, the latter provide the power ; the former is the *cybernetic* element, the latter the *dynamic*.

---

[3] Cf. *Republic*, 435A f., 509C f.; and R. L. Nettleship, *Lectures on the Republic of Plato*, chap. XI.

The word εὐγένεια is actually used towards the end of the *Republic*, 618D.

And, says Plato, since men differ so widely in their innate characteristics, they should, from childhood upwards, be subjected to tests, so that each can be educated, and eventually employed as his native gifts require. The rulers are to be men pre-eminent for their intellectual capacity or "wisdom" – "men of gold rather than of silver, iron, or brass".

Thus, for Plato the natural inequality of man is itself one of the most profound and ill-recognized of all political problems. It threatened the democracy of Athens, and it threatens the democratic state today: it is the source at once of the injustice that we must seek to correct and of the justice or civic harmony that will enable us to correct it".[4] "Plato would have his citizens believe, "as though an oracle had foretold it, that the city will perish when men of iron or brass take over its control (*loc. cit.,* 415C) : or, as he puts it elsewhere, "the ship of state is bound to founder if the unruly crew, whose job it is to manage the sails, but who are in no way 'cybernetic' (i.e. good at finding and steering a course), selfishly seize the helm" *(loc. cit.,* 488B).

Aristotle's discussion is more methodical, and issues in a more systematic classification. Here for the first times we meet a clear distinction between actual process and mere capacity or "power"[5] (δύναμις). While lecturing I am actually talking; when asleep, I have the power to talk; when newborn, "with no language but a cry", I have the power to acquire the power to talk. The distinction is of course applicable in non-psychological fields as well as psychological: as applied to the latter it is the basis of our concept of mental capacity.

In what is virtually the first textbook of psychology Aristotle substitutes a twofold classification for Plato's threefold ; and his

---

[4] Walter Pater, *Plato and Platonism*, p. 242 (the alternative title of the *Republic* is "On Justice").

[5] The regular translation "power" is perhaps a little unfortunate: δύναμαι, "I can") is "power" in the sense of "ability", not of "force". It denotes what Professor Broad has called a "dispositional property".

main contrast is drawn between what he calls the "dianoetic"[6] (cognitive or intellectual) capacities of the mind and the "orectic" (emotional and moral). The cognitive capacities manifest themselves at four successive levels – sensation, imagination, memory, and reasoning. All have the common quality of τὸ διανοητικόν[7]. There is, however, no sharp separation between the various levels or the different parts or faculties. "Soul in fact is homœo-merous, like a tissue" (i.e. it is not a collection of distinct organs) : "with Aristotle sensation is regarded as itself a discriminative capacity from which the higher acts of cognition are reached by a continuous development".[8] Throughout, it will be noted, Aristotle formulates his classification of mental activities in terms of conscious contents, and so gives it an introspective rather than a behaviouristic character – a bias which has only recently been corrected.

Cicero, in his endeavour to provide a Latin terminology for Greek philosophy, translates δύναμις by *acultas*, ὄρεξις by *appetitio* or sometimes *conatus*, and to designate διανόησις he coins a new word, rendering the Greek term almost literally by the compound "intellegentia " (i.e. interlegentia). His definition is : " Intellegentia est, per quam animus ea perspicit quae sunt".[9]

Here then we have the origin of both the concept and the term. From Aristotle and Cicero they descended to the mediaeval schoolmen; and the scholastic theories in turn developed into the cut-and-dried schemes of the faculty psychologists and their

---

[6] Liddell and Scott's *Dictionary* gives "intelligence" as the obvious rendering of this word in Plato and Aristotle. The preposition *dia-* has something of the force of the Latin *dis-*; and Aristotle notes that "sensation" *discriminates* between the qualities of things.

[7] *De Anima*, II, 3, 414a 31. Cf. *Eth. Nic.*, I, 13, 18, 1102b 30, where human excellencies are classified as "ethical" and "dianoetic".

[8] W. D. Ross, *Aristotle*, 1923, pp. 133, 136; *De Anima*, I, v, 411b 5.

[9] Cicero, *Inv. Rhet.*, II, 53. The word is sometimes coupled with *cognitio* as a synonym (Cic., *Tusc. Disp.*, V, 24). But it is used in the humblest of forms of "discernment" (e.g. taste and smell) and of "discernment" involved in practical activities (cf. *Acad. Quest.,* IV, 7, and *Inv. Rhet.,* I 29).

phrenological followers.[10]   All of them continued to contrast intellectual capacities, which they termed abilities or "faculties," with emotional or moral capacities, which they termed "propensities" ; but none recognized any "general" ability over and above the more specific faculties.   And according to the phrenologists each distinguishable mental function was due to the activity of a separate "organ" or "centre" in the brain.   The whole picture is one that Plato would instantly have repudiated, since he himself ridicules those who thought of the mind as a sort of "Trojan horse" containing within itself a collection of active homunculi, each with its own special task *(Thæetetus,* 184D). Although the later psychologists of the nineteenth century, including both associationists and their critics, were united in rejecting it, the traditional theory of faculties continued to enjoy a considerable vogue among medical and educational writers.   To this day, indeed, teachers, educational officials, school medical officers and psychiatrists constantly drop into the vocabulary of the faculty school when they attempt a character-sketch of any child or patient ; and contemporary critics of the concept of "intelligence" regularly assume that its sponsors intend it as yet another "faculty" in the sense defined by the Scottish philosophers and their physiological interpreters.

2.   Biological

In this country the conversion of psychology from a branch of philosophy into a branch of natural science was the work not of the physiologists but of the biologists, particularly the leaders of the evolutionary school – Spencer, Darwin and their disciples. Spencer, following Aristotle and the Thomists rather than Plato and Kant, recognized only two main aspects of mental life – the

---

[10] The leader of this school – the "systematizers" as they are sometimes called – was the German philosopher, Christian Wolff (1734: for his scheme, see Wundt, *Grundzüge,* p. 97).   In Britain its chief representatives were the Scottish philosophers, Reid (1780) and Stewart (1827).   The inventories of "mental powers" drawn up by these last two writers form the basis of the phrenological lists published by Gall, Spurzheim, and George Combe (*Lectures on Phrenology,* 1847).

cognitive and the affective. All cognition (he explains) involves both an analytic or discriminative and a synthetic or integrative process ; and its essential function is to enable the organism to adjust itself more effectively to a complex and ever-changing environment. During the evolution of the animal kingdom, and during the growth of the individual child (which, he assumes, briefly recapitulates the evolution of the race), the fundamental capacity of cognition becomes progressively more and more specialized and more and more comprehensive, and so differentiates into a hierarchy of cognitive abilities – sensory, perceptual, associative, and relational, much as the trunk of a tree sprouts into boughs, branches, and twigs. To designate the basic quality common to all these more specific forms he adopts the term "intelligence."[11]

Spencer's evolutionary theories were at first taken up with keener enthusiasm on the Continent than in this country. Taine, the leader of the new empirical school in France, expounded them in his monograph *De l'intelligence* (1870) ; Ribot amplified them still further in *L'heredité psychologique* (1873); and their version provided the starting point for the work of their more celebrated disciple, Alfred Binet *(L'étude expérimentale de l'intelligence,* 1903, and later papers). In Switzerland Spencer's views inspired the genetic studies of Claparède and of his pupil, Jean Piaget. Both these adopt a standpoint that is frankly biological. Piaget, in language reminiscent of Plato, contrasts the "directive" and "dynamic" elements in mental life : "every action," he says, "involves an energetic or affective aspect, and a structural, regulative, or cognitive aspect. ... Intelligence is not a faculty : it is the generic term indicating the organism's relative efficiency in organizing or structuring mental activity in order to adjust itself to changing

---

[11] H. Spencer, *Principles of Psychology*, 1870, I, esp. Pt. Iv, chaps. 1 and 3, "The Nature of Intelligence" and "The Growth of Intelligence." Spencer's account was admittedly somewhat speculative; but it has in some measure been confirmed by the work of later experimentalists (like Lloyd Morgan) and contemporary child psychologists (like C. W. Valentine).

circumstances". And he propounds, as a result of first-hand observations of the developing child, a hierarchical theory of "levels", less schematic and more exact, yet on the whole strikingly similar to that of Herbert Spencer.[12]

3. Physiological

While in France and Britain scientific psychology was regarded as a branch of biology, in Germany it was treated as a branch of physiology. The earliest experiments on cerebral localization seemed to indicate something rather like a modified phrenological theory – the functions localized in the various cortical areas being of a somewhat simpler kind than the traditional faculties. Wundt quotes with approval Spencer's principle that mental organization merely reflects the underlying neurological organization, and consequently regards *Intelligenz* as a property of the central nervous system. There is, however, no *localized* "Organ der Intelligenz" : *Intelligenz* is "simply a name for the varying degrees of efficiency in the fundamental cognitive process "– a process which he prefers to call "apperception" – i.e. "attention regarded as a process of synthesis". It operates on various levels; and he too gives a schematic diagram of the way the nervous system is organized, plainly suggested by Spencer's description .[13]

Wundt's scheme is avowedly hypothetical. But later studies of the structure and functions of the nervous system went far to confirm the general accuracy of these views. The clinical work of Hughlings Jackson and the experimental investigations of Sherrington lent strong support to the theory of a "neural hierarchy",[14] with a definite order of evolution for the various levels. Within the adult brain there are marked differences in the architecture of different parts and of the different cell layers clearly discernible under the microscope; and these differences or

---

[12] J. Piaget, *The Psychology of Intelligence* (1950), and *The Origins of Intelligence in the Child* (1953).

[13] *Grundzüge der Physiologischen Psychologie* (1874), I, pp. 380 f.

[14] The phrase is Sherrington's: cf. *The Integrative Action of the Nervous System*, 1906, pp. 314 f., and Hughlings Jackson, *Brain*, **22**, pp. 621 f.

specializations emerge progressively during the earliest months of infant life.[15]   At the same time, the examination of the cortex in mental defectives and in normal persons indicates that the quality of the nervous tissue in any given individual tends to be predominantly the same throughout.

Defectives, for example, exhibit a "general cerebral immaturity," and their nerve-cells tend to be "visibly deficient in number, branching, and regularity of arrangement in every part of the cortex".[16] After all, as Sherrington points out, much the same is true of almost every tissue of which the human frame is composed – of a man's skin, bones, hair, or muscles : each is of the same general character all over the body, although minor local variations are usually discernible.

4.   Individual Psychology

Most of the writers I have so far mentioned were interested chiefly in problems of *general* psychology.   The first to apply scientific methods to the study of *individual* psychology was Galton himself.[17]   Spencer had maintained that the basic characteristics of

---

[15] Cf. M. de Crinis, Die Entwickelung der Grosshirnrinde in ihren Beziehungen zur intellektuellen Ausriefung des Kindes, *Wiener Klinische Wochenschrift*, 1932, **45**, pp. 1163 f. J. L. Conel, *The Postnatal Development of the Human Cerbral Cortex*, 1941.

[16] J.S. Bolton, *The Brain in Health and Disease*, 1914, pp. 79 f. and Figs. 52, 53. R. J. A. Berry and R. G. Gordon, *The Mental Defective*, 1931 and ref.

[17] Galton founded an anthropometric laboratory "for the measurement of human form and faculty" as early as 1884. At first the measurements included were chiefly physical: but psychological assessments (to be obtained with tests of discrimination, reaction-time, and the like, a questionnaire on mental imagery, and rating scales for more specific qualities) were later added to his scheme: cf., for example, Inquiries into Human Faculty, 1883, and J. M. Cattell's paper on "Mental Tests and Measurements" with a note by Galton in Mind, 1890, 15, pp. 373-380. Galton's preference for the term "anthropometric" has led many to suppose that his scheme was limited to bodily measurements; but he makes it clear that he uses the word to cover all human characteristics, psychological and physiological as well as anatomical.

the human mind were innate – transmitted as part of the common racial endowment. Galton went farther and maintained that individual differences in these characteristics might also be inherited or at least inborn. When he first commenced his inquiries on mental inheritance, the prevailing hypothesis among those who attempted to describe individual differences was, as we have seen, that of the faculty school. Galton quickly became convinced that a theory of wholly specific faculties was of itself quite inadequate to account for the facts he had accumulated.

As a corrective, he introduced the distinction between what he termed "general ability" and "special aptitudes." He recognizes three main sources of individual achievement – cognitive capacities (or "abilities"), emotional or affective characteristics (such as "interest" or "zeal"), and moral or conative characteristics (notably "a will to work"). He focuses attention mainly on the first, since "natural" ability must inevitably set a limit to what interest or industry, even in the most favourable circumstances, can possibly achieve. Most writers, he argues, "lay too much stress upon apparent specialities, thinking that, because a man is devoted to some particular pursuit, he could not have succeeded in anything else; they might as well say that, because a youth has fallen in love with a brunette, he could not possibly have fallen in love with a blonde. He may or may not have had more natural liking for the former type of beauty than for the latter : but it is as probable as not that the affair was mainly or wholly due to a *general* amorousness. It is just the same with intellectual pursuits".

Galton does not deny the existence of special capacities. Indeed, he cites instances in which memory, literary ability, musical ability, and artistic talent, run through several members of the same family. In some cases the specialization may be due to family tradition or to home environment, though this could scarcely explain the prodigies of memory" ; but, in the main, he says, the pedigrees and case-studies given in his book demonstrate "in how small a degree intellectual eminence can be considered as due to purely special powers". His data suggest that individual differences in "natural ability" are distributed in accordance with the normal curve, i.e. much like differences in other human characteristics which are mainly innate, such as bodily size or stature ; and he prints a tabular classification of frequencies, which, he holds, "may apply to special just as truly as to general ability".[18]

Binet was greatly influenced by Galton's theories. Like Galton he distinguishes between *acquired* knowledge or skill (to be assessed by a "pedagogical scale") and *native* abilities (to be assessed by a "psychological scale"). Like Galton, too, he firmly believes in the notion of *general* ability, which he contrasts with "partial aptitudes". To designate this native general ability, he prefers the simple Spencerian name, "intelligence". He gives us a popular but fairly clear account of "the meaning to be given to that word, so wide and comprehensive, intelligence. ... Nearly all the phenomena with which psychology is concerned are phenomena of intelligence – sensation, perception, as much as reasoning. ... And it would seem that in the phenomena of inteligence there is a fundamental faculty, deficiency in which is of the utmost importance for practical life : this faculty", he continues, "is variously described as common sense, judgment, the capacity of adjusting oneself to circumstances" (the last is Spencer's definition). Since it enters into every cognitive process, tests of any such process might in theory be used to assess it. But, he adds, "it is neither necessary nor possible to test *all* the child's psychological processes". There is "a hierarchy among the diverse manifestations of intelligence"; the more complex and more specialized mature at later stages in a progressive order that is relatively fixed. Hence the crucial test for an individual at any given stage of development will be the hardest cognitive processes of which he is capable.[19]

---

[18] F. Galton, *Hereditary Genius*, 1869, pp. 23 f., 35 f.

[19] A. Binet, La mesure en psychologie individuelle, *Rev. Philos.*, 1898, **46**, pp. 113-123. *L'étude expérimentale de l'intelligence* (1903); (with T. Simon) Methodes nouvelles pour le diagnostic du niveau intellectuel des anormaux, *L'Année Psychologique*, 1905, **11**, pp. 191 f., 245 f. To a French psychologist the phrase "common sense" is reminiscent of the scholastic doctrine (inherited from Aristotle) of a *sensus communis*, i.e., a "*general* perceptive faculty" (as Ross translates it). "Judgement" is the term which Binet proposes in place of the term "discrimination," used by most other contemporary psychologists to designate the essential congnitive element.

Such views did not escape criticism. A hypothesis which postulated *both* a general ability *and* a number of "partial" or "special" aptitudes seemed to assume two types of capacity where one would suffice. Writers on applied psychology, including the compilers of the more popular educational and psychiatric textbooks, usually rejected the notion of a central cognitive activity as a needless philosophical abstraction, and contended that a collection of special abilities or faculties accorded best with their practical experience. On the other hand, most of the writers on pure psychology treated the doctrine of special faculties as obsolete. There was, they held, and there could be, only one form of cognitive activity, though they failed to agree about its actual nature. The older associationists, such as Mill and his followers, maintained that it was "association" – the "process by which we learn"; the younger members of the school, like Bain and Sully, maintained that it was "sensory discrimination". Of their various opponents, both the neo Kantian philosophers like Ward and the Herbartian psychologists like Stout and Adams, argued that it was "apperception" or "attention" : "when we feel, perceive, or remember a thing [says Ward] common sense thinks the object is the same, while the mental faculty differs; actually there is only a single subjective activity – attention, and what we attend to are different presentations of the object". Finally, several of Ward's disciples, like Maxwell Garnett, insisted that attention was essentially a conative process, and concluded that the apparent differences in "intelligence" were really differences in "will". Similar divergences appeared in the writings of American psychologists ; and it is these alternative interpretations that account for the discrepant opinions cropping up in the 1928 Symposium to which Dr. Heim refers.

5.　　Statistical

Down to the beginning of the present century the arguments put forward by the various disputants were largely based on everyday impressions or deductions from physiological and biological principles. What was manifestly needed, therefore, was a more direct and rigorous method of deciding between the rival views. The obvious procedure consisted in a *combination* of the two novel techniques which Galton himself had devised ; in other words, the application of the statistical method of correlation to results obtained with experimental tests.

The first to plan a systematic research on this twofold basis was J. M. Cattell. On his way back from his studies under Wundt at Leipzig, he spent some time working as Galton's assistant in the anthropometric laboratory, and the two collaborated in compiling a programme of mental tests. When Cattell returned to take up the first Chair of Psychology in the United States, he organized a scheme for testing freshmen entering Columbia and other colleges. The data thus collected were eventually analysed by one of Cattell's research students, Clark Wissler, and his investigation proved to be the first of the long series of inquiries in which correlational techniques were applied to test-results.

The primary object, so Wissler explains, was to "find a means whereby the fundamental elements of general and specific ability could be isolated and valued". The correlations, however, proved to be rather low. On the whole they appeared to indicate that whatever it is that makes for correlation in class standing seems to hold good generally ". But in Wissler's view the main lesson of the inquiry was the need for a thorough correlation of tests of all kinds based on "an exhaustive canvas of the whole field of human activity".[20]

Verification by Factorial Techniques

Here we are concerned, not with the presence or absence of "special abilities" (the subject of the long controversy between Spearman and his opponents), but solely with that of the "general factor". Taken together, the foregoing considerations –

---

[20] C. Wissler, The Correlation of Mental and Physical Tests, *Psychol. Rev. Mon. Sup.*, 1901, **3**. It is now clear that the research was wrongly planned. First, students are already selected for intelligence; and this must tend to eliminate any correlation resulting from differences in intelligence. Secondly, the processes tested were relatively simple (chiefly sensory discrimination, motor reaction, and memory), and these depend far less on intelligence than the more complex.

introspective, biological, physiological, and experimental – appeared to furnish strong presumptive evidence for a definite hypothesis which we can now formulate in the following terms : the efficiency of an individual depends largely on an abstract component or factor, termed for convenience "intelligence", which may be defined in terms of a trio of distinctions : it is (i) cognitive (in the sense already explained), and not affective or conative ; (ii) it is general, i.e. common to all cognitive activities, and not limited to a particular group ; (iii) it is innate, i.e. due to the individual's genetic constitution, not acquired as a result of opportunity or training. However, since each of these assumptions had been challenged, it seemed urgently desirable to procure, if possible, some direct empirical verification of each one.

(i) General. From the very start the point most often attacked was the assumption of an ability entering into all forms of cognitive process. To settle this question it seemed necessary to collect or construct tests of every aspect and level – i.e. motor as well as sensory, practical as well as intellectual, ranging from the simplest sensory or motor reaction to those of logical thought in its most developed forms. If, as some writers believed, the mind includes nothing but independent faculties or "group factors", such as "practical ability", "intellectual ability", and the like, the correlations between the practical tests should be positive, and the correlations between the intellectual tests should be positive, but the cross correlations between the first set and the second should be zero ; and similarly for other special abilities : if what Thorndike called the "theory of natural compensation" (or "intellectual types") was correct, then the cross correlations should be negative, because the "intellectual" type would be poor at the "practical" tests, and the "practical" type poor at the "intellectual" tests. What we actually found were *positive* correlations between *all* the processes tested. This at once put out of court the hypothesis of independent faculties or compensatory capacities, and confirmed the hypothesis of a general factor.[21]

---

[21] Cf. C. Burt, Experimental Tests of General Intelligence, *Brit. J. Psychol.*, 1909, **3**, pp. 94-177; Experimental Tests of High Mental Processes

(ii) Cognitive. The evidence I have summarized so far, however, does not of itself prove that the factor is a specifically cognitive factor ; it might be a factor common to other mental processes as well as cognitive. As we have seen, Maxwell Garnett, Pearsons' assistant and one of his ablest disciples, held that the general factor was far wider, and was in fact essentially a matter of Will, entering into moral as well as intellectual behaviour. This was at one time an extremely popular interpretation. After all, both teachers and parents have frequently doubted the existence of wide differences in sheer ability, and have assumed that, when a child makes little progress in his lessons, the cause is not so much lack of intellectual capacity as a lack of interest or effort.

In later experiments, therefore, we correlated assessments for intellectual performances with assessments for temperamental and moral qualities. This time the cross correlations, though small, were positive. But two points seemed clear : first, the correlations of intellectual performances with moral assessments were far too low to account for the high correlations *within* the intellectual performances themselves and secondly the small positive cross correlations were largely the result of a one-way influence : if the child shows no interest and exerts no effort, he naturally will not succeed ; but many a child may be keenly interested and exert himself to the utmost and yet fail to achieve success. It seems therefore that the general factor is mainly, though not perhaps wholly, cognitive.

(iii) Innate. How far the cognitive element in this factor depends on the individual's genetic constitution, and is therefore part of his unalterable endowment, is a problem about which there is far less agreement. Our ignorance of the genetic basis of mental characteristics is so great that any direct answer is scarcely practicable. We have therefore to be content with speculative inferences and indirect statistical verification.[22] But, after all, from

---

and their Relation to General Intelligence, *J. Exp. Ped.*, 1911, **1**, pp. 93-112. *The Distribution and Relations of Educational Abilities* (1917).

[22] In the first lecture I was invited to give to this *Society* (The Inheritance of Mental Characters, Eugen. Rev., 1912, **4**, pp. 168-200) I attempted to

a practical standpoint the crucial issue is that of prediction. Can we, when Tom enters the junior school at seven, or when at eleven plus it is time to allocate him to an appropriate secondary school – can we by the aid of our tests predict, not merely his intellectual efficiency during the coming years in the classroom, but his ultimate efficiency as an adult citizen? And can we, as eugenists, go still farther, and predict the kind of children he is likely to have?

To answer these questions we need "longitudinal studies" – case histories not merely of the same individuals but of the same families. I have myself been able to keep in touch, for nearly thirty years, with over 400 persons whom I first tested as children between 1915 and 1925, reassessing them from time to time, and even testing their own sons and daughters and other relatives. But before we examine the data so obtained, it is necessary to decide what precisely we wish to predict and what we are to take as the basis of our prediction.

There are in fact half a dozen varying quantities that we might seek to compare, and all are apt to be dubbed "intelligence". Much confusion would be avoided if, as I have suggested elsewhere, we extended Professor Spearman's practice and labelled each with a distinctive letter. We may perhaps distinguish them as follows:

(i)	First, intelligence in the strict technical sense – i.e. the amount of innate general cognitive efficiency possessed by any given individual – a purely hypothetical quantity: following Fisher's convention (using Greek letters to denote hypothetical quantities and Roman to denote the empirical estimates), let us call it γ : by definition it cannot be altered by any post-natal influences, though of course its observable manifestations may be.

(ii)	The actual measurement furnished by a single test or battery of tests, applied on a single occasion let us call it g_t : this is the quantity which critics evidently have in mind when they

summarize the results then obtained by these newer methods and urged the adoption of what was then a still newer approach, namely, the application of Mendelian principles to problems of mental heredity.

complain that measurements of intelligence are affected by coaching, by education, or the like.

(iii)   The adjusted assessment of the child's intelligence, reached after checking the initial test result first by the teacher's judgment and then when necessary by a different test applied on a different occasion, g_e, say ; this is what the psychologist uses (or should use) in diagnosing mental deficiency, and generally in predicting a child's future development.

(iv)   The all-round ability of adults, assessed by tests and other means, regardless of how much is due to innate or acquired components respectively, g_a, say it is this broader concept that is important in vocational guidance, and it was this that "intelligence tests" were used to measure among recruits during the recent war.[23]

(v)   The statistical "general factor", i.e., "the factor common to all tests of a given battery",[24] g_s, say; it is this more abstract quantity with which Thomson and Thurstone are concerned in their controversies with Spearman.

(vi)   "Intelligence as the layman understands the word", g_l.[25]

Which are we to choose? Most investigators[26] simply compare an initial set of test-measurements with a later set, each derived from written tests applied on a single occasion only, i.e. g_t. But the correlation between two such tests, even applied with only a minimal time interval, is still never more than about 0.85 or 0.90. Hence, much of the imperfection shown by such correlations must be due to defects in the methods of assessment ; they throw no light (as is so often alleged) on the supposed instability of γ. After

---

[23] Cf. P. E. Vernon and J. B. Parry, *Personnel Selection in the British Forces* (1949). Psychologists who are concerned chiefly with adult "intelligence" are, as a rule, sceptical of the measurability, and even the existence, of a "pure innate g." But with adults assessments of "pure innate g" are almost impossible, and nearly always irrelevant.

[24] I take this definition from R. B. Cattell, *Factor Analysis* (1952), p. 424.

[25] This is the conception preferred by Dr. Heim (*loc. cit.*, pp. 30 f.)

[26] For an impartial summary, see L. Carmichael (Ed.), *Manual of Child Psychology* (1946), pp. 586 f.

all, no experienced psychologist would diagnose a child as feebleminded on such a basis. He would invariably check the crude test-results by the child's case-history and the teacher's report, and in case of doubt retest him on a different day with one or more individual tests. Hence in what follows I shall be concerned chiefly with measurements of the third kind, g_c, i.e. assessments checked and corrected in this way. With these adjusted measurements the correlations are appreciably higher than those commonly reported for the unadjusted g_t.

For the cases I have been able to follow up, the correlations during the school period diminish progressively from 0.93 after one year to 0.74 after six years. The correlations with assessments secured in early adult life (i.e. after ten or fifteen years) average 0.61 ; and with assessments for the children of the original testees they average 0.32.

Correlations between parents and children are apt to vary somewhat erratically, in part no doubt because assessments of adult intelligence are bound to be more or less inaccurate. Let us therefore compare measurements for brothers and sisters who are all of school age. Miss Howard and I took a batch of 268 ten-year-olds each of whom had at least one sib attending school (i.e. aged eight to twelve) and who were so chosen as to be fairly representative of the total school population – (excluding pathological defectives). They were divided into four equal groups : (i) bright, (ii*a*) bright average, (ii*b*) dull average, (iii) dull; and the middle groups were pooled. When any child had more than one sib, the sibs' assessments were averaged. The bivariate frequency-distribution so obtained, expressed in the form of percentages, is shown in the table below.

TABLE I				
FREQUENCY DISTRIBUTION OF BRIGHT, AVERAGE, AND DULL SIBS				
SELECTED CHILDREN	SIBS			
	Bright	Average	Dull	Total
Bright	12.8	10.0	2.2	25.0
Average	11.2	29.6	9.2	50.0
Dull	1.3	8.9	14.8	25.0
Total	25.3	48.5	26.2	100.0

On Mendelian principles, it is easy to show[27]* that, assuming variations in intelligence are produced by a large number of genes,

---

[27] The mechanism assumed is that (except for pathological cases) intelligence, like stature, is the effect of many pairs of genes (n let us suppose), such that one in each pair, D_1, D_2, ... D_n, say, makes a small addition to the individual's intelligence while the alternative member of the pair, d_1, d_2, ... d_n, produces a small reduction. With random mating, and no one-sided dominance, the grades that could exist, and their several frequencies, would be given by the product of $(D_1 + d_1)^2 (D_2 + d_2)^2 ... (D_n + d_n)^2$; omitting subscripts, the most intelligent would be represented by D^{2n}, the next by $D^{2n-1}d$ ... and the least by d^{2n}. If n is large, the distribution will evidently tend towards that given by the normal curve. From the above formulation it also follows that, if we reclassify the total distribution, so that the proportionate frequencies are expressed by the expansion of $(\Delta + \delta)^2$, i.e., $1\Delta^2 + 2\Delta\delta + \delta^2$, then the expected results of further random matings can be deduced from a simplified model involving only a single gene pair. Cf. R. A. Fisher, *Trans. Roy Soc. Edin.*, **52**, pp. 399-433. Somewhat similar results have been reported by Dr. Fraser Roberts, starting with different proportions (*An Introduction to Medical Statistics*, 1940, pp. 233-238).

It should be added that my own figures suggest some small degree of one-sided dominance, much as has been noted in stature. But this, if present, does not disturb the main conclusion. Had the uncorrected test measurements been used, the apparent correlation would have been higher, presumably because the uncorrected test-results are to some small extent influenced by the cultural environment.

then the expected proportions in the several rows would be 4 : 4 : 1, 3 : 8 : 3, and 1: 4 : 4 respectively ; i.e., with subgroups of 25 and 50 we should expect the figures to read 11.1, 11.1, 2.8 ; 10.7, 28.6, 10.7 ; and 2.8, 11.1, 11.1. In the middle row the observed figures conform quite closely with expectation. The excess of bright sibs in the top row and of dull sibs in the bottom row is probably due to the fact that like tends to marry like. Assortative mating would obviously raise the apparent correlation. On the other hand, the inaccuracies in the assessments would tend to lower it. Allowing for such minor disturbances, the frequencies clearly suggest that we are dealing with a trait that is, in the main, the effect of multi-factor or "polygenic" inheritance.

Figures like the foregoing cannot of themselves provide conclusive proof that the characteristic we are seeking to assess is an innate and therefore permanent characteristic. But they plainly offer strong corroboration for what is, on antecedent grounds, a highly plausible hypothesis. As with most generalizations in the field of individual psychology, our acceptance of such a conclusion must rest, not on any one decisive inquiry, but on inferences reached by half a dozen different lines of approach and set forth in numerous independent researches. The evidence so far available I have summarized in some detail in other publications,[28] and accordingly I need not repeat it here.   Roughly speaking, an impartial analysis would seem to indicate that very nearly 90 per cent of the variance exhibited by assessments for a complete age-group is attributable to the genetic constitution of the various individuals and that approximately half of this (i.e. 45 per cent of the variance) is attributable to what is loosely called heredity (i.e. predictable from characteristics of near relatives).

Finally, what is the actual distribution of "intelligence" as we have defined it? Like variations in stature, variations in intelligence (γ), as Galton himself believed, follow to a close approximation the normal curve. But, what is much more important, not only is there

---

[28] Cf. Intelligence and Fertility, *Occasional Papers on Eugenics* (1946), pp. 36 f., and Ability and Income, *Brit. J. Educ. Psychol.*, 1943, 13. Pp. 88 f.

"a continuity of natural ability," but "the range of mental power between the greatest and least of English intellects is enormous."[29] Surveys carried out in London and elsewhere show that, if we take a random sample of 1,000 children aged ten by the calendar, and exclude all pathological cases, the dullest will have a mental age of only five, the brightest a mental age of approximately fifteen, and between these two extremes every intermediate grade will be found. There is a larger proportion of bright children in the upper classes and a smaller proportion in the lower, but the several classes exhibit a wide overlapping. Moreover, were we to divide the total population into the non professional and professional classes, then, simply because the former are far more numerous, I calculate that, in the former, we should find approximately three times as many "very bright" children (say, sufficiently able to pass an honours examination) as in the latter.[30]

If the views that I have put forward are correct, it is clear that these inequalities in native ability, as Plato long ago foresaw, present the democratic state with profound and far-reaching problems – problems which even today are scarcely recognized and which have been attacked only in the most tentative fashion. So far as the child is concerned, it is plainly imperative that the education authority should seek to deter mine as accurately as possible the natural potentialities of each one, and, having done so, provide him with the education best suited to his needs, and finally, before it leaves him, help to select that kind of vocation for which his gifts may seem to have marked him out. In this way, and in this way alone, can we hope to realize "that ideal polity in which the apparent injustices of nature are reconciled and harmonized by the wisdom and justice of man."

---

[29] *Hereditary Genius*, pp. 26 f.

[30] For actual figures see Ability and Income, *loc. cit. sup.*, 84 f.

Sir Julian Huxley

Courtesy of National Portrait Gallery

1962

Eugenics in Evolutionary Perspective[1]

Sir Julian Huxley, M.A., D.Sc., F.R.S.

Introduction by J.A. Beardmore

Sir Julian Huxley came from a gifted family. He was born in 1887 and displayed both academic excellence and intellectual versatility, being awarded a first in Zoology and the Newdigate Prize for English Verse in his time at Oxford.

His contributions to biology were considerable and are reflected in a large number of books, journal contributions and honours from around the world. His view of life was a broad one and he took opportunities to extend his scientific knowledge into domains of a wider nature. Thus, he collaborated with H.G. Wells and G.P. Wells to produce 'The Science of Life' (1926), became President of the Association of Scientific Workers (1930), was a member of the team which made a widely acclaimed film entitled *'The Private Life of the Gannet'* and was a regular member of the BBC *'Brains Trust'* from its inception in 1939. On the international scene he took an active part in UNESCO activities being appointed its first Director General in 1946.

Huxley was President of the forerunner of the Galton Institute, the Eugenics Society, from 1959 to 1962 and gave the Galton Lecture twice, in 1937 and 1962.

Scientifically, he was very conscious of the diversity and lack of concordance in the different strands of evolutionary thought and made significant efforts to promote the need for unification and coherence. Of most importance here was his *magnum opus* 'Evolution: The Modern Synthesis' which appeared in 1942. This pushed contemporary thought towards greater acceptance of the all-pervasive effects of natural selection though it underplays the population genetics underpinning. More controversially it reflected

---

[1] Delivered in London on June 6th 1962 and published in *The Eugenics Review*, Vol. LIV, 1962-63. Pp. 123-141.

Huxley's political and philosophical leanings (he visited the USSR twice in the 1930-1940s) and expressed "his ideological commitment to a form of humanism that looked to evolutionary biology for new moral and political guidelines" (Durant 1987). (It is, however, not clear whether he satisfactorily resolved the conflict between scientific evidence and the Lysenkoist approach dominant in the USSR at that time).

In the 1962 Galton Lecture Huxley takes an approach which emphasises 'progress' in evolution – a term which pervades much of Huxley's later writing. The breakthrough into a 'psychosocial' phase of human evolution he portrays as a turning point in human evolution. His identification of the 'knowledge explosion' over forty years ago must be seen as remarkably prescient. He saw this as having a major effect (which we are currently experiencing) on psychosocial evolution.

He draws structural parallels between the processes he sees in biological and psychosocial evolution but we now know that the timescale he assumes for human evolution needs to be greatly increased, giving significantly more opportunity for evolutionary change in both biological and psychosocial dimensions.

Huxley's discourse on the biological nature of racial diversity is an interesting exercise in itself but of more importance in this context is his discussion of natural selection and (Darwinian) fitness. For Huxley natural selection must inevitably lead to progress or improvement but not necessarily to reproductive advantage. This is a position which it would be difficult to defend now. He also is badly off target in asserting (with no supporting evidence) that "man almost certainly has the largest reservoir of genetical variance of any natural species". In fact, this statement is untrue and it is rather odd that Huxley, in recognising the power of the 'psychosocial' process failed to realise that this reduces the need for large amounts of genetic variation, especially when we consider the considerable degree of evolutionary change that can be effected through mutation in a single regulatory gene.

When Huxley turns to discussing eugenics he takes a strangely authoritarian line. His statement that approaches to dealing with 'social problem groups' might involve compulsory or semi-compulsory measures, must have excited opposition in 1962 and even more so today. The arguments he adduces for effective methods of birth control so critical for population limitation, were soon to be answered in large measure. However, his proposal for

E.I.D. (Eugenic insemination by donor) is one which betrays a lack of perception of the manifold serious problems which application of this technology would generate.

Where then does Huxley leave us? His second Galton Lecture is a stimulating if provocative product of a first rate intellect. It is a mix of good science, sensible thinking about human evolution and rather poorly thought out socio-technological engineering. It also raises, but leaves unanswered, several interesting questions relating to interactions between political thought, science and society.

The 1962 Galton Lecture: Eugenics in Evolutionary Perspective

I AM HONOURED AT having been twice asked to give the Eugenics Society's Galton Lecture. The first occasion was a quarter of a century ago, when Lord Horder was our President, and I am proud of the remarks which he and my brother Aldous made about these.

Let me begin by broadly outlining how eugenics looks in our new evolutionary perspective. Man, like all other existing organisms, is as old as life. His evolution has taken close on three billion years. During that immense period he – the line of living substance leading to *Homo sapiens* – has passed through a series of increasingly high levels of organization. His organization has been progressively improved, to use Darwin's phrase, from some submicroscopic gene-like state, through a unicellular to a two-layered and a metazoan stage, to a three-layered type with many organ-systems, including a central nervous system and simple brain, on to a chordate with notochord and gill-slits, to a jawless and limbless vertebrate, to a fish, then to an amphibian, a reptile, an unspecialized insectivorous mammal, a lemuroid, a monkey with much improved vision, heightened exploratory urge and manipulative ability, an ape-like creature, and finally through a protohominid australopith to a fully human creature, big-brained and capable of true speech.

This astonishing process of continuous advance and biological improvement has been brought about through the operation of natural selection – the differential reproduction of biologically beneficial combinations of mutant genes, leading to the persistence, improvement and multiplication of some strains, species and patterns of organization and the reduction and extinction of others, notably to a succession of so-called dominant types, each achieving a highly successful new level of organization and causing the reduction of previous dominant types inhabiting the same environment. During its period of dominance, which may last up to a hundred million years or so, the new type itself becomes markedly improved, whether by specialization of single subtypes like the horses or elephants, or by an improvement in general organization, as happened with the mammalian type in general at the end of the Oligocene. Eventually no further improvement is possible, and further advance can only occur through the breakthrough of one line to a radically new type of organization, as from reptile to mammal.

In biologically recent times, one primate line broke through from the mammalian to the human type of organization. With this, the evolutionary process passed a critical point, and entered on a new state or phase, the psychosocial phase, differing radically from the biological in its mechanism, its tempo, and its results. As a result, man has become the latest dominant type in the evolutionary process, has multiplied enormously, has achieved miracles of cultural evolution, has reduced or extinguished many other species, and has radically affected the ecology and indeed the whole evolutionary process of our planet. Yet he is a highly imperfect creature. He carries a heavy burden of genetic defects and imperfections. As a psychosocial organism, he has not undergone much improvement. Indeed, man is still very much an unfinished type, who clearly has actualized only a small fraction of his human potentialities. In addition, his genetic deterioration is being rendered probable by his social set-up, and definitely being promoted by atomic fallout. Furthermore, his economic, technical and cultural progress is threatened by the high rate of increase of world population.

The obverse of man's actual and potential further defectiveness is the vast extent of his possible future improvement. To effect this, he must first of all check the processes making for genetic deterioration. This means reducing man-made radiation to a minimum, discouraging genetically defective or inferior types from breeding, reducing human over-multiplication in general and the high differential fertility of various regions, nations and classes in particular. Then he can proceed to the much more important task of positive improvement. In the not too distant future the fuller realization of possibilities will inevitably come to provide the main motive for man's overall efforts; and a Science of Evolutionary Possibilities, which to-day is merely adumbrated, will provide a firm basis for these efforts.   Eugenics can make an important contribution to man's further evolution: but it can only do so if it considers itself as one branch of that new nascent science, and fearlessly explores all the possibilities that are open to it.

Man, let me repeat, is not a biological but a psychosocial organism. As such, he possesses a new mechanism of transmission and transformation based on the cumulative handing on of experience, ideas and attitudes. To obtain eugenic improvement, we shall need not only an understanding of what kind of selection operates in the psychosocial process, not only new scientific knowledge and new techniques in the field of human genetics and reproduction but new ideas and attitudes about reproduction and parenthood in particular and human destiny in general. One of those new ideas will be the moral imperative of Eugenics.

*   *   *

In the twenty-five years since my previous lecture, many events have occurred, and many discoveries have been made with a bearing on eugenics. Events such as the explosion of atomic and nuclear bombs, the equally sinister "population explosion," the *reductio ad horrendum* of racism by Nazi Germany, and the introduction of artificial insemination for animals and human beings, sometimes with the use of deep-frozen sperm; scientific discoveries such as that of DNA as the essential basis for heredity and evolution, of subgenic organization, of the wide spread existence of balanced polymorphic genetic systems, and of the intensity and efficacy of selection in nature; the realization that the entities which evolve are populations of phenotypes, with consequent emphasis on population genetics on the one hand, and on the interaction between genotype and environment on the other; and finally the recognition that adaptation and biological improvement are universal phenomena in life.

I do not propose to discuss these changes and discoveries now, but shall plunge directly into my subject – Eugenics in Evolutionary Perspective. I chose this title because I am sure that a proper understanding of the evolutionary process and of man's place and role in it is necessary for any adequate or satisfying view of human destiny; and eugenics must obviously play an important part in enabling man to fulfil that destiny.

As I have set forth at greater length elsewhere, in the hundred years since the publication of the *Origin of Species* there has been a "knowledge explosion" unparalleled in all previous history. It has led to an accelerated expansion of ideas, not only in the natural sciences but also in the humanistic fields of history, archaeology, and social and cultural development, and its effects on our thinking have been especially violent, not to say revolutionary, during the quarter of a century since my previous Galton Lecture. It has led to a new picture of man's relations with his own nature and with the rest of the universe, and indeed to a new and unified vision of reality, both fuller and truer than any of the insights of the past. In the light of this new vision the whole of reality is seen as a single process of evolution. For evolution can properly be defined as a natural process in time, self-varying and self transforming and generating increasing complexity and variety during its transformations; and this is precisely what has been going on for all time in all the universe. It operates everywhere and in all periods, but is divisible into a series of three sectors or successive phases, the inorganic or cosmic, the organic or biological, and the human or psychosocial, each based on and growing out of its predecessor. Each phase operates by a different main mechanism, has a different scale and a different tempo of change, and produces a different type of results.

Between the separate phases, the evolutionary process has to cross a critical threshold, passing from an old to a new state, as when water passes from the solid to the liquid state at the critical temperature-threshold of 0°C and from liquid to gaseous at that of 100°C.

The critical threshold between the inorganic and the biological phase was crossed when matter and the organisms built from it became self-reproducing, that between the biological and the psychosocial when mind and the organizations generated by it became self-reproducing in their turn.

The cosmic phase operates by random interaction, primarily physical but to a small degree chemical. Its quantitative scale is unbelievably vast both in space and time. Its visible dimensions exceed 1,000 million light-years (10^{22}km), its distances are measured by units of thousands of light-years (nearly 10^{16}km), the numbers of its visible galaxies exceed 100 million (10^8) and those of its stars run into thousands of millions of millions (10^{15}). It has operated in its present form for at least 6,000 million years, possibly much longer. Its tempo of major change is unbelievably slow, to be measured by 1,000-million-year periods. According to the physicists, its overall trend, in accord with the Second Law of Thermodynamics, is entropic, tending towards a decrease in organization and to ultimate frozen immobility; and its products reach only a very low level of organization – photons, subatomic particles, atoms, and simple inorganic compounds at one end of its size-scale, nebulae, stars and occasional planetary systems at the other.

The biological phase operates primarily by the teleonomic or ordering process of natural selection, which canalizes random variation into non-random directions of change. Its tempo of major change is somewhat less slow, measured by 100-million-instead of 1,000-million-year units of time. Its overall trend, kept going of course by solar energy, is anti-entropic, towards an increase in the amount and quality of adaptive organization, and marked by the growing importance of awareness as mediated by brains. And its results are organisms – organisms of an astonishing efficiency, complexity, and variety, almost inconceivably so until one recalls R. A. Fisher's profound paradox, that natural selection plus time is a mechanism for generating an exceedingly high degree of improbability.

In the course of biological evolution, three sub-processes are at work. The first (cladogenesis, or branching evolution) leads to divergence and greater variety; the second (anagenesis, or upward evolution) leads to improvement of all sorts, from detailed adaptations to specializations, from the greater efficiency of some major function like digestion to overall advance in general organization; the third is stasigenesis or stabilized limitation of evolution. This occurs when specialization for a particular way of life reaches a dead end as with horses, or efficiency of function attains a maximum as with hawks' vision, or an ancient type of organization persists as a living fossil like the lungfish or the tuatara.

Major advance or biological progress is always by a succession of dominant types, each step achieved by a rare breakthrough from some established type of organization to a new and more effective one, as from the amphibian to true dry-land reptilian type, or from the cold blooded egg-laying reptile to the warm-blooded self-regulating mammal with ultra-uterine development. The new dominant type multiplies at the expense of the old, which may become extinct (as did the jawless fish) or may persist in reduced numbers (as did the reptiles.)

The psychosocial phase, the latest of which we have any knowledge (though elsewhere in the universe there may have been a breakthrough to some new phase as unimaginable to us as the psychosocial phase would have been to even the most advanced Pliocene primate), is based on a self-reproducing and self-varying system of cumulative transmission of experience and culture, operating by mechanisms of psychological and social selection which we have not as yet adequately defined or analysed. Spatially it is very limited; we know of it only on this earth, and in any case it must be restricted to the surface of a small minority of planets in the small minority of stars possessing planetary systems. On our planet it is at the very beginning of its course, having begun less than one million years ago. However, its tempo is not only much faster than that of biological evolution, but manifests a new phenomenon, in the shape of a marked acceleration. Its overall trend is highly antientropic, and is characterized by a sharp increase in the operative significance of exceptional individuals and in the importance of true purpose and conscious evaluation based on reason and imagination, as against the automatic differential elimination of random variants.

The most significant element in that trend has been the growth and improved organization of tested and established knowledge. And its results are psychologically (mentally) generated organizations even more astonishingly varied and complex than biological organisms – machines, concepts, cooking, mass communications, cities, philosophies, superstitions, propaganda, armies and navies, personalities, legal systems, works of art, political and economic systems, entertainments, slavery, scientific theories, hospitals, moral codes, prisons, myths, languages, torture, games and sports, religions, record and history, poetry, civil services, marriage systems, initiation rituals, agriculture, drama, social hierarchies, schools and universities. Accordingly evolution in the human phase is no longer purely biological, based on changes in the material system of genetic transmission, but primarily cultural, based on changes in the psychosocial system of ideological and cultural transmission.

In the psychosocial phase of evolution the same three sub-processes operating in the biological phase are still at work – cladogenesis, operating to generate difference and variety within and between cultures; anagenesis, operating to produce improvement in detailed technological methods, in economic and political machinery, in administrative and educational systems, in scientific thinking and creative expression, in moral tone and religious attitude, in social and international organization; and stasigenesis, operating to limit progress and to keep old systems and attitudes, including even outworn superstitions, persisting alongside of or actually within more advanced social and intellectual systems. But there is an additional fourth sub-process, that of convergence (or at least anti-divergence), operating by diffusion – diffusion of ideas and techniques between individuals, communities, cultures and regions. This is tending to give unity to the world: but we must see to it that it does not also impose uniformity and destroy desirable variety.

As in the biological phase, major advance in the human phase is brought about by a succession of generally or locally dominant types. These, however, are not types of organism, but of cultural and ideological organization. Monotheism as against polytheism, for instance; or in the political sphere, the beginning of one-world internationalism as against competitive multinationalism. Or again, science as against magic, democracy as against tyranny, planning as against *laissez-faire,* tolerance as against intolerance, freedom of opinion and expression as against authoritarian dogma and repression.

Not only does the succession of dominant types bring about progress or advance in organization within each of the three main evolutionary phases, but it also operates, though on a grander and more decisive scale, in the evolutionary process as a whole. A biological organism possesses a higher degree of organization than any inorganic system; as soon as living organisms were produced, they became the major dominant type of organization on earth, and the course of evolution became predominantly biological and only secondarily inorganic. Similarly a psychosocial system possesses a higher degree of organization than any biological organism: accordingly man at once became the new major dominant type on earth, and the course of evolution became predominantly cultural and only secondarily biological, with inorganic methods quite subordinate.

The evolutionary perspective includes the broad background of the cosmic past. Now against this background we must face the problems of the present and the challenge of the future. Let me begin by reiterating that man is an exceedingly recent phenomenon. The earliest creatures which can properly be called men, though they must be assigned to different genera from ourselves, date from less than two million years ago, and our own species, *Homo sapiens,* from much less than half a million years. Man began to put his toe tentatively across the critical threshold leading towards evolutionary dominance perhaps a quarter of a million years ago, but took tens of thousands of years to cross it, emerging as a dominant type only during the last main glaciation, probably later than 100,000 B.C., but not becoming fully dominant until the discovery of agriculture and stock-breeding well under 10,000 years ago, and overwhelmingly so with the invention of machines and writing and organized civilization a bare five millennia before the present day, when his dominance has become so hubristic as to threaten his own future.

All new dominant types begin their career in a crude and imperfect form, which then needs drastic polishing and improvement before it can reveal its full potentialities and achieve full evolutionary success. Man is no exception to this rule. He is not merely exceedingly young; he is also exceedingly imperfect, an unfinished and often botched product of evolutionary improvisation. Teilhard de Chardin has called the transformation of an anthropoid into a man *hominisation:* it might be more accurately, though more clumsily, termed *psychosocialisation.* But whatever we call it, the process of hominisation is very far from complete, the serious study of its course, its mechanisms and its techniques has scarcely started, and only a fraction of its potential results have been realized. Man, in fact, is in urgent need of further improvement.

This is where eugenics comes into the picture. For though the psychosocial system in and by which man carries on his existence could obviously be enormously improved with great benefit to its members, the same is also true for his genetic outfit.

Severe and primarily genetic disabilities like haemophilia, colour-blindness, mongolism, some kinds of sexual deviation, much mental defect, sickle-cell anaemia, some forms of dwarfism, and Huntington's chorea are the source of much individual distress, and their reduction would remove a considerable burden from suffering humanity. But these are occasional abnormalities. Quantitatively their total effect is insignificant in comparison with the massive imperfection of man as a species, and their reduction appears as a minor operation in comparison with the large-scale positive possibilities of all-round general improvement.

Take first the problem of intelligence. It is to man's higher level of intelligence that he owes his evolutionary dominance; and yet how low that level still remains! It is now well established that the human I.Q., when properly assayed, is largely a measure of genetic endowment. Consider the difference in brain-power between the hordes of average men and women with I.Q.'s around 100 and the meagre company of Terman's so-called geniuses with I.Q.'s of 160 or over, and the much rarer true geniuses like Newton and Darwin, Tolstoy and Shakespeare, Goya and Michelangelo, Hammurabi and Confucius; and then reflect that, since the frequency curve for intelligence is approximately symmetrical, there are as many stupider people with I.Q.'s below 100 as there are abler ones with I.Q.'s above it.

Recollect also that the great and striking advances in human affairs, as much in creative art and political and military leadership as in scientific discovery and invention, are primarily due to a few exceptionally gifted individuals. Remember that on the established principles of genetics a small raising of average capacity would of necessity result in an upward shifting of the entire frequency curve, and therefore a considerable increase in the absolute numbers of such highly intelligent and well-endowed human beings that form the uppermost section of the curve (as well as a decrease in the numbers of highly stupid and feebly endowed individuals at the lower end).

Reflect further on the fact, originally pointed out by Galton, that there is already a shortage of brains capable of dealing with the complexities of modern administration, technology and planning, and that with the inevitable increase of our social and technical complexity, the greater will that shortage become. It is thus clear that for any major advance in national and international efficiency we cannot depend on haphazard tinkering with social or political symptoms or *ad hoc* patching up of the world's political machinery, or even on improving general education, but must rely increasingly on raising the genetic level of man's intellectual and practical abilities. As I shall later point out, artificial insemination by selected donors could bring about such a result in practice.

The same applies everywhere in the psychosocial process. For more and better scientists, we need the raising of the genetic level of exploratory curiosity or whatever it is that underlies single-minded investigation of the unknown and the discovery of novel facts and ideas; for more and better artists and writers, we need the raising of the genetic level for disciplined creative imagination; for more and better statesmen, that of the capacity to see social and political situations as wholes, to take long-term and total instead of only short-term and partial views; for more and better technologists and engineers, that of the passion and capacity to understand how things work and to make them work more efficiently; for more and better saints and moral leaders, that of disciplined valuation, of devotion and duty, and of the capacity to love; and for more and better leaders of thought and guides of action we need a raising of the capacity of man's vision and imagination, to form a comprehensive picture, at once reverent, assured and unafraid, of nature and man's relations with it.

These facts and ideas have an important bearing on the so-called race question and the problem of racial equality. I should rather say racial *inequality,* for up till quite recently the naïve belief in the natural inequality of races and people in general, and the inherent superiority of one's own race or people in particular, has almost universally prevailed.

To demonstrate the way in which this point of view permeated even nineteenth-century scientific thought, it is worth recalling that it was largely subscribed to by Darwin in his comments on the Fuegians in the *Voyage of the Beagle,* and in more general but more guarded terms in the *Descent of Man:* and Galton himself, against a similar background of travels among backward tribes and on the basis of his own rather curious method of assessment, concluded that different races had achieved different genetic standards, so that, for instance, "the average standard of the Negro race is two grades below our own." This type of belief, after being given a pseudo scientific backing by non-biological theoreticians like Gobineau and Houston Stewart Chamberlain, was used to justify the Nazis' "Nordic" claims to world domination and their horrible campaign for the extermination of the "inferior, non-Aryan race" of Jews, and is still employed with support from Holy Writ and the majority of the Dutch Reformed Church in South Africa, to sanction Verwoerd's denial of full human rights to non-whites.

Later investigation has conclusively demonstrated first, that there is no such thing as a "pure race." Secondly, that the obvious differences in level of achievement between different peoples and ethnic groups are primarily cultural, due to differences not in genetic equipment but in historical and environmental opportunity. And thirdly, that when the potentialities of intelligence of two major "races" or ethnic groups, such as whites and negroes or Europeans and Indians, are assessed as scientifically as possible, the frequency curves for the two groups overlap over almost the whole of their extent, so that approximately half the population of either group is genetically stupider (has a lower genetic I.Q.) than the genetically more intelligent half of the other. There are thus large differences in genetic mental endowment *within* single racial groups, but minimal ones *between* different racial groups.

Partly as a result of such studies, but also of the prevalent environmentalist views of Marxist and Western liberal thought, an anti-genetic view has recently developed about race. It is claimed that though ethnic groups obviously differ in physical characters, and that some of them, like pigmentation, nasal form, and number of sweat-glands, were originally adaptive, they do not (and sometimes even that they cannot) differ in psychological or mental characters such as intelligence, imagination, or even temperament.[2]

Against this new pseudo-scientific racial naïveté, we must set the following scientific facts and principles. First, it is clear that the major human races originated as geographical sub species of *Homo sapiens,* in adaptation to the very different environments to which they have become restricted. Later, of course, expansion and migration reversed the process of differentiation and led to an increasing degree of convergence by crossing, though considerable genetic differentiation remains. Secondly, as Professor Muller has pointed out, it is theoretically inconceivable that such marked physical differences as still persist between the main racial groups should not be accompanied by genetic differences in temperament and mental capacities, possibly of considerable extent. Finally, as

---

[2] There is the further point that races may differ considerably in body-build and that Sheldon and others have made it highly probable that body-build is correlated with temperament. Unfortunately, racial differences in body-build have not yet been analysed in terms of Sheldon's somatypes: here is an important field for research.

previously explained, advance in cultural evolution is largely and increasingly dependent on exceptionally well-endowed individuals. Thus two racial groups might overlap over almost the whole range of genetic capacity, and yet one might be capable of considerably higher achievement, not merely because of better environmental and historical opportunity, but because it contained say 2 instead of 1 per cent of exceptionally gifted men and women. So far as I know, proper scientific research on this subject has never been carried out, and possibly our present methods of investigation are not adequate for doing so, but the principle is theoretically clear and is of vital practical importance.[3]

This does not imply any belief in crude racism, with its unscientific ascription of natural and permanent superiority or inferiority to entire races. As I have just pointed out, approximately half of any large ethnic group, however superior its self-image may be, is in point of fact genetically inferior to half of the rival ethnic group with which it happens to be in social or economic competition and which it too often stigmatizes as permanently and inherently lower. Furthermore, practical experience demonstrates that every so-called race, however underdeveloped its economic and social system may happen to be, contains a vast reservoir of untapped talent, only waiting to be elicited by a combination of challenging opportunity, sound educational methods, and efficient special training. I recently attended an admirable symposium on nutrition in Nigeria where the scientific quality of the African contributions was every whit as high as that of the whites; and African politicians can be just as

---

[3] On the supposition that genetic intelligence is multifactorially (polygenically) determined and that its distribution follows a normal symmetrical curve, it can be calculated that the raising of the mean genetic I.Q. of a population by $1\frac{1}{2}$ per cent would result in a 50 per cent increase in the number of individuals with an I.Q. of 160 or over. The proportion of such highly-endowed individuals would rise from 1 in about 30,000 of the total population to 1 in about 20,000. Sir Cyril Burt informs me that if, as is possible, some types of high intelligence are determined by single genes, the increase might be still greater.

statesmanlike (and also just as unscrupulously efficient in the political game) as their European or American counterparts.

The basic fact about the races of mankind is their almost total overlap in genetic potentialities. But the most significant fact for eugenic advance is the large difference in achievement made possible by a small increase in the number of exceptional individuals.

The evolutionary biologist can point out to the social scientist and the politician that this importance of the exceptional individual for psychosocial advance is merely an enhancement of a long-established evolutionary trend. Exceptional individuals can be important for biological improvement in mammals, in birds, and possibly even in insects. New food-traditions in Japanese monkeys are established by disobedient young individuals. The utilization of milk-bottles as a new source of food by blue tits was due to the activities of a few exceptional tit geniuses in a few widely separate localities. All male satin bowerbirds construct bowers and assemble collections of stimulating bright objects at them, but only a minority deliberately paint their bowers with a mixture of berries, charcoal and saliva, and only a still smaller minority indulge the species' natural preference for blue objects by deliberately stealing bluebags to add to their display collection. And there is some evidence that even in ants, those prototypes of rigidly instinctive behaviour, a few workers are exceptionally well-endowed with the exploratory urge, and play a special role in discovering new sources of food for the colony.

But I must return to man as a species. The human species is in desperate need of genetic improvement if the whole process of psychosocial evolution which it has set in train is not to get bogged down in unplanned disorder, negated by over-multiplication, clogged up by mere complexity, or even blown to pieces by obsessional stupidity. Luckily it not only *must* but *can* be improved. It can be improved by the same type of method that has secured the improvement of life in general – from protozoan to protovertebrate, from protovertebrate to primate, from primate to human being – the method of multi-purpose selection directed towards greater achievement in the prevailing conditions of life.

On the other hand, it can *not* be improved by applying the methods of the professional stock-breeder. Indeed the whole discussion of eugenics has been bedevilled by the false analogy between artificial and natural selection. Artificial selection is intensive special-purpose selection, aimed at producing a particular excellence, whether in milk-yield in cattle, speed in race-horses or a fancy image in dogs. It produces a number of specialized pure breeds, each with a markedly lower variance than the parent species. Darwin rightly drew heavily on its results in order to demonstrate the efficacy of selection in general. But since he never occupied himself seriously with eugenics he did not point out the irrelevance of stock-breeding methods to human improvement. In fact, they are not only irrelevant, but would be disastrous. Man owes much of his evolutionary success to his unique variability. Any attempt to improve the human species must aim at retaining this fruitful diversity, while at the same time raising the level of excellence in all its desirable components, and remembering that the selectively evolved characters of organisms are always the results of compromise between different types of advantage, or between advantage and disadvantage.

Natural selection is something quite different. To start with, it is a shorthand metaphorical term coined by Darwin to denote the teleonomic or directive agencies affecting the process of evolution in nature, and operating through the differential survival and reproduction of genetical variants. It may operate between conspecific individuals, between conspecific populations, between related species, between higher taxa such as genera and families, or between still larger groups of different organizational type, such as Orders and Classes. It may also operate between predator and prey, between parasite and host, and between different synergic assemblages of species, such as symbiotic partnerships and ecological communities. It is in fact universal in its occurrence, though multiform in its mode of action.

Some over-enthusiastic geneticists appear to think that natural selection acts directly on the organism's genetic outfit or genotype. This is not so. Natural selection exerts its effects on animals and plants as working mechanisms: it can operate only on phenotypes.

Its evolutionary action in transforming the genetic outfit of a species is indirect, and depends on the simple fact pointed out by Darwin in the *Origin* that much variation is heritable – in modern terms, that there is a high degree of correlation between phenotypic and genotypic variance. The correlation, however, is never complete, and there are many cases where it is impossible without experimental analysis to determine whether a variant is modificational, due to alteration in the environment, or mutational, due to alteration in the genetic outfit. In certain cases, environmental treatment will produce so-called phenocopies which are indistinguishable from mutants in their visible appearance.

This last fact has led Waddington to an important discovery – the fact that an apparently Lamarckian mode of evolutionary transformation can be precisely simulated by what he calls genetic assimilation. To take an actual example, the rearing of fruitfly larvae on highly saline media produces a hypertrophy of their salt-excreting glands through direct modification. But if selection is practised by breeding from those individuals which show the maximum hypertrophy of their glands, then after some ten or twelve generations, individuals with somewhat hypertrophied glands appear even in cultures on non-saline media. The species has a genetic predisposition, doubtless brought by selection in the past, to react to saline conditions by glandular hypertrophy. The action of the major genes concerned in reactions of this sort can be enhanced (or inhibited) by so-called modifying genes of minor effect. Selection has simply amassed in the genetic outfit an array of such minor enhancing genes strong enough to produce glandular hypertrophy even in the absence of any environmental stimulus, it is only pseudo-Lamarckism, but no less important for that – a significant addition to the theoretical armoury of evolutionary science.

I repeat that the most important effect achieved by natural selection is biological improvement. As G. G. Simpson reminds us, it does so opportunistically, making use of whatever new combination of existing mutant genes, or less frequently of whatever new mutations, happens to confer differential survival value on its possessors. We know of numerous cases where phenotypically identical and adaptive transformations have been produced by different genes or gene-combinations.

Here I must digress a moment to discuss the concept of evolutionary fitness. The biological *avant garde* has chosen to define *fitness* as "net reproductive advantage," to use the actual words employed by Professor Medawar in his Reith Lectures on *The Future of Man*. Any strain of animal, plant, or man which leaves slightly more descendants capable of reproducing themselves than another, is then defined as "fitter." This I believe to be an unscientific and misleading definition. It disregards all scientific conventions as to priority, for it bears no resemblance to what Spencer implied or intended by his famous phrase the *survival of the fittest*.[4] It is also nonsensical in every context save the limited field of population genetics. In biology, fitness must be defined, as Darwin did with improvement, "in relation to the conditions of life" – in other words, in the context of the general evolutionary situation. I shall call it *evolutionary fitness,* in contradistinction to the purely reproductive fitness of the evangelists of geneticism, which I prefer to designate by the descriptive label of *net* or *differential reproductive advantage.*

Meanwhile, I have a strong suspicion that the genetical *avant garde* of to-day will become the rearguard of tomorrow. In my own active career I have seen a reversal of this sort in relation to natural selection and adaptation. During the first two decades of this century the biological *avant garde* dismissed topics such as cryptic or mimetic coloration, and indeed most discussion of adaptation, as mere "armchair speculation," and played down the role of natural selection in evolution, as against that of large and random mutation. Bateson's enthusiasm rebounded from his early protest against speculative phylogeny into the far more speculative suggestion made *ex cathedra* at a British Association meeting, that all evolution, whether of higher from lower, or of diversity from uniformity, had been brought about by loss mutations; and the great T. H. Morgan once permitted himself to state in print that, if

---

[4] Darwin did not use the phrase in the first edition of the *Origin of Species*, though in later editions he added it as an equivalent to natural selection.

natural selection had never operated, we should possess all the organisms that now exist and a great number of other types as well! This anti-selectionist *avant garde* of fifty years back has now come over *en masse* into the selectionist camp, leaving only a few retreating stragglers to deliver some rather ineffective parthian shots at their opponents.

Natural selection is a teleonomic or directional agency. It utilizes the inherent genetic variability of organisms provided by the raw material of random mutation and chance recombination, and it operates by the simple mechanism of differential reproductive advantage.   But on the evolutionary time-scale it produces biological improvement, resulting in a higher total and especially a higher upper level of evolutionary fitness, involving greater functional efficiency, higher degrees of organization, more effective adaptation, better self-regulating capacity, and finally more mind – in other words an enrichment of qualitative awareness coupled with more flexible behaviour.

Man almost certainly has the largest reservoir of genetical variance of any natural species: selection for the differential reproduction of desirable permutations and combinations of the elements of this huge variance could undoubtedly bring about radical improvement in the human organism, just as it has in pre-human types.   But the agency of human transformation cannot be the blind and automatic natural selection of the pre-human sector. That, as I have already stressed, has been relegated to a subsidiary role in the human phase of evolution.   Some form of psychosocial selection is needed, a selection as non-natural as are most human activities, such as wearing clothes, going to war, cooking food, or employing arbitrary systems of communication.   To be effective, such "non-natural" selection must be conscious, purposeful and planned.   And since the tempo of cultural evolution is many thousands of times faster than that of biological transformation, it must operate at a far higher speed than natural selection if it is to prevent disaster, let alone produce improvement.

Luckily there is to-day at least the possibility of meeting both these prerequisites: we now possess an accumulation of established knowledge and an array of tested methods which could make intelligent, scientific and purposeful planning possible. And we are in the process of discovering new techniques which could raise the effective speed of the selective process to a new order of magnitude. The relevant new knowledge mainly concerns the various aspects of the evolutionary process – the fact that there are no absolutes or all-or-nothing effects in evolution and that all organisms and all their phenotypic characters represent a compromise or balance between competing advantages and disadvantages; the effect of selection on populations in different environmental conditions; the origin of adaptation; and the general improvement of different evolutionary lines in relation to the conditions of their life. The notable new techniques include effective methods of birth-control, the successful development of grafted fertilized ova in new host-mothers, artificial insemination, and the conservation of function in deep-frozen gametes.

We must first keep in mind the elementary but often neglected fact that the characters of organisms which make for evolutionary success or failure, are not inherited as such. On the contrary, they develop anew in each individual, and are always the resultant of an interaction between genetic determination and environmental modification. Biologists are often asked whether heredity or environment is the more important. It cannot be too often emphasized that the question should never be asked, it is as logically improper to ask a biologist to answer it as it is for a prosecuting counsel to ask a defendant when he stopped beating his wife, it is the phenotype which is biologically significant and the phenotype is a resultant produced by the complex interaction of hereditary and environmental factors. Eugenics, in common with evolutionary biology in general, needs this phenotypic approach.

Man's evolution occurs on two different levels and by two distinct methods, the genetic, based on the transmission and variation of genes and gene-combinations, and the psychosocial or cultural, based on the transmission and variation of knowledge and ideas.

Professor Medawar, in his Reith Lectures on *The Future of Man,* while admitting in his final chapter that man possesses "a new, non genetical, system of heredity and evolution" (p. 88), claims on p. 41

that this is "a new kind of biological evolution (I emphasize, a biological evolution)." I must insist that this is incorrect. The psychosocial process – in other words, evolving man – is a new *state* of evolution, a new *phase* of the cosmic process, as radically different from the pre-human biological phase as that is from the inorganic or pre-biological phase; and this fact has important implications for eugenics.

An equally elementary but again often neglected fact is that organisms are not significant – in plain words, are meaningless – except in relation to their environment. A fish is not a thing-in-itself: it is a type of organism evolved in relation to an active life in large or medium-sized bodies of water. A cactus has biological significance only in relation to an arid habitat, a woodpecker only in relation to an arboreal one. Man, however, is in a unique situation. He must live not only in relation with the physicochemical and biological environment provided by nature, but with the psychosocial environment of material and mental habitats which he has himself created.

Man's psychosocial environment includes his beliefs and purposes, his ideals and his aims: these are concerned with what we may call the habitat of the future, and help to determine the *direction* of his further evolution. All evolution is directional and therefore relative. But whereas the direction of biological evolution is related to the continuing improvement of organisms in relation to their conditions of life, human evolution is related to the improvement of the entire psychosocial process, including the human organism, in relation to man's purposes and beliefs, long-term as well as short-term. Only in so far as those purposes and beliefs are grounded on scientific and tested knowledge, will they serve to steer human evolution in a desirable direction. In brief, biological evolution is given direction by the blind and automatic agency of natural selection operating through material mechanisms, human evolution by the agency of psychosocial guidance operating with the aid of mental awareness, notably the mechanisms of reason and imagination.

To be effective, such awareness must clearly be concerned with man's environmental situation as well as his genetic equipment. In my first Galton Lecture, I pointed out the desirability of eugenists relating their policies to the social environment. To-day I would go further, and stress the need for planning the environment in such a way as will promote our eugenic aims. By 1936, it was already clear that the net effect of present-day social policies could not be eugenic, and was in all probability dysgenic. But, as Muller has demonstrated, this was not always so. In that long period of human history during which our evolving and expanding hominid ancestors lived in small and tightly knit groups competing for territorial and technological success, the social organization promoted selection for intelligent exploration of possibilities, devotion and co-operative altruism: the cultural and the genetic systems reinforced each other. It was only much later, with the growth of bigger social units of highly organized civilizations based on status and class differentials, that the two became antagonistic; the sign of genetic transformation changed from positive to negative and definite genetic improvement and advance began to halt, and gave way to the possibility and later the probability of genetic regression and degeneration.

This probability has been very much heightened during the last century, partly by the differential multiplication of economically less favoured classes and groups in many parts of the world, partly by the progress of medicine and public health, which has permitted numbers of genetically defective human beings to survive and reproduce; and to-day it has been converted into a certainty by the series of atomic and nuclear explosions which have been set off since the end of the last war. There is still dispute as to the degree of damage this has done to man's genetic equipment. There can be no dispute as to the fact of damage: any addition to man's load of mutations can only be deleterious, even if some of them may possibly come to be utilized in neutral or even favourable new gene combinations.

Now that we have realized these portentous facts, it is up to us to reverse the process and to plan a society which will favour the increase instead of the decrease of man's desirable genetic capacities for intelligence and imagination, empathy and co-operation, and a sense of discipline and duty.

The first step must be to frame and put into operation a policy designed to reduce the rate of human increase before the quantitative claims of mere numbers override those of quality and prevent any real improvement, social and economic as much as eugenic. I would prophesy that within a quite short time, historically speaking, we shall find ourselves aiming at an absolute reduction of the population in the world in general, and in overcrowded countries like Britain, India and China, Japan, Java and Jamaica in particular; the quantitative control of population is a necessary prerequisite for qualitative improvement, whether psychosocial or genetic.

Science seems to be nearing a breakthrough to cheap and simple methods of birth-control, or reproduction-control as it should more properly be called. The immediate needs are for much increased finance for research, testing, pilot projects, motivation studies and the education of public opinion, and an organized campaign against the irrational attitudes and illiberal policies of various religious and political organizations. Simultaneously, responsible opinion must begin to think out ways in which social and economic measures can be made to promote desirable genetic trends and reproductive habits.

Many countries have instituted family allowance systems which are not graded according to number of children, and some, like France, even provide financial inducements which encourage undesirably large families. It should be easy to devise graded family allowance systems in which the allowances for the first two or three children would be really generous, but those for further children would rapidly taper off. In India, there have even been proposals to tax parents for children above a certain number, and in some provinces, men fulfilling certain conditions are paid to be vasectomized.

A powerful weapon for adequate population-control is ready to the hand of the great grant-giving and aid-providing agencies of the modern world – international agencies such as the UN and its Technical Assistance Board representing its various Specialized Agencies like F.A.O. and Unesco, the World Bank and the International Finance Corporation Administration; national agencies like the Colombo Plan and the Inter-American Development Fund; and the great private Foundations (wittily categorized as *philanthropoid* by that remarkable man Frederick Keppel) like Rockefeller and Ford, Gulbenkian, Nuffield and Carnegie.

At the moment, much of the financial and technical aid provided by these admirable bodies is being wasted by being flushed down the drain of excess population instead of into the channels of positive economic and cultural development, or is even defeating its own ends by promoting excessive and over-rapid population-increase.

Bankers do not make loans unless they are satisfied of the borrower's credit-worthiness.   Surely these powerful agencies, public or private, should not provide loans or grants or other aid unless they are satisfied of the recipient nation's demographic credit-worthiness.   If an under developed nation's birth-rate is excessive, the aid will go in providing the basic minima of food, care, shelter and education for the flood of babies, instead of the capital and the technical skills needed to achieve the breakthrough to a viable industrialization.   Wherever this is so, the aid-providing institution should insist that the nation should frame an approved policy of population-control, and that some of the aid should be devoted to the implementation of that policy and to research on the subject.   And the U.N. should, of course, take steps to prepare the way for a World Population Policy, should carry out or in any case encourage research on population-control, and should ensure that its Specialized Agencies like W.H.O., Unesco, F.A.O. and I.L.O., pay due attention to the problems of population in relation to their special fields of competence.

At last I reach my specific subject – eugenics, with its two aspects, negative and positive.   Negative eugenics aims at preventing the spread and especially the increase of defective or undesirable human genes or gene-combinations, positive eugenics at securing the reproduction and especially the increase of favourable or desirable ones.[5]

Negative eugenics has become increasingly urgent with the increase of mutations due to atomic fallout, and with the increased survival of genetically defective human beings, brought about by advances in medicine, public health, and social welfare. But it must, of course, attempt to reduce the incidence, or the manifestation, of every kind of genetic defect. Such defects include high genetic proneness to diseases such as diabetes, schizophrenia (which affects 1 per cent of the entire human population), other insanities, myopia, mental defect and very low I.Q., as well as more clear-cut defects like colour-blindness or haemophilia.

When defects depend on a single dominant gene, as with Huntington's chorea, transmission can of course be readily prevented by persuading the patient to refrain from reproducing himself. With sexlinked defects like haemophilia, Duchenne-type muscular dystrophy, or HCN "smell-blindness," this will help, but the method should be supplemented by counselling his sisters against marriage. This will be more effective and more acceptable when, as seems possible, we can distinguish carriers heterozygous for the defect from non-carriers. This is already practicable with some autosomic recessive defects, notably sickle-cell anaemia. Here, registers of carriers have been established in some regions, and they are being effectively advised against intermarriage. This will at least prevent the manifestation of the defect. The same could happen with galactosaemia, and might be applicable to relatives of patients with defects like phenylketonuria and agammoglobulinaemia.

In addition, the marked differential increase of lower-income groups, classes and communities during the last hundred years cannot possibly be eugenic in its effects. The extremely high fertility of the so-called problem group in the slums of many industrial cities is certainly anti-eugenic.

---

[5] In the past, these aims have been generally expressed in terms of defective or desirable *stocks* or *strains*. With the progress of genetics, it is better to reformulate them in terms of genes.

As Muller and others have emphasized, unless these trends can be checked or reversed, the human species is threatened with genetic deterioration, and unless this load of defects is reduced, positive eugenics cannot be successfully implemented. For this we must reduce the reproduction rate of genetically defective individuals: that is negative eugenics.

The implementation of negative eugenics can only be successful if family planning and eugenic aims are incorporated into medicine in general and into public health and other social services in particular. Its implementation in practice will depend on the use of methods of contraception or sterilization, combined where possible with A.I.D. (artificial insemination by donor) or other methods of vicarious parenthood. In any case, negative eugenics is of minor evolutionary importance and the need for it will gradually be superseded by efficient measures of positive eugenics.

In cases of specific genetic defect, voluntary sterilization is probably the best answer.[6] In the defective married male, it should be coupled with artificial parenthood (A.P.) by donor insemination (A.I.D.) as the source of children. In the defective female, the fulfilments of child rearing and family life will have to be secured by adoption until such time – which may not be very distant – as improved technique makes possible artificial parenthood by transfer of fertilized ova, which we may call A.O.D. In both cases, it must be remembered that sterilization does not prevent normal healthy and happy sexual intercourse.

Certified patients are now prevented from reproducing themselves by being confined in mental hospitals. If sterilized, they might be allowed to marry if this were considered likely to ameliorate their condition.

In the case of the so-called social problem group, somewhat different methods will be needed. By social problem group I mean the people, all too familiar to social workers in large cities, who seem to have ceased to care, and just carry on the business of bare

---

[6] It will be even more satisfactory if, as now appears likely, reversible male sterilization (vasectomy) becomes practicable.

existence in the midst of extreme poverty and squalor. All too frequently they have to be supported out of public funds, and become a burden on the community. Unfortunately they are not deterred by the conditions of existence from carrying on with the business of reproduction: and their mean family size is very high, much higher than the average for the whole country.

Intelligence and other tests have revealed that they have a very low average I.Q.; and the indications are that they are genetically subnormal in many other qualities, such as initiative, pertinacity, general exploratory urge and interest, energy, emotional intensity, and will-power. In the main, their misery and improvidence is not their fault but their misfortune. Our social system provides the soil on which they can grow and multiply, but with no prospects save poverty and squalor.

Here again, voluntary sterilization could be useful. But our best hope, I think, must lie in the perfection of new, simple and acceptable methods of birth-control, whether by an oral contraceptive or perhaps preferably by immunological methods involving injections. Compulsory or semi-compulsory vaccination, inoculation and isolation are used in respect of many public health risks: I see no reason why similar measures should not be used in respect of this grave problem, grave both for society and for the unfortunate people whose increase has been actually encouraged by our social system.

Many social scientists and social workers in the West, as well as all orthodox Marxists, are environmentalists. They seem to believe that all or most human defects, including many that western biologists would regard as genetic, can be dealt with, cured or prevented by improving social environment and social organization. Even some biologists, like Professor Medawar, agree in general with this view, though he admits a limited role for negative eugenics, in the shape of what he calls "genetic engineering." For him, the "newer solution" of the problem, which "goes some way towards making up for the inborn inequalities of man," is simply to improve the environment. With this I cannot agree. Although certain particular problems can be dealt with in this way, for instance proneness to tuberculosis by improving living conditions and preventing infection, such methods cannot cope with the general problem of genetic deterioration, because this, if not checked, will steadily increase through the accumulation of mutant genes which otherwise would have been eliminated.

It is true that many diseases or defects with a genetic basis, like diabetes or myopia, can be cured by treatment, though almost always with some expense, trouble, or discomfort to the defective person as well as to society. But if the incidence of such defects (not to mention the many others for which no cure or remedy is now known) were progressively multiplied, the burden would grow heavier and heavier and eventually wreck the social system. As in all other fields, we need to combine environmental and genetic measures, and if possible render them mutually reinforcing.

Against the threat of genetic deterioration through nuclear fall-out there are only two courses open. One is to ban all nuclear weapons and stop bomb-testing; the other is to take advantage of the fact that deep-frozen mammalian sperm will survive, with its fertilizing and genetic properties unimpaired, for a long period of time and perhaps indefinitely, and accordingly to build deep shelters for sperm-banks – collections of deep-frozen sperm from a representative sample of healthy and intelligent males. A complete answer must wait for the successful deep-freezing of ova also. But this may be achieved in the fairly near future, and in any case shelters for sperm-banks will give better genetic results than shelters for people, as well as being very much cheaper.

Positive eugenics has a far larger scope and importance than negative. It is not concerned merely to prevent genetic deterioration, but aims to raise human capacity and performance to a new level.

For this, however, it cannot rely on measures designed to produce merely a slight differential increase of genetically superior stocks, generation by generation. This is the way natural selection obtains its results, and it worked all right during the biological phase, when immense spans of time were available. But with the accelerated tempo of modern psychosocial evolution, much quicker results are essential. Luckily modern science is providing the necessary techniques, in the shape of artificial insemination and the deep-freezing of human gametes. The effects of superior germ-plasm can be multiplied ten or a hundredfold through the use of what I call E.I.D. – eugenic insemination by deliberately preferred donors – and many thousand fold if the superior sperm is deep-frozen.

This multiplicative method, harnessing man's deep desires for a better future, was first put forward by H. J. Muller and elaborated by Herbert Brewer, who invented the terms *eutelegenesis* and *agapogeny* for different aspects of it. Some such method, or what we may term Euselection – deliberate encouragement of superior genetic endowment – will produce immediate results. Couples who adopt this method of vicarious parenthood will be rewarded by children outstanding in qualities admired and preferred by the couple themselves.

When deep-frozen ova too can be successfully engrafted into women, the speed and efficiency of the process could of course be intensified.

Various critics insist on the need for far more detailed knowledge of genetics and selection before we can frame a satisfactory eugenic policy or even reach an understanding of evolution. I can only say how grateful I am that neither Galton nor Darwin shared these views, and state my own firm belief that they are not valid. Darwin knew nothing – I repeat *nothing* – *about* the actual mechanism of biological variation and inheritance: yet he was possessed of what I can only call a common-sense genius which gave him a general understanding of the biological process and enabled him to frame a theory of the process whose core remains unshaken and which has been able successfully to incorporate all the modifications and refinements of recent field study and genetic experiment.

Neither did the automatic process of natural selection "know" anything about the mechanisms of evolution. Luckily this did not prevent it from achieving a staggering degree of evolutionary transformation, including miracles of adaptation and improvement. From his seminal idea, Darwin was able to deduce important general principles, notably that natural selection would automatically tend to produce both diversification (adaptive radiation) and improvement (biological advance or progress) in organization, but that lower types of organization would inevitably survive alongside higher.

Critics of positive eugenics like Medawar inveigh against what they call *"geneticism."* However, he himself is guilty on this count, for he has swallowed the population geneticists' claim (which I have discussed earlier) that theirs is the only scientifically valid definition of *fitness;* and this in spite of his admission that one organic type can be more "advanced" than another, and that "human beings are the out come of a process which can perfectly well be described as an advancement." However, he equates advancement with mere increase in complexity of the "genetical instructions" given to the animal: if he had thought in broad evolutionary instead of restricted genetic terms he would have seen that biological advance involves improved organization of the phenotype; that fitness in the geneticismal sense is a purely reproductive fitness; and that we must also take into account immediate phenotypic fitness and long-term evolutionary fitness. To put it in a slightly different way, "fitness" as measured by differential survival of offspring is merely the mechanism by which the long-term improvement of true biological fitness is realized.

Recent genetic studies have shown the wide spread occurrence of genetic polymorphism, in animal species and man, whether in the form of sharply distinct morphs (as with colour-blindness and other sensory morphisms), in multiplicity of slightly different alleles, or merely in a very high degree of potential variance. Some critics of positive eugenics maintain that this state of affairs will prevent or at least strongly impede any large-scale genetic improvement, owing to the resistance to change offered by genetic polymorphisms maintained by means of heterozygote advantage, which appear to comprise the majority of polymorphic systems.

It has further been suggested, notably by Professor Penrose, that people heterozygous for genes determining general intellectual ability, and therefore of medium or mediocre intelligence, are reproductively "fitter" – more fertile – than those of high or low intelligence, and accordingly that, as regards genetic intelligence, the British population is in a state of natural balance. If so, it would be difficult to try to raise its average level by deliberate selective measures, and equally difficult for the level to sink automatically as the result of differential fertility of the less intelligent groups.

Although Medawar (op. cit. p. 125) appears to disagree with Penrose's main contention, he concludes that: "If a tyrant were to attempt to raise the intelligence of all of us to its present maximum, … I feel sure that his efforts would be self-defeating: the population would dwindle in numbers and, in the extreme case, might die out." It is true that he later enters a number of minor caveats, but his main conclusion remains. This to me appears incomprehensible. If selection has operated, as it certainly has done in the past, during the passage from Pithecanthropus to present-day man, to bring about a very large rise in the level of genetic intelligence, why can it not bring about a much smaller rise in the immediate future? There are no grounds for believing that modern man's system of genetic variance differs significantly from that of his early human ancestors.

As regards balanced morphisms, it is of course true that they constitute stable elements in an organism's genotype. However, when their stability is mainly due to linkage with a lethal, and therefore to double-dose disadvantage rather than to heterozygote advantage, they may be destabilized by breaking the linkage. In any case, morphisms stable in one environment may sometimes be broken up in another. This has happened, for instance, with the white-yellow sex-limited morphism of the butterfly Colias eurythema, which in high latitudes has ceased to exist, and the local population is monomorphic, all homozygous white.

Certainly some morphisms show very high stability. For instance the PTC (phenylthiocarbamide) taste morphism occurs in apparently identical form both in chimpanzees and man, and so must presumably have resisted change for something like 10 million years. However, this remarkable stability of a specific genotypic component of the primate stock has not prevented the transformation of one branch of that stock into man!

Similar arguments apply to linked polygenic systems and to the general heterozygosity in respect of small allelic differences shown by so many organisms, including man, in the former case, Mather has shown how selection can break the linkage and make the frozen variability available for new recombinations and new evolutionary change. In the latter case, the stability need not be so intense as with clear-cut morphisms.

Frequently, it appears, polymorphism depends not so much on heterotic advantage as on a varying balance of advantage between the alleles concerned in different conditions: one allele is more advantageous in certain conditions, another in other conditions. The polymorphism is therefore a form of insurance against extreme external changes and gives flexibility in a cyclically or irregularly varying environment (Huxley 1955).   Such loose polymorphic systems can readily be modified by the incorporation of new and the elimination of old mutant alleles and the incorporation of new ones in response to directional changes in environment. In any case, their widespread existence has not stood in the way of directional evolutionary change, including the transformation of a protohominid into man. Why should they stand in the way of man's further genetic evolution?

The same reasoning applies to those numerous cases where high genetic variance, actual or potential, is brought about by multiple genic polymorphism, when many genes of similar action exist, often in a number of slightly different allelic forms.

In all these cases the critics of eugenics have been guilty of that very "geneticism" which they deplore. They approach the subject from the standpoint of population genetics. If they were to look at it from an evolutionary standpoint, their difficulties would evaporate, and they would see that their objections could not be maintained.

Two further objections are often made to positive eugenics. One is by way of a question – who is to decide which type to select for? The other, which is by way of an answer to the first, is to assert that effective selection needs authoritarian methods and can only be put into operation by some form of dogmatic tyranny, usually stigmatized as intolerable or odious.

Both these objections reveal the same lack of understanding of psychosocial evolution as the genetical objections revealed about biological evolution: more simply, they demonstrate the same lack of faith in the potentialities of man that the purely genetical objections showed in the actual operative realizations of life.

For one thing, dogmatic tyranny in the modern world is becoming increasingly self-defeating: partly because it is dogmatic and therefore essentially unscientific, partly because it is tyrannical and therefore in the long run intolerable. But the chief point is that human improvement never works solely or even mainly by such methods and is doing so less and less as man commits himself more thoroughly to the process of general self-education.

Let me take an example. Birth-control resembles eugenics in being concerned with that most violent arouser of emotion and prejudice, human reproduction. However, during my own career, I have witnessed the subject break out of the dark prison of taboo into the international limelight. It was only in 1917 that Margaret Sanger was given a jail sentence for disseminating birth-control information. In the late twenties, when I was already over forty, I was summoned before the first Director-General of the B.B.C., now Lord Reith, and rebuked for having contaminated the British ether with such a shocking subject. Yet two years ago an international gathering in New York paid tribute to Margaret Sanger as one of the great women of our age. *Time* and *Life* Magazines both published long and reasoned articles on how to deal with the population explosion, and two official U.S. committees reported in favour of the U.S. conducting more research on birth-control methods and even of giving advice on the subject if requested by other nations. And to-day one can hardly open a copy of the most respectable newspapers without finding at least one reference to the grievous effects of population increase and population density on one or another aspect of human life in one or another country of the globe, including our own. Meanwhile, six nations have started official policies of family planning and population control, and many others are unofficially encouraging them.

Birth-control, in fact, has broken through – and in so doing it has changed its character and its methods.   It began as a humanitarian campaign for the relief of suffering human womanhood, conducted by a handful of heroic figures, mostly women.   It has now become an important social, economic and political campaign, led by powerful private associations, and sometimes the official or semi-official concern of national governments.   Truth, in fact, prevails – though its prevailing demands time, public opprobrium of the self-sacrificing pioneers at the outset, and public discussion, backed by massive dissemination of facts and ideas, to follow.

We can safely envisage the same sort of sequence for evolutionary eugenics, operating by what may be called Euselection, though doubtless with much difference in detail. Thus the time to achieve public breakthrough might be longer because the idea of Euselection by delegated paternity runs counter to a deep-rooted sense of proprietary parenthood.   On the other hand it might be shorter, since there is such a rapid increase in the popular understanding of science and in the agencies of mass communication and information, and above all because of the profound dissatisfaction with traditional ideas and social systems, which portends the drastic recasting of thought and attitude that I call the Humanist Revolution.

Some things, at least, are clear.   First, we need to establish the legality, the respectability, and indeed the morality of A.I.D.   It must be cleared of the stigma of sin ascribed to it by Church dignitaries like Lord Fisher when Archbishop of Canterbury, and from the legal difficulties to its practice raised by the lawyers and administrators.   Most importantly, the notion of donor secrecy must be abolished.   Parents desiring A.I.D. should have not only the right but the duty of choice.   For the time being, it may possibly be best that the name and personal identity of a donor should not be known to the acceptors, but there should certainly be a register of certified donors kept by medical men (and I would hope by the National Health Service) which would give particulars of their family histories. This would enable acceptors to exert a degree of conscious selection in choosing the father of the child they desire, and so pave the way for the supersession of blind and secrecy-ridden A.I.D. by an open-eyed and proudly accepted E.I.D. where the E stands for *Eugenic*.

The pioneers of E.I.D., whether its publicists or its practitioners, will undoubtedly suffer all kinds of abusive prejudice – they will be accused of mortal sin, of theological impropriety, of immoral and unnatural practices. But they can take heart from what has happened in the field of birth-control, and can be confident that the rational control of reproduction aimed at the prevention of human suffering and frustration and the promotion of human well-being and fulfilment will in the not too distant future come to be recognized as a moral imperative.

The answers to the questions I mentioned at the beginning of this section are now, I hope, clear. There will be no single type to be selected for, but a range of preferred types; and this will not be chosen by any single individual or committee. The choice will be a collective choice representing the varied preferences and ideals of all the couples practising euselection by E.I.D., and it will not be dogmatically imposed by any authoritarian agency, though as general acceptance of the method grows, it will be reinforced by public opinion and official leadership. The way is open for the most significant step in the progress of mankind – the deliberate improvement of the species by scientific and democratic methods.

All the objections of principle to a policy of positive eugenics fall to the ground when the subject is looked at in the embracing perspective of evolution, instead of in the limited perspective of population genetics or the short-term perspective of existing socio-political organization. Meanwhile the obvious practical difficulties in the way of its execution are being surmounted, or at least rendered surmountable, by scientific discovery and technical advance.

In evolutionary perspective, eugenics – the progressive genetic improvement of the human species – inevitably takes its place among the major aims of evolving man. What should we eugenists do in the short term to promote this long-term aim? We must of course continue to do and to encourage research on human genetics and reproduction, including methods of conception-control and sterilization. The establishment of the Darwin Research Fellowships is an important milestone in this field: I hope that we shall be able to enlarge our research activities in the future.

We must continue to support negative eugenic measures, especially perhaps in respect of the so-called Social Problem group. We should assuredly continue to be concerned about population increase, and to support all agencies and organizations aiming at sane and scientific policies of population-control. We must equally support all agencies giving eugenic advice and marriage guidance. Since significant eugenic improvement depends on donor insemination, we must do all we can to win public support for A.I.D., and to improve current practices in the subject.

In general, we must bring home to the general public the possibility of real genetic improvement, the burden it could lift off human shoulders, the hope it could kindle in human hearts. We must make people understand that social and cultural amelioration are not enough. If they are not to turn into temporary palliatives or degenerate into mere environmental tinkering, they must be combined with genetic amelioration, or at least with the hope of it in the future.

To ensure this, not only must the eugenics movement help to educate the public and especially the members of the professions – medical, educational, scientific, administrative, and others – in respect of eugenics, but it must make every effort to get the educational system improved at all levels, so as to provide everyone with the necessary minimum of biological understanding – an understanding of reproduction and population, genetics and selection, ecology and conservation, and above all of the process of evolution in its awe-inspiring sweep and of man's specific significance and responsibility in that comprehensive process.

If, as I firmly believe, man's role is to do the best he can to manage the evolutionary process on this planet and to guide its future course in a desirable direction, fuller realization of genetic possibilities becomes a major motivation for man's efforts, and eugenics is revealed as one of the basic human sciences.

REFERENCES

Baker, P. T. 1960. Climate, Culture and Evolution. *Human Biol.*, **32**, 3. (Race, environment and culture.)

Blacker, C. P. 1952. Eugenics: Galton and After. Duckworth. London. (Galton's work and views. Modern developments in eugenics.)

Boyd, W. C. 1950. *Genetics and the Races of Man.* Little, Brown. Boston (Race and evolution.)

Brewer, H. 1935. Eutelegenesis: *Eugen. Rev.,* **27**, 121.

— 1939. Eutelegenesis. *Lancet.* 1939. 1, 265.

— 1961. Ethical Parenthood and Contraception. *Balanced Living.* Brookville, Ohio. (17) 3, p. 69.

Burt, C. 1958. The Inheritance of Mental Ability. *Amer. Psychol.* **13**, 1. (Eugenics and intelligence.)

— 1959, 1961. Class Differences in General Intelligence. *Brit. J. statist. Psychol,* **12**, 15

— Intelligence and social mobility. *Ibid.,* **14**, 3. (Distribution of intelligence.)

— 1962. *The Gifted Child. Yearbook of Education, 1962.* p. 1. (Genetic intelligence.)

Carter, C. F. 1961. The Economic Use of Brains. *Advanc. Sci., Lond.,* **18**, 222. (Shortage of individuals of high ability.)

Coale, A. J. and Hoover, E. M. 1959. *Population Growth and Economic Development in Low Income Countries.* (O.U.P., Bombay.)

Count, E. W. 1950. *This is Race.* Schuman. New York. (History of racial concepts.)

Darlington, C. D. 1960. (Review of P. B. Medawar's *The Future of Man.*) *Heredity,* **15**, 44.

Dobzhansky, Th. 1962. *Mankind Evolving.* Yale Univ. Press. New Haven and London. D.N.A. (Population genetics, race, polymorphism, fitness, eugenics, cultural evolution, genotype and phenotype.)

Fisher, R. A., Ford, E. B. and Huxley, J. S. 1939. Taste-testing the anthropoid apes. *Nature,* **144**, 750. (Sensory morphisms, apes and man.)

Ford, E. B., 1949. Polymorphism. *Biol. Rev.,* **20**, 73. (Morphism, blood groups and disease.)

– 1956. *Genetics for Medical Students. Methuen.* London (Human genetics; morphism.)

Hulse, F. S. 1960. Adaptation. Selection and Plasticity in Ongoing Human Evolution. *Human Biol.,* **32**, 63. (Genetic plasticity and environment.)

Huxley, J. S. 1953. *Evolution in Action.* London and New York. Chatto and Windus (Natural selection and biological improvement.)

– 1955. Morphism and Evolution, *Heredity,* **9,** 1.

Huxley, J. S. (Ed.). 1961. *The Humanist Frame.* Allen and Unwin and Harpers. London and New York. (Introductory Chapter. General evolutionary theory.)

Kalmus, H. 1959. Genetical Variation and Sense-Perce tion. *Ciba Found. Symp., Biochem. Human Genetics,* **60.** (Sensory defects and morphisms.)

Livingstone, F. B. 1960. Natural Selection, Disease and Ongoing Human Evolution. *Human Biol.,* **32,** 17.

Mather, K. 1953. Genetical Control of Stability in Development. *Heredity,* **7,** 297. (Balanced polymor phism, stability, release of variance.)

– 1956. Polygenic Mutation and Variation in Populations. *Proc. roy. Soc.* (B), **145,** 292 (as for *op. cit.)*

McConnell, R. A. 1961. The Absolute Weapon. *Amer. Inst. biol. Sci. Bull.,* **11,** 14. (Eutelegenesis; importance of individuals of high ability.)

Medawar, P. B. 1960. *The Future of Man:* The Reith Lectures. Methuen. London.

Montague, A. 1957. *Anthropology and Human Nature.* Sargent. Boston. (Environmentalist views on race.)

Motulsky, A. G. 1960. Metabolic Polymorphisms and the Role of Infectious Diseases in Human Evolution. *Human Biol.* **32,** 29. (Morphisms and disease-resistance.)

Muller, H. J. 1929. The Method of Evolution. *Sci. Monthly,* Dec. 1929, 481. (Natural selection and directional evolution.)

— 1936. *Out of the Night.* Gollancz. London. (Eugenics and eutelegenesis.)

— 1949. The Darwinian and Modern Conceptions of Natural Selection. *Proc. Amer. Philos. Soc.,* **93,** 459. (Natural selection; fitness.)

— 1950a. Our Load of Mutations. *Amer. J. hum. Genet.* **2,** 111. (Genetic load.)

— 1950b. Radiation damage to the Genetic Material. *Amer. Scientist,* **38,** 3. (Effects of X rays, fall-out, etc.)

— 1959. The Guidance of Human Evolution. *Persp. Biol. Med.,* **3,** 1. (Eutelegenesis, deep-frozen sperm.)

— 1961a. (Review of P. B. Medawar's *The Future of Man.*) *Persp. Biol. Med.,* **4,** 377.

— 1961b. Human Evolution by Voluntary Choice of Germ-plasm. *Science,* **134,** 643. (Eutelegenesis, agapogeny.)

— 1961c. The Human Future: *The Humanist Frame,* ed. J. S. Huxley. London and New York. (Cultural and genetic evolution.)

Pettenkofer, H. J. *et. al.* 1962. *Nature,* **193**, 445. (Blood-group morphisms and disease-resistance.)

Roberts, J. A.. Fraser. 1959. *An Introduction to Medical Genetics*, 2nd Ed. O.U.P. Oxford.

Sauvy, A. 1961. *Fertility and Survival.* Chatto and Windus. London. (Over-population and economic development.)

Sheldon, W. H. 1940. *The Varieties of Human Physique.* Harpers. New York.

Sheppard, P. M. 1958. *Natural Selection and Heredity.* Hutchinson. London. (Natural selection.)

Tax, S. (Ed.). 1960. Articles by Kroeber, Washburn and Howell, Adams, Steward, et. al. in *The Evolution of Man*, Univ. of Chicago Press, Chicago. (Evolution and culture.)

Thoday, J. M. 1953. Components of Fitness. *Symp. Soc. exp. Biol. (Evolution)* **96**. (Fitness, stability, selection.)

Waddington, C. H. 1957. *The Strategy of the Genes.* Allen and Unwin. London. (Genetic assimilation; genetics and development.)

Williams, R. 1960. Why Human Genetics? *J. Hered,* **51**, 91. (Human genetic variance and environment.)

James Meade

Photograph courtesy of his family

1972

Economic Policy and the Threat of Doom[1]

J. E. Meade[2]

Introduction by David Vines[3]

This lecture is astonishing. Although given by James Meade in 1972, it is one of the very best pieces available on the current debate about global warming and the Kyoto Treaty.

In 1972, the "threat of doom" to which James Meade referred was raised by Forrester, Meadows and the Club of Rome. These scientists, analysing the global environmental problem, predicted that the world would soon run out of natural resources. Today the fear is that global warming will radically change our climate, leading to whole countries being submerged beneath the sea, and to radical changes in life for those whose homes do not disappear in this way. Thirty years ago some, at least, of the prophets of doom advocated policies which would have endangered global growth, policies which, if adopted, would have prevented the growth towards prosperity which so many people, living in the emerging-market economies, have experienced since then. Today the prophets of doom advocate the Kyoto treaty, which will, if it is to be effective,

---

[1] Bernard Benjamin, Peter R Cox and John Peel, eds., *Resources and Population* (Proceedings of the Ninth Annual Symposium of the Eugenics Society, London 1972). Academic Press, 1973.

[2] Nuffield Senior Research Fellow at Christ's College, Cambridge, England

[3] David Vines is Professor of Economics at the University of Oxford and a Fellow of Balliol College. He is also Adjunct Professor of Economics in the Research School of Pacific and Asian Studies at the Australian National University, and a Research Fellow of the Centre for Economic Policy Research. He worked closely with James Meade throughout the 1980s.

impose quite precise physical restrictions on the use of energy, to stop the release of "greenhouse gases". Many people, myself included, think that such physically imposed constraints will also endanger global growth, with damaging consequences for the next group of emerging market economies, including India and China. *Plus ca change, plus c'est la meme chose.*

What is remarkable about Meade's lecture is the clarity with which he opposed the prophets of doom in 1972. Those prophets got their central story wrong – their policies were not adopted and growth did not collapse. Today's doomsters might be wrong too, and the policies proposed in the Kyoto Treaty might cause great damage today too. James Meade's lecture contains a very clear exposition of what the prophets were getting wrong then. It also contains the clearest exposition that I have read anywhere, of how the policies being adopted as a result of the Kyoto Treaty may get things wrong too, and what we should do about this.

James Meade was awarded the Nobel Prize in Economics in 1977, for his work in international economics. But his achievements spanned the whole of the discipline. They were all informed by a strong, liberal, sense of what makes a good society. They all display Meade's determination to create an environment in which this good society can flourish – both by the design of the right incentives for private individuals and by the provision of good institutions of economic management.

Meade was born in 1907. He was educated at Malvern College, and Oriel College, Oxford. At the very beginning of his working life he spent an academic year in Cambridge, in 1930-31. Here he joined the talented group of young economists who helped John Maynard Keynes write his monumental *General Theory of Employment Interest and Money.* During the War years Meade worked in the Economic Section of the Cabinet Office. He drafted the *Full Employment White Paper* of 1944 which laid the basis for Britain's post-war economic policy. He also led those in Britain who, under Keynes direction, were planning how to run the world economy after the war. As a result, Meade participated in the British discussions with American officials on the rebuilding of the international monetary system. These deliberations led to the establishment of the *International Monetary Fund* and the *World Bank,* at a conference at Bretton Woods, in New Hampshire, in 1944. Meade also led British planning for the establishment, in 1947, of the General Agreement on Tariffs and Trade (or GATT), which was ultimately transformed, in 1994, into the World Trade

Organisation (or WTO), an institution designed to help manage moves towards a liberal regime for international trade.

In 1947 Meade became Professor of Economics at the London School of Economics, and it was here that he wrote his two great volumes on the Theory of *International Economic Policy*, for which he later received the Nobel prize.   In 1957 he moved back to Cambridge and was to spend the rest of his life there, working, without ceasing, until his death in 1995, at the age of 88.   During that time he wrote a series of books on the *Principles of Political Economy*, which, amongst other things, established the ideas on economic growth and on "externalities" which he used in the lecture reprinted below. He also led an enquiry into the UK tax system (the "Meade Committee"). Then in his last years, from 1978 onwards, he laboured to help bring about one last, but vital, transformation of macroeconomic policy-making in the United Kingdom. This was the move to the inflation-targeting regime, which the Bank of England now operates.   That regime of "constrained discretion", is, many would argue, what has underpinned the very profound improvement in economic performance in Britain in the past 15 years.   Meade played a significant part in the moves which put this in place.

Meade's lecture "Economic Policy and the Threat of Doom" is a natural product for someone whose intellectual achievement was so formidable, and whose range of view so broad.   There are five important things to say about it.

First, right from the beginning page of the lecture, Meade sets the discussion against the background of a growing world economy. This is natural; during his time in Cambridge before giving this lecture, he had been studying growth theory in detail. But he sets the stage in a revealing way. Meade writes:

"As the total world population grows and as economic development raises manufactured output per head of population, the total growth of economic activity will ... press upon [four] different kinds of constraint: first, the limited land surface of the globe; second, the limited stocks of certain irreplaceable materials such as minerals and fossil fuels; ... third, the limited ability of the environment to absorb the polluting effects of economic activity; [and] fourth, namely the available supply of man-made capital assets – machines, buildings and so on."

This summary of the sources of growth, and of the constraints upon growth, is a much more revealing one than would have been apparent from the simple Solow-Swan growth model, which was what was in the air at the time.

Second, Meade goes on to argue that any one of these four constraints may come to exert the dominant constraint on growth at any particular time, that it is quite uncertain which one will do so, and that it is quite wrong to worry about only one of these constraints at a time. That means that is wrong to worry only about the limited ability of the environment to absorb the polluting effects of economic activity (as some present- day supporters of the Kyoto treaty seem to do). To make this point, he presents a sketch of a very poor community which, because of its poverty, is unable to save more than a very small proportion of its income. If its population is growing at a high rate, its stock of capital equipment per head will begin to fall.

"At some point the availability of dwellings, schools, hospitals, tools machinery factories, etc. may become so low that output per head falls below the bare subsistence level. This human crisis might occur even although there was no shortage of natural resources and no pollution of the environment ... [but it could be] just as devastating a crisis as that due to raw material shortage or pollution."

This is, in fact, the kind of crisis that is currently facing about a sixth of humanity, who are so poor that they cannot accumulate enough equipment to be able to begin to grow. It is a crisis which Jeff Sachs and others have been labouring to resolve. (See Sachs, 2004). What Meade wishes us to do is keep an open mind as to which is the most dominant problem that we face in any circumstance. We must not, he believes, forget about the problems of development which have nothing to do with problems of the environment, or of pollution, or of a shortage of natural resources. In another example, Meade points out that we are very uncertain about how forcefully population will press upon the world. This is something which has become much more apparent in the thirty years since he gave this lecture, during which population growth has slowed to an unexpected extent in the more developed parts of the world. Slower (or faster) population growth will make the problem of global warming press less (or more) forceful over the next hundred years. Because of these kinds of uncertainty about the underlying causes of, and extent of, growth, Meade goes on to argue that we are very unsure of the costs of the pollution to the global economy, and to mankind. We cannot, says Meade, be sure that "economic development will be of a given polluting character and that technology will not be capable of introducing sufficiently non-polluting methods with sufficient speed". We are very unsure too, of the benefits to be obtained from spending resources in trying to reduce this pollution. This clarity, about being aware of the need to deal with risks, in the face of great uncertainty, is something which characterized all of Meade's work

Third, Meade argues that, in the face of these risks, we would be very unwise to impose very high costs in our efforts to reduce pollution, in search of benefits which may be of very uncertain size. This would be particularly true if those efforts to reduce pollution would harm the very poorest parts of the world, the difficulties of which have been touched on above. At the very least, we should first try to find the likely probabilities of the costs of the pollution that we are trying to avoid, before paying large sums whose likely effects in avoiding it are also not well known.

"Should one starve one person today to avert a 99 percent probability of the starvation of ten persons tomorrow? Perhaps, Yes; but should one do so to avert a 1 percent probability of the starvation of ten persons tomorrow? Perhaps certainly, No."

Fourth, Meade argues that the price mechanism should be used to help to solve the problem of pollution, in the face of such risks. The economist's "immediate reaction" is that the operation of the price mechanism can cause one activity to be substituted for another; and in this case that this price mechanism could be used so as to enable the world economy to grow in a less polluting way. Thus, he says,

"economists are often less pessimistic than natural scientists in their attitude to these problems. A large part of an economist' training revolves around the idea of a price mechanism in which that which is scarce goes up in price relative to that which is plentiful with … "substitution effects" both on the supply side and on the demand side. … How far this process will help to put off the evil day depends, of course, upon the possibilities of substitution throughout the economic system; … here [too] that economists are apt to be on the optimistic side."

Meade goes on to ask if it is "any use fiddling with the price mechanism [in this way] while the nuclear reactors burn?" (Or, we might add, whilst greenhouse gasses are spewed out?) What exactly might the price mechanism help us to achieve?

"It is in fact", says Meade, "precisely here that we need a major revolution in economic policy to make the price mechanism work. Environmental pollution is a case of what economists call 'external diseconomies' … We need politically to demand an extensive set of cost-benefit analysis of various economic activities and the imposition of taxes and levies of one kind or another at appropriate rates".

Meade carefully lists the features that would need to be studied to determine the appropriate rates at which these taxes and charges should be levied.

Meade's fifth and final contribution is the one which is most connected with current debate about the Kyoto Treaty, and I will discuss it in some detail. He argues that *taxes* on the use of fuels which pollute (e.g. by producing greenhouse gasses) are much to be preferred to the *regulation* of the amount of pollution that is produced (e.g. by regulating the emission of greenhouse gasses, as in the Kyoto treaty).

"In some cases – though these are much rarer than many administrators and technologists believe – it may be appropriate to act by a regulation rather than by a tax or a charge on pollution. … But where it is possible to define and police a noxious activity for the purpose of regulating its amount, it is possible also to define and police it for the purpose of taxing it; and normally a tax on a noxious activity will be a more efficient method of control than direct regulation."

Meade identifies one reason for this, which is known from Meade's own more general work that he did in Cambridge, which we referred to above. He writes

"Faced with a tax per unit of pollutant, those who find it cheap to reduce the pollution will reduce it more than those who find it expensive to do so; and thus a given reduction in the total pollution can be obtained at a lower cost than if each polluter was forced by regulation to reduce his pollution by the same amount."

But, the Kyoto treaty has been specifically designed to get around this objection. The Treaty brings with it the possibility of "emissions trading", in which those individuals within a country who find it cheapest to reduce pollution will be able to do a lot of this, and then sell emissions permits to others who find it more difficult to reduce emissions, thereby obtaining the efficiency improvement just described. Moreover emissions trading between countries will enable owners of emissions permits in one country, who are able to reduce pollution easily, to sell their emissions permits abroad, thus obtaining the above-discussed improvement in efficiency on a global scale.

Nevertheless Meade is right to wish to use *taxes* on the use of fuels, rather than seeking to regulate the quantity of emissions as is done in the Kyoto treaty.   The reason is central to his whole argument about dealing with risk, and it is quite surprising that he does not actually spell it out. It is clear to me that if he were here today he would certainly provide this reason. It arises as a result of the uncertainties, described in the second point above, to which Meade is so keen to draw attention.   Regulation of emissions requires an actual quantitative choice to be made, at a global level, on the amount of emissions that will be permitted. But it is a fact that the costs of restricting emissions to such a prescribed level are very, very uncertain. In particular, these costs may rise very steeply in the last stages of an attempt to reach a globally prescribed emissions target.   By contrast, although the benefits of reducing emissions are clearly uncertain, these costs-per-unit of emission are unlikely to vary greatly as emissions are reduced. That is because there is already a very large stock of greenhouse gases out there in the atmosphere, and so any additional reduction in emissions is unlikely to cause the marginal benefit of further reductions to fall significantly.

In such circumstances it is much better to tax the emissions at a level equal to the best guess of the marginal benefit of emissions reduction. As a result of doing this, the price of emissions permits would come to equal the size of the tax, and producers would choose a level of emissions at which the marginal cost of emissions would be equal to the tax rate. This outcome would end up causing the uncertainty about the marginal costs of emissions-reduction to be reflected in the quantity of emissions. If the marginal costs of emissions proved to be more than was initially thought then, in response to the imposition of a tax on emissions, there will be a smaller reduction in the amount of emissions produced. The same is true in reverse.

The alternative system, being introduced as a result of the Kyoto treaty, will have two different, and highly unpleasant, consequences. First, uncertainty in the cost of marginal reductions in emissions will not be reflected in a willingness to allow the amount of emissions to be governed by this cost. Instead, producers will be forced to carry out the required emissions control, however costly it turns out to be at the margin.   That uncertainty will come to be reflected in uncertainty about the price of emissions permits; as time rolls out this price will come to depend on the marginal cost of emissions reductions which may move in unexpected ways. Notice that this will make the effective price of fuel very volatile, since it will come to reflect the marginal price of the emissions which are associated with the use of that fuel. That will expose the community as a whole to unhelpful risks. This setup will also make the effective return to the reduction of emissions very uncertain, and so will make investment in emissions-control harder to manage. It is thus likely that less of such emissions-reducing investment will be done.

Second, if the world tries to implement the Kyoto Treaty without change, then it is possible that there will be increases in the demand for emissions permits coming from countries which grow faster than expected, and so wish to use more fuel than was predicted when the treaty was negotiated. If the marginal costs of emission-abatement are high in those countries, then they will need to purchase extra quotas from the allocations of quotas to other countries. That will require transfers of income across global boundaries: it will require these countries to export real goods and services, in order to run (possibly huge) non-oil balance of payments surpluses to pay for these quotas. The amounts of money may be very large. This is a "transfer problem" of the kind that Maynard Keynes discussed in 1929, concerning the payment of German reparations after World War I. It is clear to me that, for this reason, the Kyoto system will be no more sustainable than were German reparations payments, for reasons which Keynes analysed many years ago.

I have brought together Meade's findings in my five major points above. Meade ably summarises these findings in the following way.

Meade writes that it is a mistake to rely on models of future world events which assume a given particular flow of pollution per unit of output produced, independend of policy.

"Economic systems in the past have shown great flexibility. If we were to make the production of pollutants … really costly to those concerned, then we might see drastic changes. There is *no a priori* reason for denying that if appropriate governmental action is taken to impose the social costs on those who cause the damage, there could be dramatic changes in the more important and more threatening cases of the threat of Doom through pollution …."

This is a conclusion which should be borne in mind in today's discussions of global warming.

Meade concludes his lecture by drawing out two important international implications. This is as we might expect, from someone who was about to go on to win the Nobel prize for his work in International Economics.

First, he notes that it is essential that actions to reduce production of pollutants should not be taken in a way which so damages the growth of the world economy that it endangers the economic development of the poorest countries.   As he points out, the development of these poorest countries depends fundamentally both on maintaining the growth in demand from the more advanced countries for the exports of these poorest countries, and on sustaining the supply of capital funds from these richer countries for investment in the poorest countries.   Meade believed that policies should be resisted if they are designed to deal with problems of pollution (including those of global warming) but would have the effect of threatening these two things.

Second, Meade makes it clear that many of the policies which are needed to reduce pollution will "need international agreement and organization".   This modest five-word statement comes from someone who had helped to produce international agreement and organization for both the international monetary regime, and the international trading regime, after World War Two.   He knew the difficulties of devising such international cooperation.   And he was always determined to ensure that any such international regimes were liberal ones, consistent with, and supported by, well functioning markets and an effective price mechanism. It is not at all clear that the provisions of the Kyoto Treaty will address Meade's concerns.

References: Economic Policy and the Threat of Doom

Corden, W. M and A. Atkinson (1979) Meade, James. E. In *International Encyclopaedia of the Social Sciences, Bibliographical Supplement,* vol. 18, ed. D. L. Sills. New York, Free Press; London: Macmillan, pp 528 – 532.

Atkinson, A and M. Weale (2000) "James Edward Meade" Proceedings of the British Academy, vol. 105, Oxford: Oxford University Press

Howson, S. (2000) "James Meade" *Economic Journal* Vol 110, pp F122 - F145.

Johnson, H. (1978) "James Meade's Contribution to Economics" *Scandinavian Journal of Economics*, vol 80, pp 64 – 85.

Sachs, J. (2005) *The End of Poverty: Economic Possibilities for Our Time.* New York: Penguin

Vines, D. (1988) "Meade, James Edward". In the *Palgrave Dictionary of Economics.* London: Macmillan, pp 410 – 417.

The 1972 Galton Lecture

I am an economist with no training in the natural sciences. You must not, therefore, expect me to tell you to what extent the threat of doom is an immediate and real one. The answer to this fundamental question depends upon scientific and technological assessment of such matters as the ultimate effects of certain ecological and atmospheric disturbances, the technological prospects of substituting one material for another, and the prospects of a more direct harnessing of solar energy. There is much disagreement among highly qualified natural scientists on these questions. An economist will not grudge the natural scientists their little squabbles; but he would be foolish to try to judge between them.

That there should be considerable disagreement between the optimists and the pessimists among scientists and technologists is itself significant. The scientific and technological problems involved are very numerous; many of them are far-reaching and difficult of solution; and, above all, the interrelationships between them are exceedingly complex. What will happen to human society over the next half century depends upon a very complicated network of feedback relationships between demographic developments, industrial and economic developments, technological developments, biological and ecological developments, and psychological, political, and sociological developments. In each of the many sub-divisions of each of these separate fields experts are confronted with difficult specific problems which they have yet to solve; but in addition to these specialized problems there remains the basic problem of how the developments in these various fields react upon each other. We need to see the system as a whole; and in our present intellectual atmosphere of expert specialization it is precisely in such generalization of interrelationships that we are weakest.

Methods of studying feedback relationships in dynamic economic systems as a whole and problems of decision-making in conditions of uncertainty are matters to which economists have devoted a great deal of thought in recent years; and this must be my excuse for venturing to address you on this present occasion.

Having said that, I will beat a hasty but partial retreat. In this lecture I am going to consider only the basic economic interrelationships in discussing what we should do to meet the threat of doom. But I think that will be sufficient to give an idea of the principles involved in considering interrelationships in a dynamic social system, and it will certainly be enough for one lecture for one hour.

What then are the economic factors in the threat of doom? I take the work of Professors Forrester (1971) and Meadows (1972) at the Massachusetts Institute of Technology as the text for my sermon. As the total world population grows and as economic development raises manufactured output per head of population, the total growth of economic activity will, they argue, press upon three different kinds of constraint: first, the limited land surface of the globe; second, the limited stocks of certain irreplaceable materials such as minerals and fossil fuels; and, third, the limited ability of the environment to absorb the polluting effects of economic activity.

These are indeed three basic economic limiting factors. To these three the economist would, I think, be inclined to add a fourth, namely the available supply of man-made capital assets – machines, buildings, and so on. Each of these limiting factors has its own distinctive features: and although these features are rather obvious, I hope you will excuse me if I underline them because they have important implications for the devising of economic policies.

The first group of limiting factors, typified by land, I will call "maintainable natural resources". Consider a farm of a given quantity and quality of land. There may be room on it only for one farmer and his family at a time, if a given standard of living is to be obtained from its cultivation. But when farmer A and his family have passed on, farmer B and his family can enjoy it. There may not be room for two at a time, but there is room for an unlimited number of families provided that they succeed each other in time.

The pressure at any one time of population upon the limited amount of land and its effect in reducing output per head because of the so-called law of diminishing returns is, of course, the limiting factor which has been so prominent in classical economic analysis since the days of Malthus and Ricardo. The fact that it is an old and familiar idea does not mean that it is a false or an unimportant idea. On the contrary, it is very relevant indeed in the modern world. In addition to this straightforward economic law of diminishing returns, there are other non-economic features of the pressure of population upon the limited amount of land space which may give rise to serious human problems – for example, the psychological ills which may result from too close crowding together. As this lecture will be confined to the more or less straightforward economic problems, the tendency as population grows for output per head to fall as the amount of land per head is reduced must stand proxy for all the evils resulting from a scarcity of maintainable natural resources.

The second group of limiting factors I will call "non-maintainable natural resources". Consider a stock of 1,000,000 tons of coal. Suppose that a family must consume 10 tons of coal a year to maintain a decent standard of living and suppose that a family lives for 50 years. Then the coal stock will provide for the decent living of 2,000 families, no more and no less. Nor does it matter (provided the stock is already mined and available) whether these families exist all at the same time so that a human society of 2,000 families lasts for only 50 years or whether these families all succeed each other so that a human society of one family lasts for 100,000 years. If 10 tons of coal a year are essential for a family and if the stock of coal has a finite limit, then clearly any decent population policy through its birth control arrangements must plan, sooner or later, for the painless extinction of the human race; and, on the face of it, in so far as the supply of non-maintainable natural resources is concerned, it does not matter whether we have a large population for a short time or a small population for a long time.

In this respect "non-maintainable natural resources" are very different from "maintainable natural resources".

The distinction between maintainable and non-maintainable natural resources in the real world is not absolutely clear-cut. Land of a given quality may be maintainable if properly farmed; but it can also be mined if it is overworked or allowed to erode, so that its power to satisfy wants is, like that of a stock of coal, used up once and for all.

On the other hand, by recycling the use of certain minerals an otherwise "non-maintainable natural resource" may be capable of being used again and again provided that its users succeed each other in time.

Nor is the distinction between natural resources (whether maintainable or non-maintainable), on the one hand, and man-made capital resources such as machinery, buildings etc. a clear-cut one. Land can be improved by, for example, a man-made drainage system; it is then a mixture of a maintainable natural resource and a man-made capital asset. Coal at the bottom of a mine must be brought to the surface by human action; when it lies as an available stock in the surface coal yard, it is a mixture of a non-maintainable natural resource and a man-made capital asset.

The possible scarcity of man-made capital assets constitutes a possible limiting factor which an economist would, I think, wish to add to the Forrester-Meadows catalogue. It is clearly not such a rigid limiting factor as the fixed and immutable supplies of natural resources. But it could nevertheless in certain conditions be the decisive factor. Consider a population which has a very low standard of living and is nevertheless growing rapidly. Because its standard is low it may be unable to save more than a very small proportion of its income without reducing its standards below the barest subsistence level. This may mean that its stock of man-made capital instruments can grow at only a very low rate, since all its productive resources, such as they are, must be used to produce goods and services for immediate consumption rather than to produce goods to add to – or even to maintain – the existing stock of capital equipment. If the population is growing at a high rate, capital equipment per head will be falling. At some point the availability of dwellings, schools, hospitals, tools, machinery, factories, etc. per head of the population may become so low that output per head falls below the bare subsistence level. There is a human crisis due to a lack of man-made instruments; and this crisis which might occur even though there was no shortage of natural resources and no pollution of the environment could be just as devastating as a crisis due to those other restraining factors.

The final limiting factor on economic growth is the pollution of the environment. This subject has until recently been gravely neglected; but as so often happens in human affairs, it has, I am very glad to say, rather suddenly become the fashionable subject for academic study and for political discussion. Its study needs the co-operative work of economists, demographers, and other social scientists with biologists, chemists, ecologists, and other natural scientists. I am not qualified to discuss the technical aspects of various forms of environmental pollution. I can only consider some of the main implications for the general principles of economic policy of the existence of these problems.

In the Forrester-Meadows models of the world community this problem is treated in the following way. It is assumed that industrial production pours out a stream of pollutants of one kind or another, the flow of which into a reservoir of pollutants, as it were, varies in proportion to the level of world industrial activity; it is assumed that the natural ecological and meteorological systems drain away and eliminate a flow of pollutants out of this reservoir, this outflow depending upon the amount of pollution in the reservoir. Thus the winds disperse smog, the waterways cope with sewage, some wastes are degraded by bacterial action, and so on. Thus the degree of environmental pollution rises if the flow into the pollution reservoir from industrial and other economic activity exceeds the rate at which natural cleansing forces are evaporating the existing pool of pollution in the reservoir. But it is assumed that beyond a certain point the atmosphere becomes so polluted that the action of these natural cleansing forces is impeded. At this point the outflow of pollutants from the reservoir no longer increases as the stock of pollutants increases; on the contrary, as the flow of pollutants into the reservoir raises the level of pollution in the reservoir beyond this critical point the outflow is actually reduced; and there is then a crisis due to an explosive rise in environmental pollution which chokes economic and other human activity.

This may well be a good model of the existing relationships, though, as I have said, I have not the technical competence to express an opinion. But in any case without stretching the meaning of words too outrageously we may perhaps then talk of environmental pollution as causing shortages of certain environmental goods – for example, it causes a shortage of clean air, or a shortage of poison-free fish, and so on.

With these introductory remarks on the general nature of the four basic limitations to economic growth – namely, shortages of maintainable natural resources, of non-maintainable natural resources, of man-made capital assets, and of environmental goods – let me now present to you a much simplified model of the dynamic interrelationships between these factors. My model is in its essence of the kind constructed by Professors Forrester and Meadows; but I have modified their models in two respects. First, since my intention is no more than to give you a very general impression of the sort of way in which they are working, I have greatly simplified the model, in particular confining it to the economic relationships. Second, I have in certain respects altered the structure of their model in ways which make it rather more congenial to an economist.[4] I warn you, therefore, that when I

---

[4] Economists will, however, notice that the model which I present still has a number of glaring economic deficiencies. Quite apart from the need for greater disaggregation, which I discuss later, the production function which I use does not allow for increasing returns to scale; technical progress is an entirely exogenous factor, responding neither to learning by doing nor to investment in research and development; there is no proper savings function; the standard of living is measured by output per head and not by consumption per head; inequalities in the distribution of income are ignored; investment is assumed to be maintained at a level sufficient to give full employment; and so on.

come to criticise and to comment in detail on my model I am not necessarily commenting on the Forrester-Meadows models.

I start then in Figure 1 with a model of the production system. In my figures solid lines represent positive and broken lines negative relation ships. Thus in Fig. 1 Output per head ($^O/_N$) is assumed to be higher, (i) the higher is the amount of maintainable natural resources (or Land) per head (L/N), (ii) the higher is the remaining stock of non-maintainable (or Exhaustible) natural resources per head (E/N), (iii) the higher is the amount of man-made Kapital assets per head (K/N), (iv) the more advanced is the state of Technological knowledge (T), and (v) the the lower is the level of Pollution in the pollution reservoir (P). If X is the number of persons in the population and L is the amount of Land, then land per head (L/N) is the greater (i) the greater is L and (ii) the smaller is N; and similarly for (E/N) and (K/N).

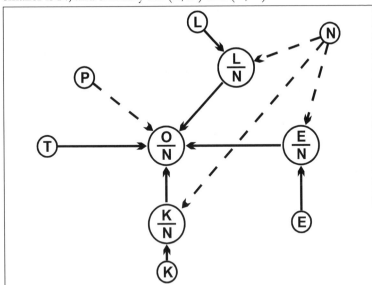

Fig. 1. The production system:
N = number of persons in the population;
L = amount of Land;
E = amount of Exhaustible resources;
K = amount of Kapital equipment;

T = state of Technical knowledge;
P = amount of environmental Pollution;
O = total Output of goods and services;
B = number of Births;
D = number of Deaths.

In my Figure 2 I add the demographic relationships. ΔN represents the rate of increase in the total population and is the greater, (i) the greater is the total number of births (B) and (ii) the smaller is the total number of deaths (D). Three factors are assumed to affect the level of births and deaths. (i) Both total births (B) and total deaths (D) will be greater, the larger is the total population (X) subject to the forces of fertility and mortality. (ii) Births (B) will be reduced and deaths (D) increased by a rise in the level of environmental pollution (F); these are some of the links whereby a possible pollution crisis would show its effect. (iii) A rise in the standard of living (O/N) will reduce mortality (D). If standards are very low, a rise from the basic subsistence level is likely to raise fertility and births; but at higher levels of the standard of living, a further rise may cause a reduction in fertility; and accordingly in my Figure 2 (O/N) is joined to (B) both by a solid and by a broken line. But if the standard of living should fall very low, then the consequential fall in births and rise in deaths will show the links whereby a crisis for human society is caused by a production crisis (a low (O/N)) due itself to a high level of pollution (F) or to low levels of maintainable natural resources per head (L/N), of non-maintainable resources per head (E/N), or of man-made capital assets per head (K/N).

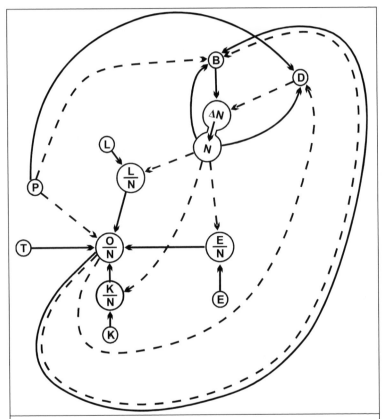

Fig. 2. The production system and the demographic relationships.

In Figure 3 I complete my simple model by showing the links whereby the total level of economic activity may react in turn upon the availability of non-maintainable natural resources, upon the stock of man made capital assets, and upon the level of environmental pollution. Total output (0) is the higher (i) the higher is the total population (N) and (ii) the higher is output per head (O/N). Non-maintainable natural resources are used up by the process of production and the rate of fall in the stock of such resources (-ΔE) will, therefore, be the higher, the higher is the level of total output (0). The stock of man made capital assets will be increased in so far as output is not consumed, but is used to invest in new capital instruments; and in so far as people save a given proportion of their real income, the rate at which the capital stock will rise (ΔK) will be the higher, the higher is the level of output and so of real income (0) from which savings can be made. But machines like human beings decay and die and so, just as a large human population (N) means that there will be many deaths (D), so a large stock of capital goods (K) will itself, through the need to replace old machines, reduce the net increase in the stock of machines resulting from any given level of newly produced machines (ΔK). Finally the rate of rise of the level of environmental pollution in the pollution reservoir (ΔP) will itself be greater, the greater is the level of total output (0). As I have already explained, we assume that with a moderately low level of pollution the cleansing forces of nature will cause a flow out of the pollution reservoir which is greater, the greater the amount of pollution in the reservoir; but after a critical point is reached, the cleansing processes may become so choked that the flow out of the reservoir is reduced by a rise in the level of pollution in the reservoir. This double possibility is shown by a solid and a broken line joining (P) to (ΔP).

The interrelationships in Figure 3 are already complex enough in spite of the great simplification of the reality which it represents. Indeed the complexities are certainly too great for it to be possible to generalize about the future course of events merely by inspection of Figure 3. But in principle one should be able to tell the future course of all the variables in Figure 3 if one knew three things:

first, the starting point, namely the present size of the population (N), the present size of the stock of non-maintainable resources (E), the present size of the stock of man-made capital assets (K), the present state of technical knowledge (T), the present state of environmental pollution (P), and the present availability of maintainable natural resources (L);

second, the form and strength of each individual relationship shown by the arrowed lines of Figure 3 – for example, the rate at which the stock of non-maintainable resources is depleted ($-\Delta E$) by the level of world output (0);

and third, the future course of technical knowledge (T).

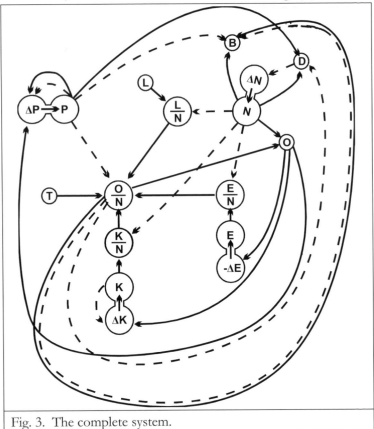

Fig. 3. The complete system.

For since one thing is assumed to lead to another in a determinate way, if we know where we start, how each individual variable affects each other individual variable, and how any outside or exogenous variables like T will behave, we should in principle be able to forecast the future movements of all the variables for an indefinite future time. We can instruct a computer to do the donkey work for us, and thus forecast the future course of world developments.

One can next examine the effect of various changes in policy by telling the computer to assume that at some particular date there is some particular change in some particular relationship – for example, that as a result of a birth control campaign there is from 1980 onwards a reduction of a given amount on the influence which the size of the population (i.e. the number of potential mothers) has upon the number of births. One can then observe the effect on the future course of all the variables of this change in policy, after taking into account all the dynamic interrelationships in the system. And this is, of course, just the sort of thing which Professors Forrester and Meadows do with their dynamic models.

It is not my intention to go through the various hair-raising scenarios for the future which they produce on various assumptions about future policies. These are important, but I must leave you to examine them for yourselves in *The Limits to Growth*. My immediate intention is only to comment on certain features of this method of studying the future.

There are some basic truths which Professors Forrester and Meadows emphasize through their work.

First, there must be an end sooner or later to exponential growth of population and output, and the limit to such growth may come upon us unexpectedly unless we are careful. The facts about the present world demographic situation which will be familiar to all of you are sufficient to illustrate the point. At present growth rates the world population doubles itself about every 30 years. If it were 3,500 million in 1970 it would be 7,000 million in 2000, 14,000 million in 2030, 28,000 million in 2060, and so on. Whatever the upper limit may be – and there obviously is *some* upper limit – we may hit it very suddenly. Indeed a mere 30 years before the final catastrophe we might be comforting ourselves with the thought that the world was after all only half full.

Second, the ultimate limit to growth may become effective either because of the exhaustion of non-maintainable natural resources, or because of pressure upon the limited supply of maintainable natural resources, or because of the choking effects of excessive environmental pollution.

It is good that these basic points should be forcibly emphasized. But it is not necessary to construct a complex dynamic model for their demonstration. Clearly scarcities of natural resources and the choking effects of an ever-increasing reservoir of pollution would set ultimate limits-to-growth. An elaborate and sophisticated dynamic model is needed not to tell us this, but to tell us how soon and how suddenly the limits will be reached, which limit will operate first, how quick and severe will be the effects of reaching a limit, how effective a given change in policy will be in mitigating these effects, and so on. It is to answer questions of this kind that there is point in trying to construct models of dynamic interrelationships of the Forrester-Meadows kind.

What will happen with any set of dynamic causal interrelationships depends in a very important way not only upon the extent to which one variable (e.g. the standard of living) affects other variables (e.g. fertility and mortality), but also upon the speed with which the various influences operate. Indeed, one very real cause for concern about the present situation is the recent changes in the relative reaction speeds in different sectors of human activity. Many changes, and in particular technological changes, have speeded up very greatly. Disease and mortality have been reduced at unprecedented rates. New synthetic chemical and other materials, as well as new technological processes, have been introduced at previously unimagined rates. As a result world population and world industrial production are growing at speeds hitherto quite unknown.

But while some variables are changing in this way at much greater speeds than before, other reactions are just as slow as ever and in some cases have become more sluggish than before. Many of the new man made chemicals and materials are slower to decompose than earlier natural substances and thus their effects (which in any case are novel and only partially understood) may be persistent and reach into the distant future.

To take another example, demographic reactions cannot be speeded up. It still takes a baby fifteen years or so of dependency before it starts to support itself; twenty years or so before it breeds, sixty years or so before it becomes an elderly dependant, and perhaps seventy years before it dies. Indeed, with the raising of school-leaving ages and with medical advances which keep people alive and active to greater ages than before, these demographic time-lags have in some respects been lengthened rather than shortened by present-day technological and social changes. Their importance may be illustrated in the following way. The continuation of high levels of fertility combined with relatively recent rapid reductions in the rates of child mortality have meant that there is an exceptionally high proportion of young children in many populations which are now growing rapidly. In these conditions population growth would continue for many years even if the fertility of women of child-bearing age were to be reduced instantaneously and without any delay whatsoever to levels which would merely replace the parents. For many years, as the present exceptionally high number of young girls grew up to motherhood, the total number of births would go on rising in spite of this immediate dramatic decline in the fertility of each individual woman. Such a population might well grow for another two or three generations and attain a size one-third greater than it was when the dramatic fall in fertility occurred.[5]

To take one more example, political delays between the observation of a change and legislative and administrative reaction to it remain as long as ever; and indeed the increasing insistence on democratic consensus in government may have lengthened the time needed to make acceptable a political decision which has obvious present disadvantages but whose future advantages are not at all obvious to the inexpert man in the street.

It is not therefore a sufficient answer to the prophets of Doom to say that their cry of Wolf has been equally relevant since the beginning of time. It has, of course, always been true that exponential growth cannot continue indefinitely. But what is

---

[5] These demographic time-lags play no role in Professor Forrester's model, where no allowance is made for changes in the age-composition of the world population. But Professor Meadows has introduced them into his Limits to Growth. I am indebted to Professor D. V. Glass and the Population Investigation Committee for the population projections which are reproduced as an appendix to this lecture and on which I have based my statement in the text of this lecture.

unique about the present situation is the unprecedentedly rapid rate of population growth and of technological innovation (which represent exceptionally rapid approaches to the finite limiting ceilings) in a situation in which the results of population growth and of technological change are at least as prolonged and as persistent as ever and in which the ultimate policy reactions to danger signals are at least as slow as ever. Such time relationships do, of course, increase the possibilities of catastrophic overshooting of safe limits; and dynamic feedback models are in principle the proper instruments for assessing the importance of the relationship between different time lags.

One must therefore sympathize with attempts to think in terms of a dynamic model of these interrelationships; but an economist can only contemplate with an amazed awe the assurance with which Professors Forrester and Meadows provide answers to our anxious questions.

The real world is a hideously complicated system and it is inevitable that any dynamic model should be highly simplified. To be useful it must, on the one hand, be sufficiently simplified to be manageable by modern techniques of analysis and computation; but, on the other hand, it must not omit any of the structural relationships which may have a fundamental effect on the outcome, and the form and quantitative importance of the relationships which are included must be reasonably accurately estimated. Furthermore, the future course of certain outside, exogenous influences must be reasonably well predicted – a hazardous undertaking since it involves predicting the future effects of scientific and technological inventions without any precise foreknowledge of the inventions themselves; for if the inventions were already well understood, they would already have been made. These are very far-reaching requirements.

Economists – or rather that special breed called econometricians, in whose arts I am myself, alas, completely incompetent – have now much experience in coping with problems of this kind in searching for answers to much more limited questions. What is it which determines the demand for new motor cars? What is it which causes money wage rates to rise rapidly?

What is it which governs businessmen's decisions to invest in new plant and machinery? And so on. But often, after the most detailed empirical enquiries, different hypotheses as to the structure of the causal relationships and as to the quantitative importance of any given factor in any assumed relationship provide conflicting results between which it is found difficult to choose even with the aid of the most refined statistical techniques. But the structure of the relationships and the numerical value of the parameters in a dynamic system can make a huge difference to the behaviour of the whole system; with one set of hypotheses the system may explode into a catastrophic breakdown and with another it may reach a stable equilibrium with or without moderate fluctuations on the way. But Professors Forrester and Meadows give results for an immensely complicated economic – social – demographic system of dynamic interrelationships for the whole world, having selected one assumed set of interrelationships and having used for each of those relationships estimates of the quantitative force of the various factors which in many cases are inevitably based on very limited empirical data.

For these reasons the conclusions drawn by Professors Forrester and Meadows are unquestionably surrounded with every kind of uncertainty. One must therefore, ask what is the moral for present policy decisions if the future results of present policies are still extremely uncertain.

This question can be put in a very sharp form by considering one of the conclusions reached by Professor Forrester (1971) in his *World Dynamics*. He very rightly emphasizes the fact that the ultimate effect of any given set of present policies depends upon dynamic interrelation ships of the kind which I have expounded. Which influences work most quickly? To what extent are the evil effects of a given influence hidden at first and then operative with a cumulative, explosive effect? and so on. Professor Forrester concludes from his model that in order to prevent a worse ultimate disaster we should seriously consider the adoption of some very tough-line present policies. I quote from his book:

> Instead of automatically attempting to cope with population growth
> national and international efforts to relieve the pressures of excess growth

must be re-examined.   Many such humanitarian impulses seem to be making matters worse in the long run. Rising pressures are necessary to hasten the day when population is stabilised. Pressures can be increased by reducing food production, reducing health services, and reducing industrialisation. Such reductions seem to have only slight effect on the quality of life in the long run. The principal effect will be in squeezing down and stopping runaway growth.

In other words we might be well advised to forget about family planning, to discourage the green revolution in agriculture and the economic development of undeveloped countries and to let poverty and undernourishment play their role in restraining economic growth in the long-run interests of human welfare.

Professor Meadows dissociates himself from these startling recommendations for which Professor Forrester alone is responsible, but this paradoxical conclusion of Professor Forrester is not necessarily nonsensical. It could well be the correct prescription. But it depends upon a number of assumptions built into Professor Forrester's dynamic model. It assumes that while a successful birth control campaign may temporarily reduce population growth and thereby raise living standards, it is not capable of preventing that rise in living standards itself from causing a subsequent renewal of population explosion. It assumes that economic development will be of a given polluting character and that technology will not be capable of introducing sufficiently non-polluting methods with sufficient speed. It assumes that the effect of pollution is not a gradual effect, but stores up a cumulative reservoir of evil, as it were, until there is a sudden explosive catastrophe. If these assumptions are correct, then we ought perhaps to adopt tough-line present policies in order to avert ultimate, total Doom.   One should perhaps be prepared deliberately to starve one person today to avert the starvation of ten people tomorrow.

But what if the outcome is uncertain? Should one starve one person today to avert a 99 per cent probability of the starvation of ten persons tomorrow? Perhaps, Yes; but should one do so to avert a 1 per cent probability of the starvation of ten persons tomorrow? Pretty certainly, No.

Much work has been done in recent years, notably by economists, on the pure theory of decision-making in conditions of uncertainty. In order to make a precise calculation as to whether a given unpleasant decision today is or is not worthwhile in view of its future potential benefits, one would in theory have to have answers to the following five sets of questions:

1. what are the different possible future outcomes of today's decision?

2. what probability should one assign to each of these possible outcomes?

3. what is the valuation – or, in economists' jargon, the utility – which future citizens will attach to each of these outcomes?

4. at what rate, if any, should we today discount the utilities of future generations?

5. what valuation or disutility to us, the present generation, is to be attributed to the unpleasant policy decision which we are contemplating?

One could then calculate whether or not the disutility to the present generation of today's unpleasant policy was greater or less than the discounted value of the weighted average of the utilities to be attached to each of the possible future outcomes, each outcome being weighted by the probability of its occurrence.

The models of Professors Forrester and Meadows are intrinsically incapable of such treatment. They are deterministic and not stochastic in form, although in fact they are steeped in uncertainty. I am not claiming that one could in any case make precise calculations of the kind which I have just outlined about the present uncertain threats of Doom; but I would claim that an appreciation of the principles of decision-making in conditions of uncertainty is helpful as a framework of ideas to inform one's hunches. My own hunch would be that the disutility of Doom to future generations would be so great that, even if we give it a low probability and even if we discount future utilities at a high rate (which I personally do not), we would be wise to be very prudent indeed in our present actions. But we should not, I think, be prepared to carry prudence to the extent of abandoning our efforts to control present births and our efforts to raise agricultural outputs and the production of other essential products in the impoverished underdeveloped countries, though we should be prepared to carry prudence to the extent of a considerable shift of emphasis in the rich developed countries away from the use of resources for rapid growth in their material outputs towards the devotion of resources to the control of pollution, to the aid of the poor, to the promotion of technologies suitable for both developed and underdeveloped economies which save irreplaceable resources and avoid pollution, and to measures for the limitation of fertility.

We may conclude that the failure to deal with uncertainties is a serious weakness of the Forrester-Meadows type of model. I turn now to a second serious weakness, namely its gross aggregation of many distinct variables. The model in my Figure 3 makes no distinction between events in different countries. It assumes only one output, making no distinction between different goods and services. It assumes only two uses of this single product, namely for personal consumption and for capital investment, allowing nothing for governmental uses for defence, space travel, supersonic aircraft, education, medicine, etc. It assumes only one form of pollution, making no distinctions between the pollution of air, water, or land or pollution by biodegradable wastes, by non-degradable wastes, by radio-active wastes, and so on.

This criticism is broadly true also of the models of Professors Forrester and Meadows, though they do both distinguish between agricultural and industrial production and Professor Meadows adds a third type, namely service industries. The introduction of this third distinction is also an important improvement. Services use up much less irreplaceable materials and cause much less pollution than does industrial production; and wealthy countries tend to spend a higher proportion of their incomes on services, thus providing a feature which mitigates somewhat the dangers of economic growth.

But all the models make no distinction between different countries, between different pollutants, or between different non-maintainable resources; and they make very little distinction between different products or different uses of products. This lack of disaggregation causes the models to exaggerate the threat of Doom in two important respects.

First, in so aggregated a model catastrophes are concentrated in their timing. Let me take the threat of a pollution crisis as an example. Let us accept the assumption that the evils of pollution often turn up unexpectedly with little forewarning when a reservoir of pollution rather suddenly reaches a critical level. In an aggregated model this must happen at the same time for every part of the world for every pollutant. *Ex hypothesi* remedial action is taken too late, and the result is, of course, catastrophic. But in fact atmospheric pollution in London rises unobserved to a crisis level in which smog kills a number of people; and belated action is taken to prevent that happening again; then the mercury danger reaches a critical level in a particular Japanese river; there is a local catastrophe; action is taken to deal with that; and so on. I have no desire to belittle these things or to deny that we should take these problems much more seriously than we have in the past. Nor, what is much more important, do I wish to deny that there may be some much more far-reaching, global dangers which are creeping up on us, such as atmospheric changes which will turn the world into an ice-box or into a fiery furnace. Natural scientists should be given every opportunity and encouragement to speed up their efforts to decide which, if any, of such evils is threatened by which of our present activities. All that I am arguing is that what in the real world might well take the form of a continuing series of local pollution disasters or of shortages of particular non-maintainable resources for which substitutes have not yet been found or of localized population control by a particular famine in a particular phase of development in a particular region are necessarily bound in an aggregated model to show up as a single collapse of the whole world system in a crisis of pollution, raw material exhaustion, or famine.

Second, an aggregated model cannot allow for substitutes between one thing and another, and some lines of economic activity use much more non-maintainable resources or produce much more pollution than do others. You may feel that I am making too much of a consideration of only secondary importance when I stress this lack of distinction in the models between different lines of production and different uses of products. Granted that there are some differences in the polluting effects and resource requirements of different lines of production and granted that economic growth may cause a shift in the relative importance of these different processes, yet, are not the shifts likely to cancel out to a large extent – some polluting processes gaining ground relatively and other polluting processes losing ground relatively? And, in any case, is not the net effect of relative shifts of economic structures of various industrial and other processes just as likely to be negative as it is to be positive on the balance sheets of pollution and resource requirements? In view of this, is it not perfectly legitimate to start with models which neglect such shifts?

An economist's immediate reaction is to point out that these models make no allowance for the operation of the price mechanism in causing one economic activity to be substituted for another. This point helps to explain why it is that economists are often less pessimistic than natural scientists in their attitude towards these problems. A large part of an economist's training revolves round the idea of a price mechanism in which that which is scarce goes up in price relatively to that which is plentiful with what in his jargon he calls "substitution effects" both on the supply side and on the demand side. Producers will turn to the production of that which is profitable because its price has gone up away from the production of that which is unprofitable because its price has fallen, while consumers or other users will turn from the consumption or use of that which has become expensive to the consumption or use of that which has fallen in price.

In so far as a mechanism of this kind is at work it means that the changes of economic structure that are brought about in the process of economic growth will not be neutral in their effects on demand for scarce resources. They will be heavily biased in favour of activities which avoid the use of scarce resources and rely on the use of more plentiful resources. How far this process will help to put off the evil day depends, of course, upon the possibilities of substitution throughout the economic system; and it is here that economists are apt to be on the optimistic side. When a raw material becomes scarce and its price goes up, it becomes profitable to work ores with a lower mineral content, to spend money on exploration of new sources, to use scrap and recycling processes more extensively, to substitute another raw material, to turn to the production of alternative final products which do not contain this particular material, and – above all – to direct Research and Development expenditure towards finding new ways of promoting these various methods of substitution. Indeed this process of substitution permeates the whole economic system. Family budgets are sensitive to relative prices; in India where labour is cheap and capital goods expensive clothes are washed by human beings but in the United States where the reverse is the case this is done by washing machines. Agriculture is intensive in the Netherlands where land is scarce and expensive and is extensive on the prairies of Canada where it is plentiful and cheap. Business enterprises succeed by finding a new process which, at current costs of the various inputs, is cheaper and therefore more profitable. Moreover – and this is of quite fundamental importance – commercial research and development is expressly geared to find new processes which economize in scarce and expensive inputs and rely on cheaper and more plentiful inputs; and technology, as we all know, can be a very powerful factor in modern society.

Some of you are probably losing your patience at this point. Is it any use fiddling with the price mechanism while the nuclear reactors burn? Has what I have just said got any relevance at all to the great problems of environmental pollution which constitute the major threat of Doom? It is in fact precisely here that we need a major revolution in economic policy to make the price mechanism work. Environmental pollution is a case of what economists call "external diseconomies". When you drive out onto the streets of London you pay neither for the damage done by the poisonous fumes from your exhaust nor for the cost of the extra delays to other travellers due to the extra congestion which you cause. When you take your seat to fly your supersonic aeroplane over my house, you are not charged for the noise you make. When you treat your farmland with artificial fertilizer, you do not pay for the damage done to my neighbouring fresh water supply. When in your upstream factory you pour your effluent into the river, you do not pay for the damage to my downstream trout fishing. When you draw water for that extra unnecessary bath, you are not charged extra on your rates – unless you live in Malvern where domestic water supplies are metered and so charged and where the inhabitants seem to live a happy and clean life with an exceptionally low consumption of water per head. When you put out that extra dustbin of waste for municipal disposal, you are not charged extra on your rates. If you were you might not merely insist on your suppliers reducing the unnecessary packaging of the products which come into your house, but you might also collect your glass bottles and offer to pay their users to come to collect them for recycled use.

I have, I fear, descended to rather homely and flippant examples. But the principle is the same for the most important and threatening examples of environmental pollution. We need politically to demand an extensive series of cost-benefit analyses of various economic activities and the imposition of taxes or levies of one kind or another at appropriate rates which correspond to the external diseconomies of these various activities. The price mechanism with its consequential process of substitution of what is cheap for what is costly could then play its part in the avoidance of environmental pollution just as it can in the economizing of scarce natural resources. Business enterprise will be induced to avoid polluting processes. Technologists will be induced to steer their research and development into the discovery of new non-polluting methods of production.

This is a vast subject fraught with difficulties with which I cannot possibly cope at all adequately in a short section of a single lecture. I can merely enumerate one or two of the main points.

First and foremost there are the problems of deciding what are the probable ultimate results of different forms of economic activity. These are matters primarily for the natural scientist and the technologist. Will the global effects on the atmosphere turn the world into an ice-box or a fiery furnace?   And what are the probabilities of these outcomes?

Second, there is the problem of evaluating the social nuisance caused by a given degree of pollution of a given kind. To make use of the classical example of a factory belching smoke, how does one measure in £ s d – or rather pounds and newpence – the cost of a given output of smoke when some people in the neighbourhood don't mind it much and others cannot abide it? Quite apart from the question how one adds up these different individual preferences, how does one discover them in the first place?

Third, a great deal of the damage done through environmental pollution is future damage. The use of DDT may confer important immediate benefits without any immediate indirect disastrous consequences; but it may be storing up great trouble for the next generation or the next generation but one. Quite apart from the technical difficulty in determining what will be the actual effects on the future of this pollutant, how does one evaluate that damage? How does one weigh the interests of future generations against the interests of the present generation?

Fourth in most cases, if not in all, it is not a question of eliminating all pollution, but of keeping pollution down to its optimal level. I illustrate once more from the economist's favourite example, namely the smoking factory chimney.   It may be prohibitively costly to eliminate all smoke, but not too costly to reduce significantly the output of smoke. To prohibit all smoke would leave the community without the smoke, but also perhaps without the product of the factory. To charge for the smoke the nuisance cost of the smoke might leave the community with some smoke nuisance, but also with the product of the factory. The latter situation might well be preferred. This is the basic reason for choosing, where possible, a policy of charging a levy or tax on the polluter which covers the social cost of the nuisance which he causes and then leaving him to decide how much pollution he will cause.

Fifth, in some cases – though these are much rarer than many administrators and technologists believe – it may be appropriate to act by a regulation rather than by a tax or charge on pollution. If the social damage is sufficiently grave, it may be wise to prohibit the activity entirely. I, for one, do not advocate discouraging murder by taxing it. But where it is possible to define and police a noxious activity for the purpose of regulating its amount, it is possible also to define and police it for the purpose of taxing it; and normally a tax on a noxious activity will be economically a much more efficient method of control than a direct regulation. Faced with a tax per unit of pollutant those who find it cheap to reduce the pollution will reduce it more than those who find it expensive to do so; and thus a given reduction in the total pollution can be obtained at a lower cost than if each polluter was forced by regulation to restrict his pollution by the same amount. Moreover, with a tax on pollution each polluter can employ the cheapest known method and, above all, will have every incentive to search for new and cheaper methods of pollution-abatement, whereas a direct regulation may well tie the polluter down to one particular method of abatement.

Sixth, in this use of fiscal incentives to avoid pollution, it is of great importance to tax that which is most noxious rather than to subsidize that which is less noxious. We all realize now that motor transport in large cities is causing intolerable congestion, noise, danger to life and limb, and atmospheric pollution. We all realize that private transport causes much more trouble per passenger-mile than does public transport. Both cause these troubles, but private transport causes more trouble than does public transport. The proper conclusion is to tax both forms of transport but to encourage public relatively to private transport by taxing private transport much more heavily than public transport. The wrong conclusion is to leave the taxation of private transport where it is, but to subsidise public transport in order to attract passengers from the private to the public sector.

Such a mistaken policy has an additional obvious disadvantage. We already need heavy tax revenue to finance desirable public expenditures, and I shall argue later that the new economic philosophy which we must evolve to meet the threat of Doom will make additional public expenditures necessary for such purposes as the redistribution of income in favour of the poorer sections of the community. The sensible thing for us to do now is to go round the whole economy taxing those activities which are noxious according to the degree of the social costs which they impose rather than starting to subsidise those competing activities which are somewhat less noxious. We can thereby help to kill two birds with one stone: we could discourage anti-social activities and at the same time raise revenue for the relief of poverty and for those other desirable public activities which we shall need to promote.

I have confined the points raised in this lecture to the use of taxes or other regulations to discourage economic activities which pollute the environment. In principle the same types of tax or regulation could be used to discourage economic processes which use up exhaustible materials; but I leave undiscussed in this lecture the question whether it is necessary in this case to supplement the influence of the market price mechanism which will in any case raise the cost of scarce materials. There is not time in one lecture to deal with every question.

To summarize, it is a mistake to rely on models of future world events which assume a constant flow of pollution or a constant absorption of exhaustible materials per unit of output produced. Economic systems in the past have shown great flexibility. If we were to make the production of pollutants and the use of exhaustible materials really costly to those concerned, we might see dramatic changes. Indeed, there have already been some marked improvements in the cleansing of local atmospheres and waterways in those cases where the first steps of governmental action have been taken. There is no *a priori* reason for denying that if appropriate governmental action is taken to impose the social costs on those who cause the damage, there could be dramatic changes also in the more important and more threatening cases of the threat of Doom through pollution or through the exhaustion of resources.

Such is the first fundamental reorientation which we need in our economic policies, namely to set the stage by fiscal measures or by governmental regulation which will give a commercial incentive to free enterprise to select a structure of economic activities which avoids environmental pollution and the excessive use of exhaustible resources. But given the structural pattern of the economy, pollution and the exhaustion of natural resources will also be affected by the absolute level of total economic activity; and this means that there must be restraint over both the rate of growth of population and, at least in the developed countries, over the rate of growth of consumption per head.

This last consideration points to the need for a second fundamental change of emphasis in economic policies in the rich developed countries. Much modern competitive business seeks new profitable openings for business by commercial advertising which aims at generating new wants or at making consumers desire to discard an old model of a product in order to acquire a new model of what is basically the same product. Thus the desire for higher levels of consumption of unnecessary gadgets and of new models to replace existing equipment is stimulated at the expense of taking out the blessings of increased productivity in the form of increased leisure. I have for long disliked the moral atmosphere of restless discontent which this creates. The discouragement of commercial advertisement by means of heavy tax on such advertisement and the return to broadcasting systems which are not basically the organs for the stimulation of new wants by advertisement could be helpful moves in the right direction. Moreover, some steps could be taken to give incentives to producers to produce more durable products rather than objects expressly designed to need rapid replacement. For example, if cars were taxed much more heavily in the first years than in the later years of their life, consumers would demand cars which were durable and did not need rapid replacement. In general, if a heavy tax is laid on the purchase of a piece of equipment and if this discouragement to purchase is offset by a reduction in the rate of interest at which the funds needed to finance the purchase can be borrowed, there will be an incentive to go for durability in the equipment. Less frequent replacement will mean a lower tax bill, and at the same time the value of the equipment's yield in the more distant future will be discounted at a relatively low rate.

The need to set some restraints on the levels of total production suggests yet a third basic change of emphasis in our economic policies. If we wish to improve the lot of the poorest sections of humanity, then either we must rely on rapid and far-reaching growth of output per head or we must rely on the redistribution of income from the rich to the poor. In recent years both for the relief of domestic poverty and for the closing of the hideous gap between standards of living of the rich, developed countries and of the poor, under-developed countries the emphasis has been on economic growth. The extension of social services for the relief of poverty at home has, we have been told by our politicians, been impeded by the slow rate of growth of total output, it being assumed that any relief of poverty must come out of increased total production so that all classes may gain simultaneously. The raising of standards in the under-developed countries must, we have all assumed, come basically out of the growth of total world output, so that standards in the developed countries can be raised simultaneously with those in the under-developed countries.

I have no intention of asserting that we should avoid further economic growth. Indeed a rise in output per head, hopefully of a less noxious form than in recent years, is an essential ingredient in the relief of world poverty. A glance at the arithmetic of national incomes is sufficient to show that it cannot possibly be achieved simply by a redistribution of income from rich to poor countries. But I am asserting that we would be wise to shift the emphasis significantly from a mere boosting of growth to a serious reliance on a more equal distribution of what we do produce, although we must face the fact that this inevitably multiplies possibilities of conflict of interest between different classes in society.

But as soon as we emphasize redistribution we are faced with a very difficult dilemma.   Anyone who studies the financial arithmetic of poverty in this country – and I have recently undertaken a fairly intensive study of that subject – is driven inevitably to the conclusion that if anything effective and manageable is to be done more help must be given to the large than to the small family. However one may do this, whether by higher family allowances or by more indirect and disguised means, it necessarily involves subsidising the production of children. If we aim at shifting our philosophy from a mad scramble for ever higher levels of production and consumption of goods, however unnecessary they may be, to a more humane and compassionate society in which basic needs are assured, if necessary at the expense of inessential luxuries, we come up against the thought that our children, who by the way never asked to be born, are also human beings with basic needs and that the more there are of them in a family the greater the total needs of that family if every member is to be given a proper start in life.

The same basic dilemma shows itself in a somewhat different form when we consider the closing of the gap between the rich and the poor countries. It is the poor countries with the highest rates of population growth which will be in the greatest need of foreign aid and technical assistance in order to undertake those projects of capital development, (building new schools, new hospitals, new houses, new machines, new tools and so on), which are necessary simply in order to prevent a decline in the amount of capital equipment per head of the population. However disguised, does not this amount to the international subsidisation of those countries which are producing the most children?

Restraint on consumption per head is a means of restraining total demands on scarce resources which necessarily involves restraints on standards of living. On the contrary, restraint of population growth is a means of restraining total demands without any fall in standards of living. Population control may for this reason be put high on the order of priority for action to meet the threat of Doom, though it raises a basic ethical question which I cannot discuss today. At what level is it legitimate to maintain standards for the born by denying existence at current standards to those whose births are prevented? It would appear to me that, however one might answer this basic ethical question, the population explosion is now such that restraints on fertility should constitute our first priority as a means for restraining the growth of total demands on scarce resources of land, materials, and environment.

In many of the poorer underdeveloped countries the rate of population growth is exceptionally high; and their need for restraint is, therefore, exceptionally obvious. But there is need for restraint also of the less rapidly growing richer populations; and it should not be forgotten that one more American citizen because of his high level of consumption puts an immensely greater strain on world resources than does one more Indian peasant.

But while the control of population might make the most desirable contribution to the control of the total demand on resources, it presents in one way the most difficulty in its achievement. The price mechanism together with a proper, extensive system of pollution taxes by imposing appropriate pecuniary penalties can be used to restrain scarcities of material and environmental goods; these instruments provide powerful negative feedbacks in the total dynamic system. As the demands on material and environmental resources become excessive, so prices and charges rise to discourage demand and encourage supply. But with population, alas, it seems that we must introduce a vicious positive feedback. We wish to discourage large families; but on distributional grounds the larger the family the more we must subsidise it.

There is only one possible way out of this dilemma and that is to devise population policies which restrain population growth by means other than pecuniary penalties on the production of children. The first thing obviously is to enable everyone to avoid having more children than they want. Sterilization and abortion on demand, the development of family planning advice and services in all maternity hospitals, the complete incorporation of universal and free family planning into the National Health Service, the provision of extensive domiciliary family planning services, school education which inculcates that sexual intercourse should never take place without contraception unless a child is positively planned, governmental promotion of research into contraceptive methods – these are the first types of action to which we must devote resources to match any help which we give to large families. Whether or not we shall in the end be driven to consider more authoritarian methods is a question which need not be raised until we have fully explored the effects of a fully developed attempt at voluntary family planning.

I have, I fear, subjected you to a rapid and superficial survey of a large number of economic issues; and yet there is one vast section of my subject matter which I have hardly mentioned, namely the international implications of these problems. Before I sit down, I would like briefly to indicate one or two of the most important issues in this field.

First and foremost, there is the distinction between the rich and the poor nations. The less developed countries fear that the concern of the richer countries with the quality of the environment – a luxury which the rich can well afford – will for various reasons impede economic growth in the less developed countries – a necessity which the poor cannot do without. Past experience has shown that a recession of economic activity in the United States and other developed countries has hit the under-developed countries by reducing the demand for their exports and by reducing the amount of capital funds available in the rich countries for investment in the poorer countries. Might not a planned restraint on the growth of real income in the rich countries have similar effects in reducing their demand for imports, their foreign aid, and the capital funds available for the development of the poorer countries and, indeed, in leading in general to an attitude unfavourable to industrialization and growth in the poorer countries?

This fear must be exorcized. The stimulation of output per head in the poor countries is an absolute necessity for dealing with poverty in those countries. Such economic development is not incompatible with increased emphasis on population control, pollution control, and the recycling of materials. These things must not be confounded with policies to keep down the standards of living in the poorer countries.

A second set of major international problems arises from the fact that many of the problems which I have discussed cut across national frontiers. The supersonic aircraft of country A pollutes the atmosphere for country B. The whalers of country C reduce the catch for the whalers of country D. Country E may pollute a river, lake, or sea on which country F is also situated. Many of the controls which I have discussed will need international agreement and organization.

And finally there is the problem of international disarmament. It is not merely that nuclear, chemical, and biological weapons of war would, if used, represent the ultimate pollution of the environment. There is a much more mundane day-to-day consideration. The production of armaments itself constitutes an appreciable proportion of industrial output in the developed countries; and it is concentrated in sectors of the economy which make heavy demands on material and environmental resources.   Moreover, there is a very heavy concentration in the richer countries of governmental research and development on weapons of war which, if turned to such topics as the control of the environment, might transform the outlook.   Disarmament could make a major contribution to our problem.

The development of the will and the institutions for international action in these three fields is essential for the successful moulding of any set of effective economic policies to meet the threat of Doom.

References

Forrester, J. W. (1971). *World Dynamics*. Massachusetts: Wright-Allen Press Inc.
Meadows, D. L. (1972). *The Limits to Growth*. London: Earth Island.

Appendix

The Population Investigation Committee has in the following two tables made projections of the future population (1) in a country such as India in 1961 and (2) in a country such as England and Wales in 1961. Thus Table I shows what would happen to a population which started with the age structure of the Indian population in 1961 (i.e. with 41.2 per cent under 15 years of age) and with the Net Reproduction Rate of the Indian population in 1961 (i.e. with the N.R.R. = 1.865) on various assumptions about the speed with which the Net Reproduction Rate was reduced to unity from its 1961 level of 1 865. Table II carries out a similar exercise for a population which started with the age structure of the population of England and Wales in 1961 (i.e. 21.7 per cent of the population under 15 years of age) and with the Net Reproduction Rate of the population of England and Wales in 1961 (i.e. with the N.R.R. = 1.323).

TABLE I

India Type of Population (Age Structure of India, 1961: estimated N.R.R. India, 1961= 1.858). Projections assuming varying speeds of decline of N.R.R. to 1.0. single sex population, 1 million at point of initiation

N.R.R. 1.0 from:	Initial population	Subsequent population (millions) in					
	1 million	30 yrs	50 yrs	75 yrs	100 yrs	150 yrs	200 yrs
Immediately	1 million	1.275	1.331	1.329	1.331*	1.331	1.331
In 15 years	1 million	1.434	1.537	1.558	1.559*	1.559	1.559
In 30 years	1 million	1.532	1.771	1.843	1.843	1.844*	1.844
In 50 years	1 million	1.695	2.135	2.501	2.585	2.589*	2.589

* Point from which population is stationary.

TABLE II

England and Wales Type of Population (Age Structure of England & Wales, 1961 = 1.323). Projections assuming varying speeds of decline of N.R.R. to 1.0. Single sex population, 1 million at point of initiation

N.R.R. 1.0 from:	Initial population 1 million	Subsequent population (millions) in					
		30 yrs	50 yrs	75 yrs	100 yrs	150 yrs	200 yrs
Immediately	1 million	1.018	1.027	1.030*	1.030	1.030	1.030
In 15 years	1 million	1.066	1.093	1.111*	1.111	1.111	1.111
In 30 years	1 million	1.094	1.155	1.196	1.198*	1.198	1.198
In 50 years	1 million	1.128	1.228	1.356	2.585	1.396*	1.396

* Point from which population is stationary.

It should be remembered that the N.R.R. of 1.323 in 1961 is not realistic as a measure of marriage cohort or birth cohort replacement. The conventional N.R.R. yields too high a figure, being affected by age at marriage and proportions married: A more realistic rate would be lower and thus the population increases associated with slower rates of decline in fertility would be smaller than are indicated by the projections.

Alex Comfort

Reproduced by permission of The Kinsey Institute for Research in Sex, Gender, and Reproduction, Inc. Photograph by Bill Dellenback, staff photographer.

1976

Sexuality in Old Age[1]

Alex Comfort[2]

Introduction by Dr Kevan R Wylie[3]

Alex Comfort has been variously described as a physician, a poet, a novelist, an anarchist and a pacifist. *The Joy of Sex; a gourmet guide to lovemaking* was published in 1972. This provided one of the first ever sex manuals. It sold almost 12 million copies and whilst originals remain around the many libraries and sex clinics of the world, it continues to resell in various guises. During the 1970's Comfort lived in Santa Barbara, California, before retiring to England in 1985 where after he gave his Galton lecture. The Galton Lecture in 1976 was certainly ahead of its time and in many ways remains an aspiration for many. What is fascinating in Comfort's academic career was his wide interests in research and writing themes and by the late 1960's he had a senior role in the British Society for Research on Ageing.

Comfort graduated from Trinity College in Cambridge reading natural science. It was not until the 1950s that he concentrated more on aspects of ageing which coincided with various insightful works on ageism and sex. His first book was an American Travel Guide written at the age of 18 with his last book at the age of 77 being a sex book. He wrote another 48 books ranging from anarchist and pacifist monographs to highly respected studies looking at the normal ageing process and the Roman Emperor Nero.

Perhaps one of the most insightful physicians and psychiatrists of his time, in 1961his book on *Darwin and the Naked Lady* looking at Indian erotology and his book on *Koka Shastra and other medieval Indian writings on love* in 1964 predated his book on T*he Joy of Sex*.

---

[1] Originally published in Chester, Robert and Peel, John, eds., *Equalitites and Inequalities in Family Life: Proceedings of the Thirteenth Annual Symposium of the Eugenics Society, London 1976*, Academic Press, London, 1977.

[2] Institute for Higher Studies, Santa Barbara, California. USA

[3] Consultant in Sexual Medicine

Themes of fear and rejection of sex and older age remain prevalent in society today.   His insight and concerns have exerted only moderate influence and change in modern society. Of course there have been movies portraying sexual activity between older people but still the rights of older people are rarely publicly debated or explicitly insisted upon by either care providers, the individuals themselves or often those who pay for the care.

The 1972 best seller was based on a previous book of cooking which acted as an inspiration for his own manual. Although his methods of investigation may now be frowned upon anecdotal evidence would suggest that his statement that sex should be free from guilt, free from fear of disease and mutually satisfying if not a little bit racy was something that was evident in his work and which was clearly proposed throughout the decades of life for everyone. Some of his most famous quotes respected and idealised women to the extent that 'a woman's greatest asset is her beauty' and 'a meal can be an erotic experience in itself', both virtues which he described as pertaining in older life when indeed women and men were often free from many of the pressures of life.

Unfortunately even now our knowledge about sexual behaviour in the older person is limited and is much more likely to be described in the male than in women. Ageism remains prevalent and many belief systems and attitudes suggest that sexual behaviour is not only inappropriate but repugnant or abnormal in older age. Perhaps one of the most worrying aspects is that much of this remains self imposed.   Comfort argued that the increasing education and freedom of the public will eventually play an active part in liberating the sexual lives of older people but the likelihood is that for many this is some decades away. Although many older couples will be and remain sexually active it remains unclear why those who are not choose or accept this state. For some it may be physiological or due to medical factors but if intimacy and motivational issues remain unaddressed and help unavailable then with increasing longevity these individuals and couples have a long and potentially unhappy time ahead of them.

The 1976 Galton Lecture: Sexuality in Old Age

Aging induces some changes in human sexual performance. These are chiefly in the male, where orgasm becomes less frequent and where more direct physical stimulation is required to produce erection; but compared with age changes in other fields such as muscular strength or vital capacity these changes are functionally minimal. Sexuality, in other words, lasts in humans of both sexes much better than most or many other functional systems. In fact, in the absence of disease, sexual requirement and capacity are lifelong, and even if and when actual intercourse fails through infirmity the need for other aspects of sexual relationship such as closeness, sensuality and being valued persist. This is totally contrary to folklore and to the preconceptions of hospital and nursing home administrators, some of whom seem to dislike sexuality even among staff. It is even contrary to the beliefs of many older people themselves – they have been in a sense hocussed out of continuing sexual activity by a society which disallowed it for the old, exactly as they have been hocussed out of so many other valuable activities of which they are fully capable such as useful work, social involvement (in the name of disengagement) and even continued life, through being wished away by well-meaning relatives. You recall Tom Lehrer, "In all probability I'll lose my virility – and you your fertility and desirability" … The odd thing is that the hocussing has not been more successful. We have remarked elsewhere that in our experience old folks stop having sex for the same reasons they stop riding a bicycle, ie. general infirmity, thinking it looks ridiculous, and no bicycle. Of these the greatest is the social image of the dirty old man and the asexual, undesirable older woman. We have been dealing with aging in what has been very much a sexually handicapped society.

As in so many other sexual contexts, the handicap has been self renewing and self-maintaining until lately. Old people were not asked about sexual activity because they were assumed to have none, and assumed to have none because they were not asked. Such questions were excluded from histories because they might cause embarrassment, and they continued to cause embarrassment (though much less to the patient than the doctor) because they were not normally included. Our fantasy of the asexual senior when we are younger becomes a blueprint for our own aging when we get older, and is a classical process of bewitchment by social expectation.

In fact, as Simone de Beauvoir (1972) pointed out, the facts were there all along, as they were over other sexual matters such as the normality of masturbation, but they had undergone the invisibility usual to facts which do not fit a social preconception.

Statistical studies on the sexual activity of old people are instructive as they tend to show that old people have always been sexually active, but that this activity has been reinforced as the attitude of the culture has become less negative. We need to bear in mind that those now aged 80 had the sexual indoctrination of the year 1905. In America that was pretty varied as between New England and, say, New Orleans, and the differences between what the Japanese call the "front" and the "back" cultures were great. As far back as 1926 Raymond Pearl recorded that nearly 4 per cent of males between 70-79 having intercourse every third day and nearly 9 per cent more were having it weekly (Pearl, 1930). Kinsey's figures pointed to a decline in coital frequency in both sexes with age, but these figures were cross-sectional. In 1959 Finkle and his co-workers questioned 101 men aged 56 to 86, ambulant patients with no complaint likely to affect potency, and found 65 per cent under age 69 and 34 per cent over 70 still potent, with two out of five over 80 averaging ten copulations a year. When investigated further they found that some in the sample had never had intercourse. Others, though potent, had no partner. In the over-70 group the main reason given for sexual inactivity was "no desire" and, of all the men over 65, only three gave as reason "no erection". Newman and Nichols (1960) questioned men and women from 60 to 93 years of age and found 54 per cent active overall. No significant decline was found under 75. Among those over 75, 25 per cent were still active and the fall was accounted for chiefly by illness of self or spouse.

> Those who rated sexual urges as strongest in youth rated them as moderate in old age; most who described sexual feelings as weak to moderate in youth described themselves as without sexual feelings in old age.

confirming Pearl's 1926 finding that early starters are late finishers. Pfeiffer *et al.* (1968) at Duke University studied 254 people of both sexes and found that the median age for stopping "sexual activity" (presumably coitus, not masturbation) was 68 in men, range 49-90, and 60 in women with a high record of 81, the difference being due to the age differential (average four years) between spouses. The figures for regular and frequent intercourse were 47 per cent between 60 and 71 and 15 per cent age 78 and over. The most interesting part of this study is that unlike previous examinations it was longitudinal not cross-sectional. Over a five-year period 16 per cent of propositi reported a falling off of activity but 14 per cent reported an increase. What we are seeing in cross-sectional studies, therefore, is a mixture of high and low sexually-active individuals, in which those whose sexual "set" is low for physical or attitudinal reasons drop out early – often using age as a justification for laying down what has for them been an anxious business. Social pressure, ill health and the ill health of a partner, and lack of a partner take some toll among the others, but among the sexually active and sexually unanxious when young, aging abolishes neither the need, nor the capacity for intercourse. A generation which has lived sexually, viewed sexual activity positively and has aged, not in the expectation of asexuality and impotence but of continuing as long as possible in the style they have known, will quite certainly sample very much higher than the propositi in these studies. Today, individual variation is large, continuance of sex activity depends on the set and the life-pattern of each patient, and older people experience the changes in normal sexual physiology which I have described, but that is all. The negative picture is folklore; part of the negative folklore of aging, it is self-fulfilling, and it is preventable if we set the record straight.

Bearing in mind that these figures include those whose sex lives were never vigorous, or who laid down sexuality willingly as an embarrassing burden, those still active are probably sexually unanxious people whose valuation of sexuality has run counter to society's constant attempts at castration.

Exactly the same has happened, incidentally, over performance and intelligence with age. Preconceived ideas have realized themselves, helped by confusion between longitudinal and cross-sectional work, and between aging and age-linked pathologies such as atherosclerosis. It has taken the careful work of Eisdorfer and others to show how little is the age-decline in performance intrinsic and how much it depends on self-fulfilling prophecy. So long as we treat the old as asexual, ineducable, unemployable and unintelligent some of them will oblige by being so. The next "old", however, will not. They, incidentally, will be us and I doubt if we shall let society impose on us the patterns it imposed on our grandfathers.

Bearing in mind that people who are now 80 were born in 1897, I think we can anticipate that our, and future generations, whose valuation of sexuality is higher and whose anxieties about it are less, will go much less gently into that good night, a fact which nursing home administrators must take to heart.

For those who are old now, sexuality, if it can be maintained, or revived without impertinent interference, or at least not condemned, mocked or obstructed, is a solace, a continued source of self-value, and a preservative. Not all will wish to have it pressed upon them, but at least we could stop turning it off. Surgeons could stop doing radical prostatic and other pelvic operations which compromise potency on the assumption that after sixty it will not be needed, or suggesting that for certain conditions the vagina of elderly women should simply be sewn up. The idea of providing petting rooms in hospitals is well-meaning but is part of the patronizing view of the old which we would not much like if it were offered to us. They need not petting but privacy. We have to impress this on society, despite its Freudian anxieties about parental intercourse, that all humans are sexual beings retaining the same needs until they die. If we can do it without applying evangelistic pressures, we have to get it through the head of the old and the aging that loving and being loved, both in their full physical expression, are never inaesthetic nor contemptible if they are appropriate. To quote Richard Burton:

Ancient Men will dote in this kind sometimes as well as the rest; the heat of love will thaw their frozen Affections, dissolve the ice of age, and so enable them, though they be three score Years of age above the girdle, to be scarce thirty beneath. (It is interesting that for Burton, a man of sixty, is considered aged.) Otherwise it is most odious, when

an old Acherontick Dizard, that hath one foot in his Grave, shall
flicker after a lusty wench...

Even Burton was clearly not fully aware of the active sexuality of
the old. Few authors, indeed, have been until our own day; the old
were aware of it, if one asked them, but kept their own counsel for
fear of hostile comment. Burton's traditional view is easier for
men to accept. It has been cruelly remarked that women have a
menopause, but men do not have a womenopause. Now women
are as conscious of their needs and their capacity as are men, but
they fear rejection and the state of being not desired or not
desirable. They have not been helped by the social image of
competition for youth, but I think this situation will change. It will
change because our valuation of sexuality is changing, and because
of the growing number of older people. I do not believe that the
movies of twenty years from now will all be about young lovers.
Many are going to be about older lovers. There will be an
interregnum when promotion switches to the middle-aged, an
interregnum of plastic surgery and rejuvenation exploitation, but I
also think that this will pass. The remedy for it lies in an increasing
social awareness of the falsity of the sex-object game which women
have been induced to play, and have sometimes played willingly,
and the growing acceptance of people as people, the rise of the
elders which my colleague Harvey Wheeler at the Institute for
Higher Studies, has described. I think the demographic shortage of
women in some cohorts will help, even though the traditional male
expedient is to raid younger age groups for mates. In fact I think
we would agree that really experienced males are happy to have
intercourse with a woman of any age who experiences herself as a
fully sexual person.

It is important, especially in view of the creation of "postmature
ejaculation" or "ejaculatory incapacity" as a label, to explain to
older males that they will probably not ejaculate vaginally at every
act if intercourse is frequent. Ejaculation can usually be produced
by masturbation if desired, but frequent masturbation at this time
may reduce sensitivity. The slower response of older men can be
seen as an improvement of function, given the short coital times
reported at earlier ages.

A related syndrome is seen in older couples when the post-menopausal woman is put on hormone maintenance therapy. In this case lubrication may be greatly increased, the male cannot reach orgasm, and fears he is becoming impotent. Explanation and dose adjustment are indicated.

Sexual activity prolongs life in rats. There is no hard evidence that it does so in people. It would however be very interesting to compare the sexual frequencies reported by coronary and matched non-coronary males in the late 50s, on the basis that short bursts of tachycardia such as those experienced during coitus have been recommended by some exercise physiologists as a protective against heart attack. The role of sexual activity and sexual frustration in producing or preventing prostatic disease has also never been investigated. With a decrease in patient reticence and doctor embarrassment, such studies are now possible.

The value of hormone supplements in women has been much debated. In men, they may lower orgasmic threshold, but the main action of androgens seems to be in improving well-being and hence response generally. Mesterolone is probably the agent of choice, since it is not "read" by the hypothalamus as testosterone, and administration does not cut off endogenous androgen production. Androgen levels in age vary, and are only rarely deficient.

My general conclusions are these. Geriatricians need to support and encourage the sexuality of the old without embarrassing or evangelizing them. It is a mental, social, and probably a physical, preservative of their status as persons, which our society already attacks in so many cruel ways. Abram Maslow stressed long ago the relation of sexual activity to dominance and to peak experiences: it has a function in ego-preservation. We can at least stop mocking, governessing and segregating the old and the aging: it is to their sexuality, after all, that we owe our own existence, and that sexuality is honorable. Generations which have grown up with full and unanxious sex lives are not going to drop them at the whim of a nursing-home administrator or at an arbitrary chronological age.

How far the sexuality of the old can be rekindled or encouraged depends on them, and their wishes and feelings, but as with the disabled, who have been similarly victims of black social magic, we can do a lot by non-discouragement. This includes the avoidance of medical, surgical or social castration. Early counselling is needed to neutralize the jinx which faces many people as they age as is research into, and repetition of, the facts about continued male potency and female capacity. In some cases active therapy with hormones, decent and judicious cosmetic surgery, and counselling will also be necessary. Old men need to be warned of the risk of "sexual disuse atrophy" rather as they are warned against bed rest. Obesity is a common cause of impotence. Alcohol is a powerful sedative and quite a usual contributor to impotence at all ages. Slightly younger men need information about the normal decline in orgasm frequency; they should be encouraged to enjoy the extra mileage, and their partners briefed about the need for more direct tactile stimulation. Older people seem to profit from instruction in cultivating some of the gentler and less specifically genital forms of sensuality and sexual expression, and are often very ready for them. If their sex lives have been full and their sensuality not blocked by anxiety or convention, sexuality in old age becomes a different and a quieter experience but not less sexual and no less an experience than in youth. Nor is it ever too late to learn; one hears of anorgasmic women who in their late 60s or even their 70s have learned to masturbate and then to progress to coital orgasm for the first time in their lives. Their motive in coming for treatment was that they did not want to die without the full experience of womanhood. As to the fear of rejection by each other, or by others, as ridiculous or oversexed, anyone who has watched many people making love (and very few sex pundits have) would agree that people of all ages look more beautiful and less absurd doing that than doing almost anything else, such as playing golf. There are many simple, procedures which can help. For example, conservative prostatic surgery, treatment of prolapse and senile vaginitis, correction of pendulous breasts and other minor gynaecological problems and treatment for depression, diabetes, obesity, and alcoholism.

Some drugs like DOET, which alter the backdrop of consciousness, may also be of use, but we can probably help most by not hindering, and not letting others hinder, the normal continuance of a normal and necessary function which stays fully effective in its relational and recreational uses, and statistically its main uses in humans, long after its reproductive functions are over. Most people can and should expect to have sex long after they no longer wish to ride bicycles. Such people need fewer tranquillizers, less institutionalization, and live richer lives.

I have said we need to help without impertinent interference. In the case of the disabled we were always told that reference to their sex needs could embarrass them, in fact; when counselling was offered, they beat a path to the door. I suspect the same would happen with the old. Some of that counselling will come from the regular physician, but he may not always have the requisite sexual know-how. Quite a feasible arrangement is that sexuality be allowed or gently encouraged to come up in group discussion among couples, and that can move on to more individual sensuality training of the same kind which helps some people of any age. The fact of peer discussion alone is a reassurance and a help to very many people; not infrequently when it has become really frank and any initial embarrassments have been overcome, people solve each other's problems. This is certainly true of the disabled and I expect it would be true of the old. Discussion also serves to create a climate of renewed sexual interest and hope which can quite transform the atmosphere of a home for the disabled, and could, I think, do so even more for a retirement home where people are not disabled, only very often discouraged. What the institutional old require is not the provision of petting rooms, but the privacy and autonomy which other adults enjoy in choosing or rejecting sexual options. The wish to exercise that option is not evidence of senility, and its exercise is worth more than medication in re-establishing and maintaining the sense of self. A really good book on sex for the older citizen could be a big start as a nonsense-corrective. It is rather nice that many older people have been resexualized or even fully sexualized for the first time, by aware sons and daughters. This service for them in the recreational and relational use of sex compensates in part for the service they did us in its reproductive use.

References

de Beauvoir, S. (1972). *Old Age.* New York: Putnam.

Finkle, A. L., Moyers, T. G., Tobenkin, M. I. and Karg, S. J. (1959). Sexual potency in aging males. I. Frequency of coitus among clinic patients. *Journal of the Amercian Medical Association,* 170, 1391-1393.

Newman, G. and Nichols, C. R. (1960). Sexual activities and attitudes in older persons. *Journal of the American Medical Association,* 173, 33-35.

Pearl, R. (1930). *The Biology of Population Growth.* New York: Knopf.
Pfeiffer, E., Werwoerdt, A. and Wang, H. S. (1968). Sexual behaviour in aged men and women. *Archives of General Psychiatry,* 19, 753-758.

Paul H Gebhard

Reproduced by permission of The Kinsey Institute for
Research in Sex, Gender, and Reproduction, Inc. Photograph
by Bill Dellenback, staff photographer.

1978

Sexuality in the Post-Kinsey Era[1]

Paul H. Gebhard[2]

Introduction by Lesley A. Hall[3]

This paper provides us with an intriguing historical insight as one of Kinsey's closest collaborators examined the situation shortly after the supposed 'Sexual Revolution' of the late 1960s. Gebhard drew a picture that differs perhaps less from that pertaining nearly thirty years later than he seems to have anticipated being the case. He touched on a number of issues that are still far from being resolved: far from having become of purely historical interest, they remain of continuing relevance.

Some of the topics addressed by Gebhard do now seem of historical interest. He comments on the prevalence of 'petting', a concept that seems to have vanished from the sexual vocabulary of the 21st century, in spite of the strong evidence for the continuing prevalence of practices involving (hetero-)sexual interaction without penile penetration of the vagina (although there is Presidential warrant for considering that these are somehow 'not sex'). It seems almost quaint that he perceived 'venereal disease [as] not the plague it was before antibiotics', and that he saw the main remaining concern to be the prevalence of gonorrhoea attributable to the reservoir of asymptomatic cases. At the very time that he was writing panic was already rising about the epidemic levels of herpes, previously a minor player in the world of STDs, among the general population. According to an article published in the *British Medical Journal* in the very same year this, 'once a rare, occupational

[1] Originally published in Armytage, W.H.G., Chester, R and Peel, John (eds.). *Changing Patterns of Sexual Behaviour: Proceedings of the Fifteenth Annual Symposium of the Eugenics Society*, London 1978. (London, 1980: Academic Press)

[2] Institute for Sex Research, Indiana University, Bloomington, Indiana, USA

[3] Wellcome Library for the History and Understanding of Medicine

disease of prostitutes' had become 'a serious, common, infection'.[4] And, of course, not yet risen above the horizon, HIV/AIDS was shortly to change the whole picture.

On the whole Gebhard took a confident and Whiggish view of the changes that he perceived to be in progress and indeed deemed them 'worthy of the name "revolution".' Some of these remain as major, even if, in the current climate of opinion in the USA, seriously contested, developments. 'Extramarital coitus' and cohabitation are widespread and (even if censured by some influential groups) are generally considered to be acceptable practices. Homosexuality is far more visible, and the increased social acceptance of homosexuality, if it has not caused more individuals to become so, has certainly facilitated the possibility of living a life proclaiming this identity, rather than concealing it or seeking to be 'cured'. One might, however, in the light of more recent considerations of issues of desire and identity and self-fashioning, be somewhat critical of Gebhard's assertion that 'no-one chooses to be homosexual', eliding the existence of same-sex desire with social identity.

There seems to be an underlying belief that the changes Gebhard observed were relatively rapid and recent. However, the walls of the citadels of morality that he saw crumbling to dust in the sixties and seventies had been under siege for very much longer. These much longer historical roots are half-acknowledged in the mention that changes in laws had emerged from 'respected older persons and impeccable organizations': these had finally caught up with recommendations being made from more radical directions from the later nineteenth century. But there are a number of places where an adequate historical grounding is lacking, not surprising given that the historical analysis of sexuality was still only beginning to emerge as a distinctive field of study in the late seventies. And especially given the continuing relative lack of attention to the sexual attitudes and behaviour of the 'normal heterosexual man' it is perhaps not remarkable that Gebhard made the mistake of assuming that male anxieties and dysfunctions were the product of the emancipation of women and the demands made upon men to be satisfactory partners, rather than that these silent sufferings were gradually becoming articulated in an era of greater sexual openness.

---

[4] 'Genital herpes and cervical carcinoma', *British Medical Journal* 1978 (1), p. 807.

Gebhard observed 'evidence of a renaissance of sexual repression', which he attributed to the 'backlash response' to 'changes which are too drastic and too rapid', but he also suggested that it was the manifestation of widespread underlying conservative attitudes, being self-interestedly manipulated by politicians. Even so, he held out hope that 'tolerance and rationality will prevail' and placed his hope in the 'the myriad options... through learning and conditioning' to modify attitudes and behaviour.

While the HIV/AIDS epidemic, which commenced only a few years later, has stimulated further investigations into sexual attitudes and behaviour, it remains regrettably the case that, as Gebhard claimed, 'there is no cheap and easy way to obtain good data on human sexuality', and studies such as those collected in the 1998 volume, *Researching Sexual Behavior: Methodological Issues*, edited by John Bancroft, the recent director of the Kinsey Institute,[5] demonstrate the continuing truth of this. This collection also underscores Gebhard's point about the enormous potential in such work for misunderstandings about the meanings of terminology and resultant miscommunication and confusion, exacerbated across different cultures.

In the early twenty-first century, 'the protracted period of strife and litigation' fomented by very different views of the place of sexuality in society, predicted by Gebhard, still continues and shows no sign of achieving any simple or early resolution.

The 1978 Galton Lecture: Sexuality in the Post-Kinsey Era

I initially chose a broad title for my presentation with the idea of leaving myself a wide latitude of choice of topic. Time passed, procrastination continued, and when I finally addressed myself to the preparation of this lecture I realized I had irrevocably committed myself to an impossibly vast subject. The only solution to this dilemma is to speak in generalities rather than specifics and to try to present a synthesis and overview. You will probably welcome this solution to my problem because it means I will not be burdening you with only the statistics of the numerous surveys and research projects which have proliferated at an exponential rate

---

[5] John Bancroft (ed.), *Researching Sexual Behavior: Methodological Issues* (Bloomington, IN.: Indiana University Press, 1998).

since it has become safe, if not wholly respectable, to indulge in sexology. The quality of research in sexual behaviour and attitudes ranges from good to adequate to execrable and regrettably some of the latter have received wide publicity. The commonest defect is that of sampling. For example, surveys conducted by two popular magazines, *Redbook* (Levin and Levin, 1975) and *Psychology Today* (Athanasiou *et al,* 1970) consisted of questionnaires printed in these magazines with an exhortation to fill them out and mail them in. While the roughly 100,000 returns received by *Redbook* seems mightily impressive, one must realize this constitutes a return of less than 5 per cent of the magazines distributed that month. Moreover, the 100,000 questionnaires proved too much to process, and so only 10,000 – one in ten – were utilized to form the basis of the report. This constitutes one-half of one per cent of those who received the questionnaire. Similarly, the *Hite Report* (Hite, 1976) on women, and the male counterpart produced by Dr Pietropinto and Ms Simenauer (1977) depended wholly on self-selection: only those who were motivated by who knows what reasons responded to the questionnaires which were handed out at supermarkets and other gathering places or which were simply mailed to an unknown population of respondents. Some of the Swedish studies were excellent in this respect; for example, Zetterberg (1969) used census data to select 2,156 persons aged 18 to 60 to constitute a representative cross-section of Sweden, and all but 153 responded. In the USA, the studies of Zelnik and Kantner on young people (1977) and Westoff's study of married persons (Westoff and Ryder, 1977) approach this ideal. At the risk of seeming vain, I will cite the Institute for Sex Research studies as examples of good research. The bitter fact is that there is no cheap and easy way to obtain good data on human sexuality.

At this juncture let me confess to a strong bias in favour of interviewing rather than self-administered questionnaires. If a question, no matter how carefully written, can be misconstrued, it will be. Kinsey learned this early in his career when he experimented with a questionnaire (Kinsey *et at.,* 1948). One of his questions to college males was "Are both of your testicles descended?" To his profound amazement a substantial percentage replied "No". When he inquired personally, he received the reply, "Well, one seems to be descended, but the other hasn't come down as far." A similar case resulted in Dr Schmidt's questionnaire given to West German college students. He asked males what percentage of their premarital coitus resulted in ejaculation, and was taken aback to learn that about one-fifth of the young men suffered from ejaculatory impotence – that is, they had coitus, but did not ejaculate. Interviews with these young men revealed that they were in universities far from their usual female partners and on those rare occasions when they were reunited they tried to make up for lost time. Consequently in the first night of reunion, they would ejaculate during the first and second coitus, but run dry by the third or fourth. This scarcely constitutes impotence!

Taking the good studies along with the bad and attempting to discern general proportions and trends, one finds enough agreement to permit one to make the following generalizations.

Masturbation evidently has changed little in prevalence and frequency over the past few decades except that it is becoming more common in females now that they are increasingly recognizing that they are entitled to have sexual desires and needs. While the ever-never incidence of masturbation in males approaches 100 per cent (as it always has) and while there has been an increase in females to at least the two-thirds level, masturbation still suffers from taboo. While all educated people will stoutly maintain that it will not cause insanity and that it is a normal and natural function, no one wants their spouse or sexual partner to know of it.

Orgasm during sleep suffers not from taboo, but from almost total neglect. So few researchers have inquired about this subject one can make no 'guesstimate' as to whether it is increasing or decreasing. I find this neglect fascinating: it suggests that an involuntary act has no moral or ethical significance and hence does not merit our consideration. This, I believe, reflects our obsession with sin. Note that in the realm of sexual behaviour the public is primarily interested in fornication and adultery, our primary sources of sin and gossip.

There is little to say regarding trends in premarital petting. A phenomenon so near to being universal cannot change appreciably unless it were to decrease, which is close to an impossibility in European-American society. However, there have been changes in petting techniques. Larger numbers of persons at ever younger ages are experiencing (or should I say, enjoying) manual and oral stimulation of the genitalia. These more sophisticated techniques have naturally caused an increase in the number of persons who reach orgasm in petting. For example, about a quarter of the unmarried college females interviewed during the Kinsey era had reached orgasm in petting by age 20, whereas an Institute survey in 1967 revealed that about half had done so. The percentage of unmarried persons having mouth-genital contact has risen steadily from under 20 per cent in Kinsey's time to nearly one-third in the late 1960s, and the *Playboy* survey (Hunt, 1974) reported over 80 per cent. This increase is in keeping with the suggestions, or even commands, found in current marriage manuals and magazines.

Premarital coitus has always been the focus of attention in our twentieth century western society obsessed with penile penetration. We deem a female virginal despite digital or lingual penetration of the vagina, but a partial penile penetration of a few seconds is sufficient to put the female in a totally new category: that of non-virgin. Note that the legal definition of rape in the USA is always a matter of penile penetration no matter how slight or brief.

In examining the various studies, nearly all being of college populations, it is clear that there has been a progressive increase in premarital coitus in the USA and in northern and western Europe. This has not been a sexual revolution, but simply the continuation of a trend visible since the beginning of this century. For example, the Kinsey data reveal that 8 per cent of the females born before 1900 had had premarital coitus by age 20 (Kinsey *et al.,* 1948, 1953), and this percentage gradually rose until among women born between 1910-19 some 23 per cent had had premarital coitus by age 20. Both Packard's 1968 study entitled *The Sexual Wilderness* and our own 1967 college study showed that at that date 33 per cent of the unmarried college females were no longer virgins by age 20. The slightly later *Psychology Today* survey reported 78 per cent of their female readers had had premarital coitus. Finally the *Playboy* survey in the early l970s offers some more useful data. Taking only those who had married and hence ended their premarital life, the investigators found that 31 per cent of their oldest group of females (55 or older) had had premarital coitus, but each younger cohort had higher figures until their youngest group reported 81 per cent. The *Redbook* survey gave somewhat higher percentages and again found the behaviour most common among the younger generations. Figures for males are higher than those for females, but the differences are decreasing with each generation. Ultimately we shall arrive at the point now reached in Sweden where roughly 95 per cent of both males and females have experienced coitus before marriage (Zetterberg, 1969).

It is clear that as a part of the general emancipation of women they have gradually become recognized as humans with their own sexual needs and rights. Beyond this, many women are now striving for the same degree of sexual freedom previously accorded only to males. This trend toward egalitarianism when coupled with the continual exhortations of magazines and marriage manuals has caused females to demand sexual satisfaction from their husbands and lovers. This feminine expectation of sexual competence in males has made many males feel an uncomfortable sense of obligation. For them coitus has become a test of competence and manhood, and this in some cases has engendered worry and impotence. It is one thing to have coitus with a virgin or near virgin; it is quite different to have sex with an experienced woman who not only has high expectations, but is in a position to make invidious comparisons. Comparisons can now be made almost instantaneously in certain situations thanks to a recent change in law or at least in law enforcement. In a number of places such as Sandstone Lodge in Los Angeles and Plato's Retreat in New York the members can enjoy coitus in full view of anyone who cares to watch.

The increase in premarital coitus has several beneficial aspects: it is biologically and psychologically healthy in the sense that we are all sexual beings whose imperative needs cannot be postponed with impunity for up to a decade between puberty and the legal age of adulthood. Moreover, we tend to forget that some people marry late or never, and we cannot expect chastity from them. We are always guilty of thinking of premarital coitus as being confined to the teens and early twenties. Premarital coitus causes marriages to be contracted on bases other than just sexual accessibility: in the past there was an unfortunate custom of bartering one's body for a wedding ring. Now young people marry for other and more rational reasons. True, divorce rates are higher, but this is not because of premarital coitus, but of higher expectations of marriage and the removal of the condemnation which formerly applied to divorcees.

On the other hand, the increase in premarital coitus has brought with it an increase in premarital pregnancies and venereal disease. Zelnik and Kantner's non-college white females had a 22 per cent incidence of pregnancy by age 19, and of Sorenson's sample of non-virgins aged 13-19 essentially the same percentage had conceived before wedlock. While a fair number of these pregnancies terminate in marriage, many of these marriages forced early in life result in unhappiness and educational and occupational disability. Most of these unwanted pregnancies are not the result of contraceptive failure, but of failure to use contraception. In the aforementioned Zelnik and Kantner study, only 20 per cent of the girls used contraception regularly and fewer than half had used any in their most recent coitus. It seems incredibly irrational not to use the extremely effective and readily available contraceptives – and that is precisely the problem. The girls are emotional rather than logical: they do not wish to acknowledge to themselves or to others that they want or at least expect coitus; they fear that by using contraceptives they will make the male think they are promiscuous; and many of them complain that premeditated contraception spoils what they would like to believe is romantic spontaneity. Still others think that not having contraceptives available will prevent them from yielding to temptation. Lastly, there is always the thought that just this one time won't make me pregnant. The males are also remiss in assuming that contraception is the female's responsibility. To add to the problem are the numerous myths about the time of fertility, the idea that female orgasm is a prerequisite for conception, etc.

While venereal disease is not the devastating plague it was before antibiotics, it is common for two reasons. One reason is simply the increase in the number of sexually active persons. The second reason is the recognition of many diseases not previously considered venereal. The commonest sexually transmitted disease is now non-gonorrhoeal urethritis. Venereal warts and herpes genitalis vie for second place. Syphilis is no longer considered by venereal disease specialists as important: it is easily cured and many people inadvertantly cure themselves by taking antibiotics for colds and other infections. The big concern of the venereal disease specialists is gonorrhoea. We know now that as much as half of the disease is without symptoms in females and the same may be true for 10 or 15 per cent of the males. This great reservoir of undetected cases will keep the disease common until a vaccine is developed or until some totalitarian government forces everyone simultaneously to receive a massive dose of antibiotic.

I will devote little time to the subject of marital coitus since it has been remarkably stable in both incidence and frequency. The only consequential change appears to be a higher rate of female orgasm and the use of a greater variety of foreplay techniques and coital positions. The male-above female-supine position is no longer the only position suitable for decent folk, and mouth-genital and anal contact are no longer considered the monopoly of the French or of deviants. The *Psychology Today* and *Redbook* surveys found 80 to 90 per cent of their married females reporting mouth-genital contact. The incidence of anal coitus given by the *Playboy* survey was 25 per cent among couples under age 35, and *Red book* reported an unbelievable 47 per cent. While I mistrust these figures, I believe that an increase has occurred since the Kinsey era in these techniques, possibly as single experimental trials.

Like other forms of heterosexual activity, extramarital coitus (adultery) has increased among females. The Kinsey figure of 26 per cent (Kinsey *et al.,* 1953) has now risen to 30 per cent according to *Redbook,* or 36 per cent according to *Psychology Today.* The male figure seems to have changed but little, hovering between 40 and

50 per cent. The number of extramarital partners for females seems to have remained constant: nearly half of the women confined themselves to one partner and an equal proportion limited themselves to between two to five men. Lastly, while no one has good data, it is my impression that extramarital petting has also increased and in its milder forms has become standard procedure at parties.

Homosexual activity, despite the great publicity accorded it in recent decades, does not seem to have increased. This is what one should have anticipated, for with the exception of a few females who try lesbianism as a political gesture of independence from men and except for a few male prostitutes, no one chooses to be homosexual. One's sexual orientation is beyond one's volition and the die seems to have been cast in childhood or early adolescence. Consequently, homosexuality seems little influenced by fads, fashions, and changing morality.

Similarly the paraphilias such as fetishism and sadomasochism seem largely independent of social change, and what little evidence we have does not indicate any real increase. There may be more temporary experimentation motivated by curiosity or a desire for novelty, but paraphilias as regular behaviour seem not to have become more prevalent despite their greater exposure in the mass media.

Now let us turn from behaviour and examine the changes in attitudes and *mores*. Here there have been changes worthy of the term 'revolution' for they have been vast and rapid.

Cohabitation is one such change. In my young adult years only lower socio-economic level couples lived together without benefit of clergy; married or divorced young people were excluded from high schools and colleges; college women had to return to their segregated quarters by specified times; and coitus constituted grounds for dismissal. Now unmarried couples of any social class live together with little censure, and some of our most famous actresses and models not only cohabit, but unabashedly reproduce. I must add that many of these cohabitations eventually metamorphose into conventional legal marriages, and they represent the trial marriages advocated many years ago by free-thinkers.

Sex education in the schools, although delayed and impeded, is another change. Society has in the main grudgingly accepted the need for some sexual instruction prior to marriage. The term 'grudgingly' is apt: in my own state of Indiana until last year the State Board of Education specified that in sex education courses in grammar and high schools there should be no mention of masturbation, homosexuality, sexual techniques, abortion, or contraception. There was and still is great resistance to sex education below the college level. Many otherwise reasonable people cling to the idea that children are sexless innocents who would never have a sexual thought or impulse unless some adult had spoiled their purity with premature knowledge.

Gay liberation certainly represents a great change and a sudden one. Rather than leading secretive and hypocritical lives, many homosexuals are now revealing themselves and some are politically active, marching with placards, holding public meetings, forming openly gay organizations, and publishing their own magazines and newspapers. Famous and/or respected people are proclaiming their sexual orientation. Some gay groups have established a continuing meeting and dialogue with the police and clergy. In colleges we now have Gay Liberation groups conducting meetings in college buildings. In Kinsey's day a known homosexual student was immediately expelled and a gay faculty member was forced to resign quietly at the end of the semester.

With the change toward a permissive society, a host of previously hidden persons have emerged into public view and are publishing their own specialized magazines and advertisements. Swingers, spouse traders, transvestites, sadomasochists, and others are now in the open. Even in the highly taboo area of paedophilia there are organizations which hold public meetings and publish. The prostitutes have formed an organization named 'Coyote', an acronym for 'call off your old tired ethics', and are politically active in some areas. Accompanying this outburst of freedom have come some publications so highly specialized as to be almost humorous. Recently there appeared a magazine devoted entirely to 'fisting': the insertion of the hand or even arm into the rectum. Or, to be accurate, I should say into the colon. We researchers presumed this technique to be an innovation until it was drawn to my attention that this act was depicted by Michaelangelo and still graces the ceiling of the Sistine Chapel. The emergence of all these hithertofore hidden deviations has profoundly shocked many people.

Perhaps the greatest change of all has been the rapid collapse of censorship. In the United States today there is no censorship of the written word, theatre, photography, graphic art, or cinema. The only media retaining strict control are radio and television, and even here control is weakening during the late hours of the night. Change has been so rapid that we at the Institute for Sex Research are in the absurd position of having locked away in steel cabinets books and magazines which are on open display in the local reputable bookstores. The degree of change is illustrated equally dramatically by my clear recollection that in 1948 a newspaper man who visited us following the publication of our first volume regretfully stated that he could not write about our work because he represented a family newspaper in which a word such as 'masturbation' could not appear. Some enterprising businessmen have produced sales catalogues of not only sadomasochistic apparatus, but sadomasochistic jewellery: rings for pierced foreskins and pierced labia. This conjures up the fantasy of someone saying, "Excuse me dear, but you forgot to take off your ring." While foreskin rings have a respectable antiquity, going back to Roman times, their appearance in publicly available catalogues strikes me as a change if not an innovation.

All of the changes in behaviour and attitude have necessarily had repercussions in the fields of ethics and religion. Theologians are now being forced to re-examine previously unquestioned tenets. Is fornication or adultery always a sin? Can a homosexual be a good Christian? Are contraception and abortion sins against God and nature? Pandora's box has been opened on the altar.

Medicine, too, has had to revise its thinking. Many medical men are debating if the things we thought were sexual pathologies might not really be unusual adaptations or perhaps only the extremes of the range of normalcy. The American Psychiatric Association has removed homosexuality from its list of disorders. In transsexual operations surgeons now perform the previously forbidden act of removing healthy tissue. Contraceptives and abortions are now not only freely available, but available to minors without parental consent. At present there is heated debate over the ethics of using surrogate partners (or even the therapist) in treating sexual dysfunction. Ethical problems hithertofore unimagined have arisen in the past few decades; for example, should a male infant with a microphallus be raised as a deficient male or given an operation and raised as a functional, albeit sterile, female?

Law, usually the slowest to respond to social change, has changed markedly and rather rapidly in regard to sex. I have already mentioned the collapse of censorship and the making of abortion legal. In addition, in the USA nineteen states have changed their sex laws so that what consenting adults do sexually in private is no longer subject to legal sanctions. Various municipalities have enacted ordinances prohibiting discrimination against homosexuals even though homosexual activity was a felony a few years ago. Mouth-genital contact, once included in the sodomy statutes, is currently protected by a Supreme Court ruling that marriage brings an aura of sexual privacy which the law cannot invade. The changes in our laws were not instigated by young radicals, but by respected older persons in impeccable organizations such as the American Law Institute and, in Britain, the Wolfenden Committee. A number of model penal codes have been devised which are refreshingly rational in their sexual aspects. For example, no longer do they observe the old dichotomy of adult and minor, but have graduated crimes and punishments depending not upon some absolute age, but upon the age discrepancy between the individuals involved. Another welcome development is the abolition of ancient, vague, and poorly defined sex offences which could be interpreted so as to indict almost anyone. There were until recently some fantastic examples. One state defined sodomy as the insertion, however slight, of the penis into any 'unnatural orifice' of the body. Setting aside the problem of what bodily orifice is unnatural, a strict interpretation of that law would mean that a man who, in impetuous haste, missed the vulva and struck the navel would be guilty of sodomy. One of the broadest and most common of these vague laws was the one against contributing to the delinquency of a minor, under which in some states a male aged 21 could be convicted for petting with his 20-year-old fiancée. A number of legal scholars have suggested that there need be only three sex laws: one to forbid acts involving force, duress, or trickery; one to forbid the sexual exploitation of children by adults; and one to prevent offensive public behaviour.

Our advances in law since Kinsey's day have given rise to some knotty problems. Allow me a series of rhetorical questions. Does the 'consenting adults in private' law legalize prostitution? Does it allow consenting sadomasochists to inflict substantial physical damage? Does it negate adultery as grounds for divorce? And what of incest between consenting adults? If homosexuality is no longer a crime, can it be brought up in divorces where there is a battle over child custody? Lastly, the legal problems resulting from the transsexual operations boggle the mind. Our society has been based on a male-female dichotomy, and any gender reversal utterly confounds our sacrosanct record system. Does a divorced man escape alimony by becoming a divorced woman? Can a female-to-male transsexual marry a woman? Would an adoption agency give them children? The possibilities of confusion are endless until society accepts some new definition of genders.

In concluding this section on law, I believe law is slowly being forced to face a major question: is physical sexual expression a natural human right? If so, does this right extend to children, the mentally deficient or insane, and to prisoners? Beyond this is an even more difficult question to which I am sure you have devoted much thought: is reproduction a natural human right? Ultimately I feel this question must be answered in the negative, for irresponsible procreation infringes upon the well-being of others (Gebhard *et al.,* 1965).

Up to this point I have concerned myself with change in the sense of the modification or abandonment of previously normative behaviours and attitudes. Now let us examine reverse change, that is, rejection of recent changes and a return to former *mores.* It is an anthropological axiom that changes which are too drastic and/or rapid cannot be accommodated by a society, and there will be a backlash response. We are now seeing this clearly in the United States. Numerous local and some national anti-pornography groups have been formed and are vigorously seeking the re-establishment of censorship. They have been rather successful, particularly since some greedy pornographers ventured into the field of child-adult sex ('kiddie porn') and caused a violent revulsion even in those with liberal viewpoints. Our Supreme Court has reversed its erosion of censorship and has in essence made censorship a matter of local option. In consequence, the producers of and actors in explicitly sexual motion pictures have been successfully prosecuted in a number of cities, and even theatre owners and projectionists have not been immune. At the risk of seeming paranoid, I must say that everywhere I look I see evidence of a renaissance of sexual repression. The Supreme Court has refused to review a federal District Court's ruling in Virginia which upheld a sodomy statute. New York modified its 'consenting adult' law to make homosexuality a misdemeanour, and Idaho revoked its 'consenting adult' law entirely. Anita Bryant has launched her anti-homosexual campaign labelled 'Save Our Children' and has received the enthusiastic support of religious fundamentalists and right-wing conservatives. Recent referenda in Wichita, Kansas; Eugene, Oregon; St. Paul, Minnesota; Moscow, Idaho; and Dade County, Florida have abolished the ordinances designed to prevent discrimination against homosexuals. The Roman Catholic Church has reaffirmed its stand against abortion and most contraception, and stressed its condemnation of any orgasm-producing act save for marital coitus and orgasm while sleeping. Resistance to sex education persists. Our federal government has made abortion difficult for the poor, and Louisiana has surrounded abortion with almost insuperable restrictions, Senator Proxmire and his staff, in ferreting out the waste of taxpayers's money, has attacked a number of sex research projects, and an Illinois politician followed his example and succeeded in terminating a federally funded sex research project in the southern part of that state. Even we at the Institute have been receiving ominous inquiries as to the sources of our grants and the amounts of money involved. Johns Hopkins Hospital has evidently ceased, or greatly curtailed, transsexual operations. The Equal Rights Amendment faces defeat in no small measure due to the sexual liberality of its proponents. I predict a protracted period of strife and litigation which will be exacerbated as politicians seize upon sexual issues to win votes. The Institute for Sex Research has conducted a national survey of attitudes which reveals that the majority of adults are strongly opposed to homosexuality and adultery, and do not accept premarital coitus even between adults. Politicians sense this conservatism and make use of it. The battles I predict will involve not only the conservative traditionalists and the ultra-liberals, but will engage many sincere and thoughtful citizens who hold strongly opposing views. We can hope that ultimately tolerance and rationality will prevail though the cost be Churchillian blood, sweat and tears. Since I am addressing a eugenics society, it is fitting that I conclude on an appropriate note: the proper relationship between sexuality and population. I think it is obvious that any objective and intelligent person who is not hampered by religious or nationalistic constraints must conclude that the greatest danger facing mankind is overpopulation. Uncontrolled reproduction must rapidly deplete our finite resources and pollute our environment. It will negate many of our efforts toward the betterment of the human condition. It will lead to struggle and possibly warfare between the 'haves' and the 'have-nots'. Uncontrolled reproduction, like uncontrolled cellular growth, is ultimately lethal. Advances in science and technology can only delay the inevitable. Even nuclear war cannot be viewed as a horrible solution to the problem for it will simply reduce the habitable space for the survivors. We must abandon our age-old goal and biological imperative to be fruitful and multiply freely. Distasteful as the idea is, we cannot rely upon the voluntary co-operation of humans to hold constant or reduce population. While the intelligent persons with consciousness of the problem will co-operate, these persons are far outnumbered by the uneducated, less intelligent, and selfish. I doubt if we have the time to educate and persuade this majority which will grow larger as those who appreciate the problem reproduce less. Reproduction must become a privilege and not a right, and birth limitation must be imposed by adjustments in taxation policy, the rewarding of minimal reproduction, delaying marriage, and devising ways to appeal to self-interest. We must, as someone succinctly put it, make sex more recreational and less procreational.

What of our chances of waging a successful campaign against overpopulation before we are all living in a crowded polluted world on a subsistence economy? I am somewhat pessimistic since I agree with the neurophysiologists who point out that our newly evolved neocortex has not yet established control over our primitive brain. We remain more creatures of emotion and habit than of logic, and this is especially true of sex, for it is an inherent genetically determined phenomenon. On the other hand, evolution holds some hope. While most other life forms have their sexual behaviour rigorously programmed, the higher life forms are progressively emancipated from the control of hormones, pheromones, and patterned behaviour. The human female, for example, is the only mammalian female without an oestrus cycle: she can be sexually aroused and functional at any time. We are freer than any other animal to determine our sexual lives. This shift from problem-free machine-like sexual functioning determined by chemical substances to the myriad options available to us through learning and conditioning, holds the possibility of our modifying our attitudes and behaviour to insure our survival and well-being.

References

Athanasiou, R., Shaver, P. and Tavris, C. (1970). Sex. *Psychology Today,* 4, 39-52.

Gebhard, P. H., Pomeroy, W. B., Martin, C. E. and Christenson, C. V. (1958). *Pregnancy, Birth and Abortion.* New York: Harper-Hoeber. London: William Heinemann (Medical Books).

Gebhard, P. H., Gagnon, J. H., Pomeroy, W. B. and Christenson, C. V. (1965). *Sex Offenders: An Analysis of Types.* New York: Harper-Hoeber.

Hite, S. D. (1976). *The Hite Report: A Nationwide Study on Female Sexuality.* New York: Macmillan.

Hunt, M. M. (1974). *Sexual Behavior in the 1970s.* Chicago: Playboy Press.

Kinsey, A. C., Pomeroy, W. B. and Martin, C. E. (1948). *Sexual Behavior in the Human Male.* Philadelphia and London: W. B. Saunders.

Kinsey, A. C., Pomeroy, W. B., Martin, C. E. and Gebhard, P. H. (1953). *Sexual Behavior in the Human Female*. Philadelphia and London: W. B. Saunders.

Levin, R. J. and Levin, A. (1975). Sexual pleasure: the surprising preferences of 100,000 women. *Redbook*, 145, 5 1-58.

Packard, V. O. (1968). *The Sexual Wilderness; the Contemporary Upheaval in Male-Female Relationships*. New York: D. McKay. London: Longmans.

Pietropinto, A. and Simenauer, J. (1977). Beyond the Male Myth: What Women Want to Know About Men's Sexuality: A Nationwide Survey. New York: Times Books.

Westoff, C. F. and Ryder, N. B. (1977). *The Contraceptive Revolution*. Princeton, New Jersey: Princeton University Press.

Zelnik, M. and Kantner,J. F. (1977). Sexual and contraceptive experience of young unmarried women in the United States, 1976 and 1971. *Family Planning Perspectives*, 9, 55-71.

Zetterberg, H. L. (1969). *Om Sexuallivet i Sverige*. Stockholm: Nordiska Bokhandeln.

Hunt, M. M. (1974). *Sexual Behavior in the 1970s*. Chicago: Playboy Press.

Kinsey, A. C., Pomeroy, W. B. and Martin, C. E. (1948). *Sexual Behavior in the Human Male*. Philadelphia and London: W. B. Saunders.

R G Edwards

The Current Clinical and Ethical Situation of Human Conception *In Vitro*[1]

R. G. Edwards[2]

Introduction by Peter R Brinsden [3]

The contribution that Professor Robert Edwards has made to the field of human assisted conception is without equal in the World; justly is he hailed as "the father of *in vitro* fertilisation".

It was as a result of his early pioneering research on reproduction in mice in the early 1950s, progressing to humans in the early 1960s, that led to his teaming up with gynaecologist Mr Patrick Steptoe, and later Jean Purdy, a nurse. The three of them worked together in the face of great adversity, due to a lack of facilities, funding and hostility from colleagues and the Press. They achieved, after eight years of research, the world's first human pregnancy from *in vitro* fertilisation (IVF) – only to discover that the pregnancy was ectopic. It was a further two years before they were able to announce the birth of Louise Brown on 25 July 1978, the first birth of a child conceived through IVF. This event is accepted as being one of the most significant medical – scientific achievements of the Twentieth Century. In the following 27 years this technology, which very many critics and sceptics said would never become an accepted or ethically acceptable treatment for infertility, has been responsible for the birth of approaching two million babies worldwide.

---

[1] Originally published in Carter, C.O., ed., *Developments in Human Reproduction and their Eugenic, Ethical Implications: Proceedings of the Nineteenth Annual Symposium of the Eugenics Society London 1982*, Academic Press, London 1983

[2] Physiological Laboratory, University of Cambridge, Cambridge and Bourn Hall, Cambridge

[3] Medical Director, Bourn Hall Clinic, Cambridge

Reading in 2005 "Bob" Edwards' paper which he presented to the then Eugenics Society in 1982, allows one to fully appreciate the real passion he felt then to help infertile couples to have children. However, as interesting in this paper and in many other of his earlier writings, Professor Edwards showed his amazing, almost uncanny, ability to forecast the future clinical and scientific directions in which the field of human assisted conception would progress. Among the advances that he predicted, many of which are now in everyday use, are: the maturation of human oocytes *in vitro*, pre-implantation genetic diagnosis of embryos, sex selection, the therapeutic use of embryonic stem cells, nuclear transfer, human cloning, blastocyst culture, IVF surrogacy, gamete intrafallopian transfer, the importance of avoiding multiple pregnancies, and the cryopreservation of human oocytes and embryos.

To many of his admirers, one of the most significant attributes demonstrated by Professor Edwards during the past five decades of his career has been his willingness and enthusiasm to address "head on" the ethical implications and consequences of his life's work. In the seminal paper written by him and David Sharpe in the journal Nature in 1971, they show an amazing thoughtfulness, sensitivity and far sightedness about many of the ethical issues surrounding IVF and related techniques that are as relevant and important to Society today as they were then. This remarkable insight into the need for ethics committees, as well as sensible and reasonable regulation, is also brilliantly addressed in the following reissued version of Professor Edwards' 1982 lecture to the Eugenics Society. We, his scientific and clinical colleagues and friends, acknowledge the truly remarkable contribution that Bob has made in his chosen field, for which we all salute you. What greater testament could there be to a lifetime's dedicated work than to have been responsible in very large measure for the births of approaching two million children!

The 1982 Galton Lecture: The Current Clinical and Ethical Situation of Human Conception *In Vitro*

Many babies have now been born after the fertilization of human eggs *in vitro,* in the UK, Australia, USA, France, Israel, Germany and Austria. It is 4 years since the birth of Louise Brown. Fifty-six babies, all normal, have been delivered from our clinic in Bourn Hall during the last year. More and more clinics are opening to introduce *in vitro* fertilization on a wide scale in many countries. What a contrast to the situation in the 1960s and 1970s, when surrounded by scepticism and doubts, very few people thought the technique would work, let alone have a realistic clinical application.

I wish to discuss several aspects of human conception *in vitro,* dealing mostly with our own work. My lecture is divided into three parts, first, somewhat whimsical, recalling wonderful events over a period of 15 years which were full of incident, culminating in the birth of Louise Brown (Edwards *et al.,* 1978; Steptoe *et al.,* 1980; Edwards and Steptoe, 1980). I will then be factual, describing current results at Bourn Hall and elsewhere and, lastly, my talk will discuss extensively some of the current ethical issues associated with the fertilization of human eggs *in vitro.*

The History of *In Vitro* Fertilization

My interest in human oocytes and the possibility of fertilization *in vitro* began in the late 1950s and early 1960s. At that time, I became increasingly fascinated with the *in vitro* maturation of oocytes of various mammals, including man. My interest was aroused by work on the superovulation of mice and the precise timing of oocyte maturation in that species (Fowler and Edwards, 1957; Edwards and Gates, 1959), and it was stimulated too by the explosion of knowledge of human chromosomes and especially the presence of chromosomal anomalies in many handicapped children.

In those days, the field was almost completely unexplored. In the 1930s, Pincus and Enzmann (1935) had reported their attempts to mature human oocytes *in vitro,* and believed that all the post-dictyate stages of meiosis occurred during an interval of 12 h, as in rabbit oocytes. My own work did not support this conclusion at all, and it took some years to discover that no visible change occurred in maturing human oocytes for approximately 24 h, when diakinesis began, and maturation was only completed after 36 h approximately (Fig. 1; Table 1) (Edwards, 1962; 1965a,b). Some other pioneers, Menkin and Rock (1948), Shettles (1955) and Hayashi (1963) also made contributions to the field by collecting human oocytes or embryos from the female tract, and attempting to fertilize or culture them *in vitro*. But their work was not established on any fundamental knowledge of oocyte maturation, fertilization *in vitro* and the culture of mammalian embryos *in vitro*. Without such understanding, progress was doomed to be very limited and no authentic examples of fertilization can be accepted (Thibault, 1969). There was little point, for example, in collecting oocytes from the oviduct, because there would be no prior knowledge on the time of ovulation and the oocytes rapidly become degenerate. The fundamental principle in these early stages of the work was to identify the stages of the first meiotic division in maturing human oocytes, which would give a clear indication that the process of maturation had begun, and then to find the successive stages of meiosis leading to the metaphase of the second meiotic division and the extrusion of the first polar body. To the best of my knowledge, this was first reported in 1965 (Edwards, 1965a,b).

Table I

Duration of meiosis in human oocytes (Edwards, 1965b)

	Hours after release of oocytes from follicles
Germinal vesicle	0-24
Diakinesis	25-28
Metaphase-I	26-35
Metaphase-II/polar body	36-43

Much of the fundamental work on oocyte maturation and some occasional examples of the fertilization of these oocytes *in vitro,* had been achieved by 1966. I still recall working then with Dr Howard Jones in Baltimore, operating on a rhesus monkey to place human spermatozoa and mature human oocytes in the oviduct, in an attempt to obtain fertilization (Edwards *et al.,* 1966). In 1968, I met Patrick Steptoe and Jean Purdy, and once this team of three was formed, progress was steady and very exciting. Yet the difficulties were immense, even before we had begun to work.

Patrick Steptoe was a Consultant in the National Health Service (NHS), working in the Oldham General Hospital. Jean and I worked in Cambridge University, separated from Oldham by 180 miles. Our intentions were to attempt fertilization *in vitro* and the culture of embryos, in order to alleviate some forms of infertility, and to study the origin of inherited defects. This was a massive undertaking at such a distance. Our laudable aims initially attracted grant support, which declined after 2 or 3 years. One reason for the decline was the belief that infertility should not be treated because the world was overpopulated! We have always rejected this cynical stance, which penalised one unfortunate section of the community for the over-fertility of the others, a stance that is even advocated by some people with several children of their own. Other reasons for the difficulty in grant support lay in the belief that the whole procedure was unattainable, or that it was premature and would result in gross defects in the children. I have never accepted that there was an increased risk of deformities in children conceived through fertilization *in vitro,* and have never found any evidence from large numbers of studies on animal embryos to sustain this fear.

We were fortunate in obtaining just sufficient funds to continue the collaborative work between Cambridge and Oldham. These precious sums had to be used for travel to Oldham, first to the Oldham General Hospital, to a tiny room in the Pathology Laboratory, and then to a converted waste disposal room next to the operating theatre. From 1970, we travelled to Kershaw's Hospital, Royton, near Oldham, where the local Health Authority had kindly given us space to carry on our work and, officially, just two beds! But we had facilities there: an operating theatre, a culture room and a small preparation room. There were numerous journeys to this hospital, often in a great hurry after a 9 o'clock lecture in Cambridge University, following a practical class, interrupting a piece of research or a laboratory meeting. The journeys were made in hired cars, paid for out of our Cambridge research grants. Our limited resources had to be extended to cover all the equipment, media, and disposables needed, and to pay for board and lodging when we stayed overnight in Kershaw's Hospital, which was frequent. So much for the myth that the National Health Service paid all our expenses! It paid for virtually none until the birth of Louise Brown was imminent. Patrick

Steptoe was partly covered by the NHS in his practice in the hospital, although he bought much of his operating theatre equipment.

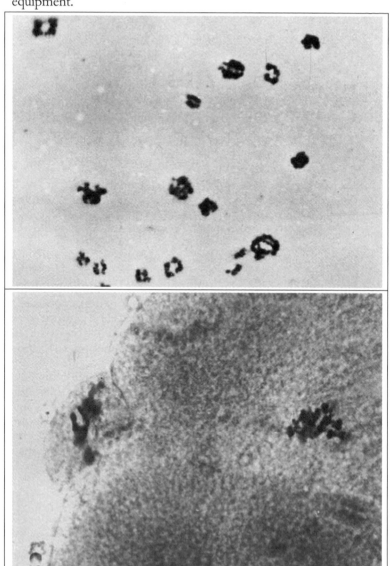

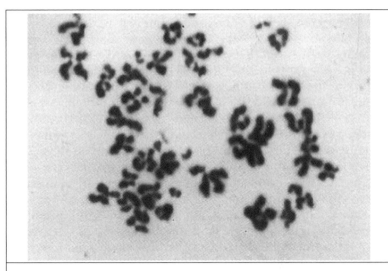

FIG. 1.   Stages of meiosis in maturing human oocytes. (a) Diakinesis (detail). This stage is critical to indicate oocyte maturation, its brief duration being a clear marker of an ongoing stage in meiosis. (b) First polar body and metaphase of the second meiotic division (metaphase-II). (c) Chromosomes (detail) in metaphase II.

The full procedure of oocyte aspiration, fertilization and cleavage *in vitro* and the replacement of embryos into the mother was initiated in the late 1960s and 1970s, and is followed today by every clinic in practice.   It was essential to collect maturing human oocytes from the ovary just before ovulation occurred, because the entire process of maturation *in vitro* might be incompatible with normal embryonic growth after fertilization (Chang, 1955).   In the early days, it was essential to use hormones to stimulate follicle growth, usually human menopausal gonadotrophin (HMG) to stimulate two or more follicles, and human chorionic gonadotrophin (HCG) to induce the follicular changes initiating oocyte maturation and ovulation (Fig. 2) (Steptoe and Edwards, 1978).   Our preliminary tests on clomiphene were discouraging, because few oligomenarrhoeic patients became pregnant in each cycle of treatment and occasional luteinizing hormone (LH) discharges were seen during the cycle, and we abandoned this treatment in favour of HMG (Edwards, 1973).   Correct timing was essential to ensure that preovulatory oocytes were aspirated. As in other species, oocyte maturation follows a rigid timetable, and ovulation can be predicted with great accuracy after an injection of HCG. Our observations on the maturation of human oocytes *in vitro* had been confirmed in oocytes taken from excised ovaries of some patients given HCG (Jagiello *et al.,* 1968). Patrick was confident that preovulatory oocytes could be collected from Graafian follicles by laparoscopy, and this was achieved very quickly using our cheap home-made aspirator, which is still in use today (Steptoe and Edwards, 1978). We sent a manuscript to a journal, describing this innocent equipment, only to have the paper rejected on ethical grounds!

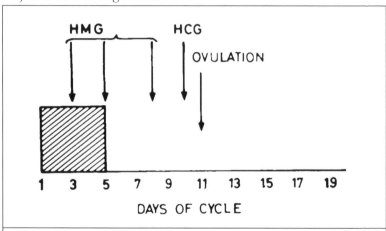

FIG. 2   Simplified schedule for injecting HMG and HCG. The injection of HCG was usually given a day or two later.

The discovery of the first meiotic division in some maturing oocytes collected by laparoscopy from the ovary showed that our techniques were feasible. We knew that preovulatory oocytes could be obtained – a vital need for normal embryonic growth after fertilization, and we had a shrewd idea of the timing of human ovulation, confirmed soon afterwards to begin 37 h after the injection of HCG (Table II) (Edwards and Steptoe, 1975; Edwards *et al.,* 1970). We knew then that the optimal time for laparoscopy for the collection of oocytes would be between 32 and 36 h after the injection of HCG. The next step was to fertilize the eggs *in vitro*.

Table II

Timing of ovulation after HMG or clomiphene, followed by HCG (Edwards and Steptoe, 1975)

Time after HCG (h)	No. of patients	No. ovulated
29-31	59	1
32-35	59	2?
35-37	5	1
37-38½	7	3
40-42	3	2
44	6[a]	4

[a] Talbot et al. (personal communication)

At that time, in 1968 and 1969, fertilization *in vitro* had been achieved using simple procedures in only one mammalian species – the hamster (Yanagimachi and Chang, 1964). It was known that changes occurred in the spermatozoa before they could penetrate oocytes, and these changes became known as capacitation, following the work of Austin (1951) and Chang (1951). Most work had been carried out on the rabbit and there was a deep-seated belief that spermatozoa had to be collected from the female reproductive tract before fertilization *in vitro* was possible (Thibault, 1969). For some reason, the hamster was regarded as an exception, and the rabbit was paid considerable attention. Yet the hamster work was to be our guide during an essential year of work, most of it carried out in Cambridge.

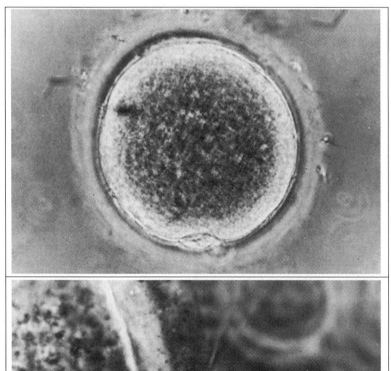

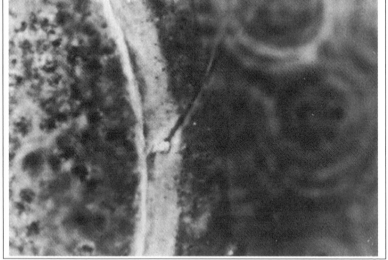

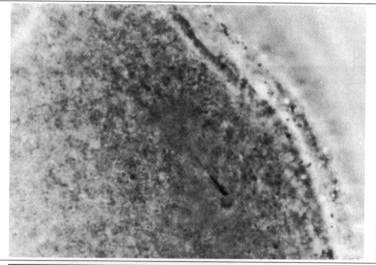

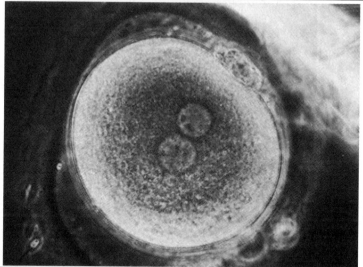

FIG. 3   Stages of fertilization of human eggs *in vitro*. (a) Unfertilised living egg with first polar body. (b) A spermatozoon has passed the zona pellucida and is touching the vitellus of the oocyte. (c) The sperm head is swelling inside the oocyte, and the mid-piece and tail can be seen in this fixed preparation. (d) Two pronuclei and polar bodies in a living oocyte.

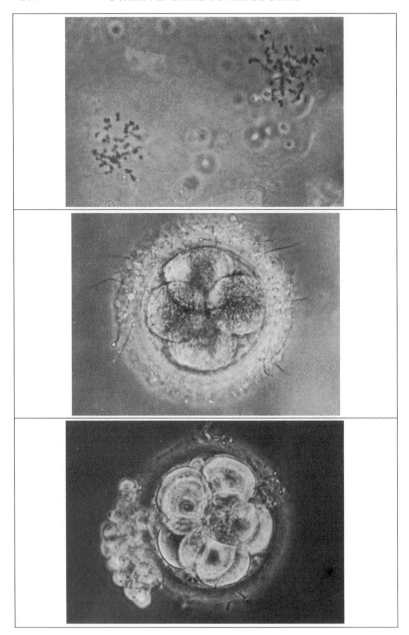

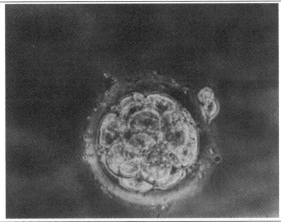

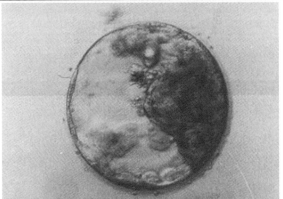

FIG. 4   Cleaving human embryos *in vitro*.   (a) Two mitosis in a 2-cell embryo.   (c) 8-cell.   (d) 16-cell.   (e) Blastocyst, with inner cell mass, blastocele and zona pellucida.

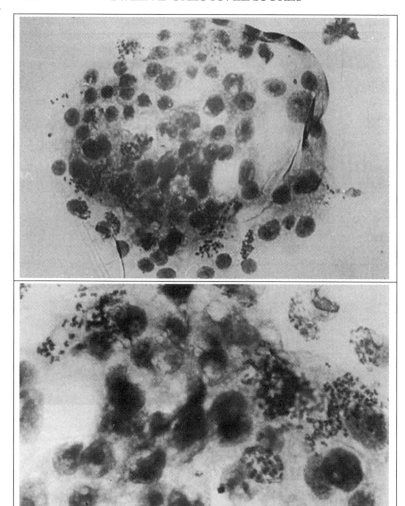

FIG. 5   Stained preparation of a human blastocyst. (a) Entire blastocyst. (b) Detail of nuclei and chromosomes.

We had seen a few examples of sperm penetration and pronucleus formation in our studies before 1969, but our collaboration with B. D. Bavister (1969), then working for his Ph.D. on fertilization *in vitro* in hamsters, proved decisive. Using his modified Tyrode medium, containing pyruvate and albumin, we obtained high rates of fertilization of human oocytes that had matured *in vitro*. We had to mature human eggs *in vitro* in Cambridge, collected from ovaries excised for other clinical reasons, because co-operation of the kind enjoyed with Patrick Steptoe in Oldham was not available. Some of the fertilized eggs were abnormal, to be expected when oocytes matured *in vitro* are used (Edwards *et al.,* 1969; Bavister *et al.,* 1969). The medium was very simple, and ejaculated human spermatozoa were used for fertilization after their gentle centrifugation to remove seminal plasma. Once again, as so frequently before and since, our publication stimulated the disbelievers, doubters and critics to decry the occurrence of fertilization on the grounds that the spermatozoa had not been capacitated, even though this phenomenon was highly obscure! Yet our results were undeniable, because all the stages of fertilization were identified and photographed (Fig. 3; Table 3), and it was clear that this difficult stage in the procedure had been successfully passed. The next step was to obtain the cleavage of embryos *in vitro*.

Table III
Timing of human fertilization in vitro (Bavister et al., 1969)

Hours after insemination	Unpenetrated	Details of the eggs		
		Spermatozoa in zona or perivitelline space	Enlarging spermhead in vitellus	Pronucleate
6-6½	3	0	0	0
7-10½	5	6	0	0
11 and later	12	6	1	11

Several media were tested to support cleaving embryos *in vitro,* and Ham's F10, supplemented with human serum, proved to be the best (Edwards *et al.,* 1970). Once again, we achieved major success with human research while the work on animals was insecure. At that time, the rabbit was virtually the only mammal in which cleavage of the embryo *in vitro* could be attained. There was considerable interest in mouse embryos, and the importance of pyruvate and lactate as energy sources had been recognized (Brinster, 1965). The human embryos proved adaptable and co-operative, and within 12 months they were developing to expanding blastocysts in culture, almost the final stage of their preimplantation growth (Fig. 4) (Steptoe *et al.,* 1971). These observations on the growth of embryos *in vitro* were sufficient to complete the opening phases of our work. We intended to replace 8-cell or 16-cell embryos into patients, but it was essential to know that the embryos were capable of developing considerably further *in vitro* and that their development was normal. Some embryos had to be examined histologically for their nuclear morphology and chromosomal contribution, and the chromosomal spreads were not excellent because there were so few mitoses and so few embryos to study (Fig. 5). But the chromosomes could be seen in more than twelve, and we knew at least that the embryos were approximately diploid and certainly not triploid, confirming that fertilization was monospermic in our cultures (Edwards, 1973: Edwards and Steptoe, 1973).

At this time, in 1970-71, no other group was working on human conception *in vitro.* Indeed, we did not see any illustrations of cleaving human embryos and blastocysts reported from any other clinic or laboratory until 1981, at a meeting in Berlin. There were no scientific or medical studies to compare with ours, so we were unable to exchange ideas on the work with any other practising group. Yet, in 1970, all those observations on human embryos *in vitro* showed clearly that morulae or blastocysts could be replaced into the mother or a donor, raising ethical issues which were debated at the time and have suddenly come into prominence again recently.

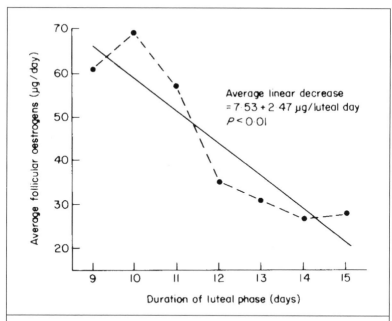

FIG. 6 Duration of the luteal phase in relation to the total amounts of urinary oestrogens during the follicular phase of patients given HMG and HCG (Edwards *et al.*, 1980).

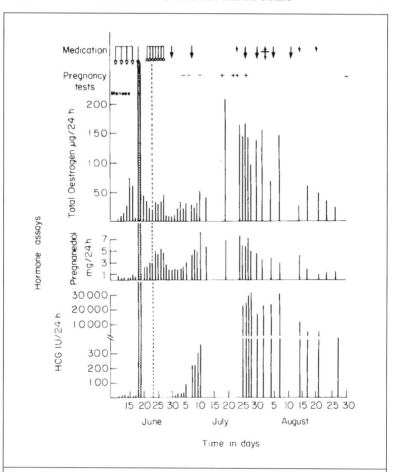

FIG. 7 The first pregnancy established by fertilization *in vitro*. The blastocyst was replaced after fertilization in cleavage *in vitro*, following the use of HMG and HCG to stimulate follicular growth and ovulation. Rising levels of HCG indicated that the pregnancy was normal, and this was confirmed by ultrasound. Progestogen supplements were given throughout the luteal phase. The embryo was found later to have implanted in the oviduct (Steptoe and Edwards, 1976). ⟶ HMG. ⟶ HCG. ⟶ Primulot depot 500 mg. ⟶ Primulot depot 250 mg. ⊢⊢⟶ Ethinyl oestradiol 0.1 mg. ⟶o Norethisterone orally. – Negative pregnancy test. + Positive pregnancy test. ▦▦▦▦ Interval between HCG and laparoscopy; luteinisation would occur around the time of laparoscopy. Reimplantation of embryo.

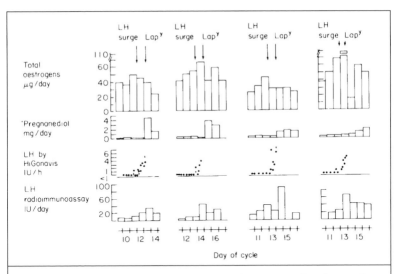

FIG. 8 Monitoring the natural menstrual cycle. Twetny-four hour urinary oestrogens were used to monitor follicular growth, and urinary LH was assayed to detect the surge which indicated the onset of follicular maturation. Laparoscopy was usually performed 24-26 h after the surge of LH. Rising levels of urinary pregnanediol showed that luteinization had occurred (Edwards *et al.*, 1980).

Discussions in the early 1970s with many of our colleagues culturing animal embryos *in vitro,* on the safety of embryo transfer, decided us to replace cultured human embryos into their mother. A pattern was soon established: Patrick gave three or four injections of HMG to patients to stimulate follicle growth, which was assessed by measuring urinary oestrogens. When oestrogen levels rose sufficiently, HCG was given to induce oocyte maturation, and we arrived in our hired car at Kershaw's 30 hours later to prepare for oocyte collection and fertilization; and replaced embryos in the mother 2½–5½ days later. This decision to replace embryos signalled the onset of a long and frustrating period for us. Despite repeated journeys to Oldham, none of the replaced embryos would implant. Embryonic growth *in vitro* was excellent, but the use of HMG to induce follicular growth was disturbing the luteal phase of the patients, reducing it to a very brief period – sometimes as little as 8 or 9 days (Fig. 6) (Edwards, 1973; Edwards *et al.,* 1978). The length of the luteal phase became progressively shorter as the amount of follicular oestrogens rose, i.e. patients with the highest levels of oestrogens and the best response to HMG had the shortest luteal phase. When the dose of HMG was reduced, few or no eggs were obtained, and the luteal phase, although slightly longer, was still too brief.

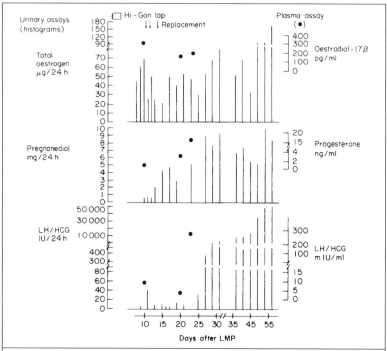

FIG. 9   Pregnancy established by replacing an embryo after fertilization and cleavage *in vitro*, when the natural cycle of the mother had been monitored (Edwards *et al.*, 1980).

At this time, a report from de Kretzer *et al.* (1973) showed that another group was following our lead by replacing embryos grown *in vitro* into the mother. But cleavage in their system was irregular, and the reported rise in levels of HCG could not have been embryonic because it occurred so soon after replacement — perhaps it was an LH discharge induced by clomiphene. We saw no other report on embryos cleaving *in vitro* until after the birth of

Louise Brown.

There was an obvious need to supplement the luteal phase, to overcome the progesterone deficiency and to stimulate the uterus for implantation to occur. At long last, in 1975, the first successful pregnancy was established with endocrine assays and scanning revealing the growth of a fetus (Fig. 7) (Steptoe and Edwards, 1976).

What a wonderful moment! But it ended in disappointment, because it was an ectopic pregnancy, implanted in the oviduct, and the fetus died and had to be removed.

But this was a wonderful stimulus to us, even though the pregnancy ended tragically. We knew that our embryos were capable of implanting, that they could attach themselves to the wall of the uterus and were capable of sustained fetal growth. We had been concerned then that subtle changes might be induced in the embryos by our culture media, that the embryos may be "running out of steam" or could not escape from the zona pellucida or some other reason was interfering with their growth. Now we knew that at least some embryos were capable of implanting, and this knowledge gave us the stimulus to continue. Even so, further work using many stimulants in the luteal phase, yielded only two other short-lived pregnancies (Edwards *et al.,* 1980).

One alternative approach tested in 1976 was to store embryos at low temperatures, with the intention of replacing them in the mother during a subsequent natural cycle. Some oocytes and cleaving embryos were frozen to -190°C and thawed out a few days later. Some retained their morphology, but none displayed any more cleavages *in vitro* (Edwards and Steptoe, 1980). Another approach was needed.

It was then, in 1977, that we decided to change to the natural cycle, to monitor follicle growth and the LH surge, and collect the single preovulatory oocyte that was maturing in the ovary (Fig. 8). We could only attempt this because of our considerable experience built up in earlier years. As the world knows, our second patient was Leslie Brown (Steptoe and Edwards, 1978). It was wonderful to collect the single egg, fertilize it *in vitro,* and watch it grow to an

8-cell embryo, when it was replaced into its mother. We obtained four pregnancies during 9 months work (Fig. 9) four critical pregnancies because Patrick had reached the age of retirement in the NHS and, anyway, we could not continue with our endless journeys to Oldham from Cambridge. The birth of Louise Brown and two other children gave us great hope for full support to continue our work, even though another fetus had proved to be triploid and aborted at 10½ weeks. We felt confident now that State money could become available for our work.

Sadly, there was still no support. We needed a complete clinic, an operating theatre with sterile air, facilities for setting up a small laboratory next to the operating theatre, and the opportunity to carry out laparoscopy whenever required. Unfortunately, these conditions were not forthcoming, and we had to resort to building our own clinic, financed by our own private money, and by funds that were borrowed from wherever we could. This was how our work at Bourn Hall began, in our clinic opened more than 2 years after the birth of Louise Brown; two years of frustration when no collaboration was possible between us, when no work was carried out at all.

During this interval, our work began to be copied abroad. These initial phases presented major difficulties to some groups, with successful replacements being rare, and only one child being born (Lopata, 1980). We believed these difficulties arose because the correct scientific methods of embryo culture were not applied, that the importance of strict technique and knowledge of mammalian embryology were overlooked. Some clinicians believed that embryologists were an unnecessary luxury, and attempted the whole procedure without them. This attitude was adopted even though several embryologists were available who were fully trained in these procedures. Pregnancies were soon established elsewhere once the balance of scientific/medical collaboration was established (Trounson et al., 1981; Wood et al., 1981), confirming for us the value of our own team work among three colleagues for many years in Oldham.

Clinical Results on the Alleviation of Infertility 1981-82

Our work on *in vitro* fertilization resumed at Bourn Hall in Cambridge, which opened in October, 1980. I would like to describe our results obtained during the period between January 1st, 1981, and January 14th, 1982, when one set of work was completed. Some of the patients treated during this period are still pregnant, and we are awaiting the outcome of these pregnancies before the data can be finally evaluated. We have saluted elsewhere the work of other clinics now being established (Edwards and Purdy, 1982), and have presented their detailed results and discussions with ours. I would like to present brief details of the work as it has developed; full details have been published elsewhere (Edwards, 1981; Edwards and Fishel, 1982; Edwards and Purdy, 1982; Edwards *et al.,* 1983a, 1983b; Fishel and Edwards, 1982; Fishel etal., 1983a, 1983b; Steptoe and Webster, 1982).

FOLLICULAR GROWTH, OOCYTE COLLECTION, AND FERTILIZATION AND CLEAVAGE *IN VITRO*

In Bourn Hall, as in Oldham, we decided to monitor the natural cycle of some patients, using assays of urinary oestrogens and LH. Other patients, especially those with difficult access to the ovary or with fertilization problems have been given clomiphene as a follicular stimulant, since this treatment was successfully reintroduced by Wood and colleagues (1981). Urinary hormones were also used to assess the response of patients to this treatment. After receiving clomiphene, many patients discharge their own LH surge to induce follicular and oocyte maturation. Some patients do not produce an LH surge after treatment with clomiphene (Fig. 10), and HCG must be given before their follicles become atretic; for this reason, we give all patients HCG when their urinary oestrogens reach 150 µg/24h or more, after considering the day of the cycle and previous menstrual history, and provided that ultrasonic scans have revealed growing follicles. Some patients are given combined treatment with clomiphene and HMG, as in the earlier work in Oldham.

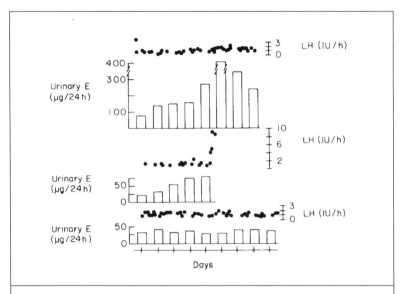

FIG. 10 Response of patients to clomiphene (Edwards, 1981). (a) A considerable rise in levels of urinary oestrogens was not followed by an LH surge. The pituitary response to oestrogens had evidently been impaired, perhaps by the anti-oestrogenic action of clomiphene. The levels of urinary oestrogens declined as the follicles became atretic. (b) A weak rise in urinary oestrogens was followed by an LH surge. (c) No distinct rise in levels of urinary oestrogens, and no LH surge occurred in this patient.

Success with the laparoscopic collection of preovulatory oocytes is high (Table IV), and fertilization and cleavage *in vitro* have remained consistently good. True rates might be even higher, because we assume that all oocytes surrounded by the typical viscous fluid are preovulatory, whereas some may have been non-ovulatory.

After initial work in the opening months, we decided to restrict the culture to Earle's medium, reinforced with pyruvate, and containing human serum (8% v/v for fertilization, and 15% v/v to support cleavage), and only one antibiotic, penicillin. An osmotic pressure of 285 m Osmol/kg approximately and pH of 72 were identical to those used since the early days of the work in Oldham.

Table IV
Assessment of laparoscopy
30 September, 1981 – 14 January, 1982
(Edwards et al., 1983a)

Patients	No.	
Laparoscopies	166	
Failed laparoscopies	21	
Oocyte recovery	145	(87%)
No. of ruptured follicles	3	(2%)
Method failure	5	(3%)
Oocyte recovery without laparoscopic complications[a]	153	(95%)

[a] Complications include encephaloid ovaries (1), substantial adhesions (7), cystic response to stimulation (2), severe endometriosis (1), many tiny follicles (2).

Fertilization rates *in vitro* are very high with "satisfactory" spermatozoa, i.e. with numerous live spermatozoa and good motility (Table V). I will discuss below the problems arising with fertilization *in vitro* when there is evidence of antibodies or inflammation in the male reproductive tract, and in cases of oligospermia. The cleavage of embryos *in vitro* is excellent. The embryos were grown for between 2½ and 4½ days *in vitro,* when they reached various stages of growth between the 4-cell and the early blastocyst. Only a few (<5%) display a disordered growth which precluded their replacement in the mother. Embryos have been replaced in 90% of patients with one or more preovulatory oocytes, and subsequent pregnancies have been identified by rising levels of HCGP, ultrasound and the clinical symptoms of pregnancy.

All embryos were replaced into the mother via the cervix, mostly without anaesthesia, in either the lithotomy or the knee-chest position. Special catheters have been devised, some made of extruded nylon and others of polyethylene, and the problems of traversing the cervical canal with fine catheters containing an embryo have been largely overcome. Difficulties are seldom encountered now during this phase of the treatment.

Table Va
Total number of patients
January 1, 1981 – January 14, 1982
(Edwards et al., 1983a)

Patients	No.
Laparoscopies	649
With > 1 oocyte	538
With > 1 fertilized	420
Replacements	414
Clinical pregnancies	76 (18%)[a]
Elevated HCGβ	12 +

[a] Percentage of replacements

Table Vb
Total number of patients
September 30, 1981 – January 14, 1982
(Edwards et al., 1983a)

Patients	No.
Laparoscopies	166
Oocyte recovery	145
Fertilization	127
Replacements	126
Clinical pregnancies	28 (22%)[a]
Elevated HCGβ	2

[a] Percentage of replacements

PREGNANCIES FOLLOWING THE REPLACEMENT OF EMBRYOS

The overall results on all patients during this period are shown in Table V. These data include all the patients treated, whatever their cause of infertility. The majority had tubal occlusion, although some had idiopathic infertility, and others suffered from oligospermia. In rare cases, evidence of antibodies against spermatozoa were found in either the husband or the wife, and a few patients had endometriosis or luteal phase deficiencies, which became apparent only when they were undergoing treatment.

Table VI

Overall success rates using the natural menstrual cycle
(Edwards et al., 1983a)

Patients	1/1/81 – 14/1/82	1/10/81 – 14/1/82
Laparoscopies	382	35
With > 1 oocyte	312	29
With >1 fertilized	236	25
Replacements	232	24
Clinical pregnancies	37 (16%)[a]	6 (25%)[a]
Elevated HCGβ	5 +	0

[a] Percentage of replacements

Table VI

Overall success rates with clomiphene and a natural LH surge
(Edwards et al., 1983a)

Patients	1/1/81 – 14/1/82	1/10/81 – 14/1/82
Laparoscopies	144	61
With > 1 oocyte	133	50
With >1 fertilized	85	40
Replacements	83	40
Clinical pregnancies	18 (22%)[a]	9 (23%)[a]
Elevated HCGβ	1 +	1 +

[a] Percentage of replacements

Table VIII

Overall success rates with clomiphene and HCG
(Edwards et al., 1983a)

Patients	1/1/81 – 14/1/82	1/10/81 – 14/1/82
Laparoscopies	123	70
With > 1 oocyte	113	66
With > fertilised	99	62
Replacements	99	62
Clinical pregnancies	21 (21%)[a]	13 (21%)[a]
Elevated HCGβ	6 +	1 +

[a] Percentage of replacements.

The first question to consider is whether our methods are improving with time. The overall data have been subdivided into the periods between January, 1981, and January 14th, 1982, and between September, 1981, and January 14th, 1982, in Tables VI–VIII. There are variations between different treatments in the rates of implantation. The initial work at Bourn Hall involved patients being treated during the natural cycle, and success rates improved with better techniques (Table VI). Clomiphene was introduced later, when the methods were established, and success rates with this method have remained steady (Tables VII and VIII). The embryos appear to cleave more rapidly after patients are given clomiphene and HCG (Table IX and X), but this might also be due to the introduction of clomiphene when our methods had been well established. At the present time, it appears that no treatment is superior to the others, for the greater chance of obtaining embryos following stimulation by clomiphene appears to be balanced by a slightly higher chance of obtaining pregnancy during the natural cycle.

Table IX
Cleavage rate of the human embryo to the 4 cell stage in vitro
(Fishel et al., *1983a)*

		Hours post-insemination			
Cycle	Total no. of embryos	50	$50\frac{1}{2}$-55	$55\frac{1}{2}$-60	$60\frac{1}{2}$
Natural cycle	21	29	48	19 (96%)[a]	1
Clomid/LH	44	39	39	11 (89%)[a]	11
Clomid/HCG	41	46	51	2 (99%)[a]	

[a] Accumulative percentage

Many of the pregnancies have been uneventful, and have resulted in birth or in continuing pregnancy (Table XIa). The incidence of abortion in relation to maternal age is given in Table XIb; most abortions occurred in the first 10 weeks of gestation, as occurs after conception *in vitro*. Some pregnancies may last very briefly. We have noticed some transient rises in levels of HCGβ in urine during the period after embryos were replaced; the significance of this discovery is uncertain. Similar observations of such brief pregnancies have been reported after conception *in vivo* (Batzer *et al.,* 1981) and *in vitro* (Edwards and Purdy, 1982), and these pregnancies are sometimes referred to as "biochemical pregnancies". They may arise through the stimulation of the uterus by the catheters used for replacing embryos, but they could represent a distinct group of early abortions. We currently place them in a distinct category, separate from clinical pregnancies, and their importance will be assessed in later work.

Table X
Cleavage rate of human embryos to the 8 cell stage in vitro
(Fishel et al.*, 1983a)*

Cycle	Total no. of embryos	Hours post-insemination				
		<55	55½-65	65½-75	75½-85	<85½
Natural Cycle	23	26	13	22 (61%)[a]	35	0
Clomid/LH	11	36	27	0 (63%)[a]	27	9
Clomid/HCG	17	65	12	12 (89%)[a]	12	0

[a]Accumulative percentage.

It is necessary to standardize methods and procedures during fertilization *in vitro,* and to identify the optimum conditions of each stage. These targets are not simple, and we can barely identify some of the most pertinent conditions even after establishing more than 100 pregnancies. There are literally too many parameters to analyse, despite our attempts to reduce the number of variables by standardizing an Earle's medium for fertilizing and embryo culture *in vitro,* timing replacements of embryos from 17.00h, and ensuring that numerous procedures are followed strictly (Purdy, 1982a).

Some variables were tentatively identified, including the use of different catheters. Those made of extruded nylon or polyethylene, especially the latter, initially proved more successful (Table XII), and they pass easily through the cervical canal. The replacement of two embryos rather than one also appears to raise the chance of implantation (Wood *et al.,* 1981), although the reason is far from clear (Table XIII). There may be a lower chance of the mechanical loss of the embryo if two are replaced, e.g. less chance of accidentally withdrawing the embryo from the uterus as the catheter is withdrawn. The endocrine conditions for implantation might be superior in patients with two or more embryos because the luteal phase is superior in those with two or more follicles. Implantation rates could also be higher with twin replacements because there is a greater chance that one of them is normal.

Table XIa
Analysis of first 101 pregnancies at Bourn Hall
(Fishel et al., *1983b)*

Patients delivered	57
Babies born	59
Third trimester	3
Abortions	26 (30%)[a]
"Biochemical"	15 (15%)[b]

[a] Percentage of 86 clinical pregnancies. [b] Percentage of 101 pregnancies

Table XIb
Effect of age on the rate of abortion (Fishel et al., *1983b)*

	Mean patient age	Years				
		20-25	26-29	30-34	35-39	40
Ongoing pregnancy	33	1	9	27	22	1
Abortion	33	0	2 (18%)	14 (34%)	9 (29%)	1

Table XII
Pregnancies in relation to the type of catheter used for replacement (Fishel et al., *1983a)*

Catheter	Patients	Pregnancies
"Bourn"	50	10 (20%)
Edwards/Wallace IIA	55	15 (27%)
Edwards/Wallace IIB	47	5 (11%)
Edwards/Wallace III	16	5 (31%)
Double	34	9[a] (27%)

[a] Six "biochemical"

The level of circulating oestrogens may also influence the chance of pregnancy. Patients given clomiphene who have higher levels of urinary oestrogens before HCG is given, or before the endogenous LH surge begins, appear to have a greater chance of pregnancy. Each of these indicators is still tentative, because so many other variables are involved in the work that many hundreds of pregnancies will have to be analysed before any clear markers emerge.

At present, we have apparently established more than half of the pregnancies and births so far reported in the world, but this situation will change rapidly as many new clinics open. At the present time, 56 babies have been born from Bourn Hall and 3 more from Oldham. No serious complications have been reported. Follow-up studies will be needed to confirm that the children are growing normally and detailed examinations on them might be needed as they grow, although the risks of abnormal growth appear to be similar to those occurring after conception *in vivo*. Eventually, a child will be born after *in vitro* fertilization suffering from trisomy, monosomy or another inherited defect typical of the disturbances that characterize human births. This will almost certainly not be due to conception *in vitro,* but to the known risks of fetal anomalies. Trisomic and monosomic abortuses have been identified after fertilization *in vitro* (Frydman, 1982), and a triploid fetus aborted during our Oldham work (Steptoe and Edwards, 1978). We have not so far found any more examples of chromosomal imbalance in the few abortuses where samples were obtained for cytogenic analysis.

Scientific Studies on Human Conception

Before discussing the ethics of *in vitro* fertilization, I would like to describe three of the scientific observations which are implicit in our work. Studies on the endocrinology of the menstrual cycle are providing knowledge on the timing of the LH surge in women, we now have a greater understanding of the problems arising with some spermatozoa during fertilization *in vitro,* and some unusual but very preliminary observations have been made on the timing of implantation in a few pregnancies.

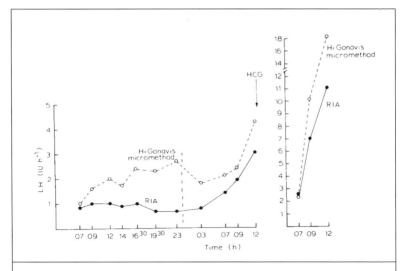

FIG. 11   Assays of urinary LH in patients by Hi-Gonavis and radioimmunoassay. Both assays coincide, and reveal the LH surge beginning in early morning (Edwards and Purdy, 1982).

TIMING OF THE BEGINNING OF THE LH SURGE IN WOMEN

Most assays for LH are carried out on urine, using the kit Hi-Gonavis® (Mochida Pharmaceuticals) as in Oldham, and the urine of a number of patients has also been assayed for LH using a radioimmunoassay kit. The two sets of data coincide completely: some examples are shown in Fig. 11. Notice that in these patients, levels of LH began to rise to surge levels from about 0300 h in the morning. We have examined a large number of patients by now, and most of them begin to discharge their LH surge during the early morning hours. A frequency distribution of the beginning of the LH surge in groups of our patients is shown in Fig. 12; similar results have been obtained with patients examined during their natural cycle and in those given clomiphene. The daily rhythm is less distinct in Summer and Autumn than in Winter and Spring, possibly due to the longer light period. Our estimates of the beginning of the LH surge will be late because our assays are based on urinary levels, and the surge in plasma will presumably occur some 3–4 h earlier. We also time the beginning of the LH surge from the first rising assay; the mid-point between that and the previous low assay would obviously give a better time of the first rise in LH. The LH surge in plasma would therefore begin approximately 6 h before our assays indicate.

There appears to be a remarkable diurnal rhythm in the timing of the beginning of the LH surge in women. There is a "critical period" before the beginning of the discharge of LH, just as in rats (Everett *et al.,* 1949). The essential difference between the two species is that the critical period in women occurs at 0300 h, whereas in rats it occurs at 1500 h. The LH rhythm in women is related to their cortisol rhythm; all those beginning their LH surge in the morning showed a typical rise of the urinary cortisol to be expected at this time of day (Fig. 13). Interestingly, the few patients we have examined who began their LH discharge in the afternoon also had a secondary discharge of urinary cortisol at this time.

Just as in women, the cortisol and LH rhythms appear to be related in rats (Buckingham *et al.,* 1978). Data from Goddard (unpublished) confirms that the critical period begins in mice during the afternoon, and this is the time that their diurnal adrenal activity begins (Nichols and Chevins, 1981). Females of the three species are identical in that their cortisol and LH rhythms are interlinked, but they have chosen opposite ends of the day to begin their endocrine activity. Rat females without a clear diurnal adrenal rhythm displayed irregular oestrous cycles (Ramaley, 1974). We do not know if a similar correlation occurs in women.

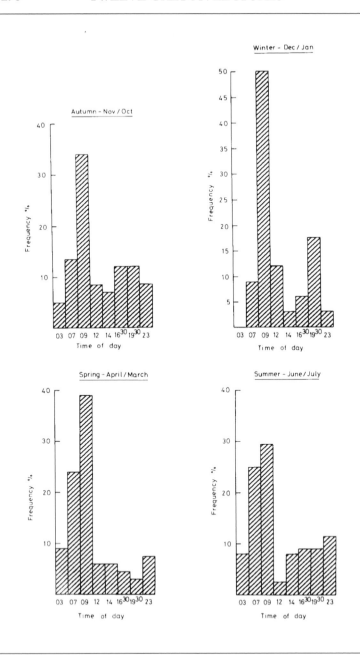

FIG. 12   Frequency distribution of the beginning of the LH surge in > 200 British patients throughout the year (autumn 1981 – summer 1982). These provisional results include data from patients given clomiphene and those monitored during their natural menstrual cycle. Notice the rhythm becomes weaker in summer, and this persists into autumn; this effect is presumably due to the long daylight hours.

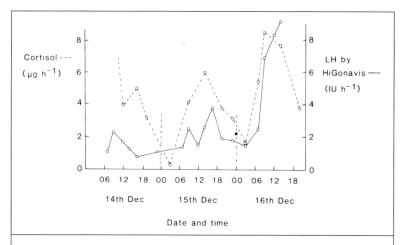

FIG. 13   Relationship between the morning rise in urinary cortisol and the beginning of the LH surge in one patient (Edwards and Purdy, 1982).

We can predict the time of human ovulation from our data on the beginning of the LH surge. It shows that the majority of women will undergo ovulation from about 10 a.m. until 4 p.m. (Fig. 14). This has implications for human conception *in vivo*. Assuming that intercourse occurs in the evening following ovulation, the oocytes of many women will be approximately 12 h old before fertilization occurs. Should intercourse occur on the next night, then the oocytes will be 36 h old. The quality of cervical mucus should permit sperm transport 12 h after ovulation, and may also do so at 36 h, so the spermatozoa will be able to reach the ampulla. We know from our studies on oocytes maintained *in vitro* that they can be incubated for 12 h or more, then be fertilized *in vitro* and develop into a full-term infant. Delayed fertilization should therefore be possible *in vivo* following an ovulation occurring during the day.

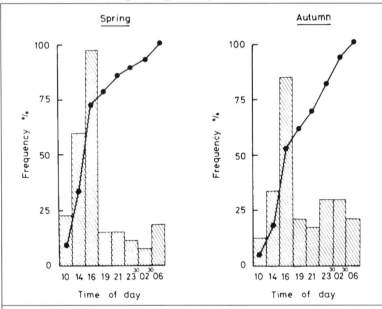

FIG. 14   Estimated timing of ovulation in patients in Bourn Hall (solid line). This has been derived by estimating the mid-point between the last tonic level of LH and the first rising assay, and allowing a period of 4 h between the rising levels of LH in plasma and urine. An interval of 37 h is expected between the plasma LH surge and ovulation (see Table II).

Several other consequences follow from these observations. In animals, delayed fertilization is a common cause of triploidy, and this may be one reason for the high incidence of this condition in many human fetuses which undergo abortion after conception *in vivo*. We do not know at present if delayed fertilization can lead to trisomy, and so be the cause of the high rate of abortion and the birth of children with chromosomal imbalance. We suspect, however, that the incidence of trisomy will not be raised because its origins lie in the meiotic prophase of the first meiotic division, either through asynapsis which occurs in the fetal ovary, or desynapsis during the long follicular phase of oocyte growth (Henderson and Edwards, 1968; Hassold and Matsuyama, 1978).

Delayed fertilization is therefore unlikely to exert major effects on the incidence of trisomy, although it might raise the chance of dispermy which is a frequent cause of triploidy (Jacobs *et al.,* 1978).

The daily rhythm in the timing of ovulation also has implications for the safe method of contraception. Ovulation is entrained to a daily rhythm, as in rats; if it fails to occur at the expected time on one day, it must begin 24h later, not a few hours later. The error in timing ovulation for the rhythm method is thus 24 h, which could account for the high failure rate.

IDIOPATHIC INFERTILITY, OLIGOSPERMIA AND OTHER PROBLEMATICAL SPERMATOZOA

The second example I would like to describe concerns problems with fertilization. We can classify our patients according to the properties of their spermatozoa. Most men produce spermatozoa which are "satisfactory", this conclusion being drawn from observations on motility and the absence of deleterious conditions such as clumping. Spermatozoa from these men give very high rates of fertilization, approaching 90 per cent or more, and probably higher because some of the oocytes may not have been fully preovulatory at insemination. Other men produce samples of spermatozoa which are not satisfactory. These are shown in Table XIV. Some conditions in the semen, e.g. the presence of many inflammatory cells in the ejaculate or massive agglutination of spermatozoa depress overall rates of fertilization. Other conditions, such as viscous seminal plasma, small amounts of agglutination, and minor clumping, do not appear to be incompatible with high rates of fertilization.

It is also clear that fertilization rates can be high in couples with idiopathic infertility and oligospermia. Neither of these conditions, even extreme oligospermia, are incompatible with the establishment of pregnancy through fertilization *in vitro*. Data on rates of fertilization *in vitro* are given in Table XV. Fertilization rates in several different types of patients are good and are only lowered if other factors are involved such as the suspected presence of antibodies or inflammation. We have not seen any evidence of abnormal fertilization in any of these patients. The chance of pregnancy following the replacement of an embryo is similar in each type of patient, except perhaps in women with immunological infertility, hence all of them share the same opportunity of pregnancy following successful fertilization *in vitro*. Any improvement in the rates of implantation, still the major hurdle to the full development of conception *in vitro,* would benefit all of these patients equally.

Table XIV
Fertilization rates in vitro *(Edwards et al., 1983a)*

Spermatozoa	Total no. of patients	No. with 1 fertilised oocyte	% Oocytes fertilised
Satisfactory	95	87 (92%)	85%
Head clumps, viscous seminal plasma	11	10 (90%)	95%
Some cells/debris	25	20 (80%)	70%
Many immotile sluggish/erratic	20	12 (60%)	50%
Massive clumping	10	5 (50%)	45%
Tail agglutn., many immotile	12	5 (41%)	41%
Massive cells/debris	7	2 (30%)	30%

Table XV
In vitro *fertilization, oligospermia and idiopathic infertility*

Patients	Sperm/ml	Motility	Oocytes	No. fertilized
Oligospermia {	$5\text{-}25 \times 10^6$	20%	18	13 (72%)
	very few [a]	–	10	7 (70%)
	Very few [a] + cells	–	6	2 (33%)
"Idiopathic"	–	–	18	15 (83%)

[a] Less than 4×10^6 in total. Whole sample had to be used for *in vitro* fertilization

DOES DELAYED IMPLANTATION OCCUR IN WOMEN?

I would like, lastly, to consider one aspect of the implantation of embryos. The great majority of our pregnancies have shown similar endocrine characteristics, with rising levels of urinary HCGβ from day 11 of pregnancy. Some examples of these rising levels are shown in Fig. 15. In two pregnancies, the initial measurements of urinary HCGβ suggested that implantation had not occurred, because the levels remained very low, and then began to rise several days later than expected. Both of these pregnancies have passed uneventfully, and two normal children have been born.

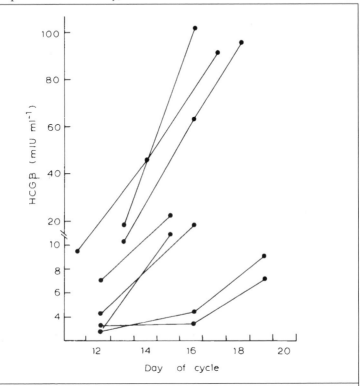

FIG. 15 Rising levels of urinary HCGβ in pregnancies established in Bourn Hall. Notice that the rise was delayed in two patients who have since given birth to a child.

We do not know the cause of this delay in the rising levels of HCGβ. It could be due to the weak development of trophoblast and its secretion of HCG, or to the delayed implantation of an embryo. Delayed implantation is well known in many animal species (Psychoyos, 1973), but there is no information as to whether it exists in man. The analysis of further pregnancies could prove of considerable interest in the study of human reproductive physiology.

The Ethics of *In Vitro* Fertilization

In the third part of this lecture, I would like to discuss the ethics of *in vitro* fertilization. This discussion is timely, since a great deal of interest has been raised recently in this topic. We have been sensitive to the ethical implications of our work since it began, and have made numerous contributions to it over the years (Edwards, 1971, 1972, 1974, 1980; Edwards and Sharpe, 1971; Edwards and Steptoe, 1973; Kennedy and Edwards, 1975). Recent discussions on the relationship between ethical principles and *in vitro* fertilization have been presented by Dunstan, 1974, and Kuhse (1982).

THE BASIS OF ETHICS

What are ethics? This branch of philosophy embraces the study of standards of judgements and behaviour at all levels in a society — the individual, the corporate body and the state. Some ethicists search for absolute values, for a received ethic based for example on Greek, biblical or political beliefs. Others offer a more practical set of values, such as the concept of utilitarianism. To many scientists, many modern debates on new ethical issues appear to ignore the more ancient concepts, relying instead on practical and pragmatic decisions. A change seems to have occurred, placing more emphasis on widespread debate and choice within a community rather than on the acceptance of authoritarian edicts. Challenges to established standards during the last century, for example, reduced the impact of Church and State on ethical standards in relation to contraception and sterilization. Today, Papal pronouncements, for example on divorce and abortion, do not carry the same commanding weight as before, even among many Catholics who emphasize their right to consult their own conscience.

Ethical debates at the present time often seem to be restricted to the pros and cons of a particular situation, each "situation" being decided independently of other ethical problems. Nevertheless, it would be a mistake to overlook the contribution of earlier fundamental debates in ethics to the current values of society, and to assess properly the existing balance in present day moral issues. The underlying principles of standards and behaviour in Christian societies, and in others, remain as clear as they have always been, even if no longer cloaked in theocratic terms. They are still based on Greek and Judeao-Christian beliefs, and for many people biblical inspiration fulfills the same role today as earlier, even if modern ethical debates seem to be based on factual and even technical standards. It is important not to be misled, to accept too easily that there is a new modern "received ethic", based on finding a balance between what can be done and what should be done in a rapidly-changing technological society. Such debate is superficial, because it cloaks the essential base of the ancient spiritual and ethical attitudes underlying it.

This dependence on fundamental beliefs holds even though modern ethical problems concern issues never discussed before, such as genetic engineering and transplantation surgery. The traditional practitioners of ethics, e.g. in the Church or humanities, have no guide to rely on in the Bible or elsewhere; the situation has changed because there are no guidelines, such as there have been for centuries on issues such as abortion or incest. Many modern situations are so novel that the professions who used to set ethical standards might even have no knowledge of the work or its consequences. Decisions on how to progress are increasingly left to those who establish the work, e.g. scientists and doctors, and the regulation of it to politicians and lawyers who must frame the necessary legislation. But despite this apparent shift in emphasis, decisions on new ethical issues are still based on the traditional theological and social values of society, which stand as a guide in making essential decisions.

Whatever the underlying principles might be, ethical standards must be based on a rational set of values, capable of scientific verification or impartial judgement if at all possible. Standards can change if new circumstances arise. Concepts such as "rational" and "value" are not simple terms to define: they each have different meanings to different people, depending on their personal set of experiences. Each of us will have our own ethical standards, even though the general framework of a moral code may be shared by large numbers of people in a given society. For this reason, injunctions to "Do unto others as you would have them do unto you", will be interpreted in numerous ways, and thus provide only a narrow basis for fundamental reasoning. The moral outlook of individual practitioners will influence their ethical decisions, for example on the prescription of contraceptives for teenagers.

How do individuals attain their own morals and behaviour? Political philosophers in the last century stressed the importance of social position, and psychoanalysists in the present century have identified successive stages in the development of self, conflicts arising in each phase being resolved during subsequent growth, e.g. in the emergence of sexual behaviour. Today, some ethologists suggest that responses and behaviour are the product of previous experiences, that beliefs are limited by earlier events and experiences in life. It is essential that anyone taking decisions in a critical ethical situation must be aware of such discussions on the basis of individuality, as well as being informed on the philosophical basis of ethics and the technical complexities of decision taking in a modern society. Taking such decisions involves a considerable responsibility, e.g. introducing ablative chemoradiotherapy in the treatment of malignancy, or replacing the first embryo in an *in vitro* fertilization programme knowing that the child will live for many years.

Each of us can arrange our lives according to our individual standards until large ethical conflicts arise involving groups of people, e.g. of different religions or professions. Establishing standards within a profession and a society then involves compromises among the opinions of its individual members, and between professions. The actions of the individual are restricted, in the shared interests of the wider group. In a sense, Ethical Committees or Commissions actually decide on such limitations, reducing a large number of possible actions to an acceptable few. They establish a course of action which is permissible, even though not necessarily defined legally. This view of the role of Ethical Committees is somewhat similar to the "convention" of acceptable behaviour in a society, far wider in scope than that covered by law, as defined by Dunstan (1974).

Ethical standards are usually established today as a welter of individual viewpoints, which are encompassed into a norm acceptable to a majority in society. Many conventions and laws are obeyed almost without question, whereas others, such as the acceptance of abortion, are constantly under debate and disagreement. Most of the more novel and intricate ethical dilemmas arise in the major professions, e.g. theology, law, politics, medicine, science, and individual members of these professions, and their corporate bodies, will obviously have much to contribute in solving their own ethical problems. Sometimes a general and relevant principle can be identified underlying debates on several issues, enabling contributors without a special training in a profession to add their opinions. This neutral viewpoint can be invaluable, because ethical standards might vary amongst different professions, e.g. a medical doctor might be unwilling to divulge information regarded as essential by a journalist. They might also vary within a profession, e.g. doctors differ in their approach to abortion.

Some ethical standards are coded in a framework of law, but in fast-moving areas of research in practice, scientists and doctors might have to work without help from the law. The work is not illegal: there is simply no law directly relevant to it, although some law might apply to part of it. This situation perhaps occurred during early stages of work on organ transplantation, when there was but little legal discussion on the issues, and doctors were, and still are, divided amongst themselves. The treatment and perhaps the fate of handicapped newborn children was, until recently, another example where decisions on life and death were evidently left largely in the hands of individual doctors, where the legal profession had not been fully involved. Under these circumstances, the recommendations of professional bodies can set a responsible ethical standard, before any law has been framed to deal with a new situation.

In rapidly changing situations, as in the advances of modern science, standards of judgement and behaviour established at one period may have to change with new discovery or with new thinking. The overriding problem is how to assess an imminent advance in knowledge or methods, how to cope with a new dilemma. Obviously, the risks of any new approach must be evaluated and carefully weighed against the predicted benefits; this is a matter for investigation. The impact of new advances on the ethical standards of society must also be anticipated and judged in its widest sense, and this evaluation may be a matter of opinion. Decisions are not easy. New ideas mean that a choice must be made between the old and the new; to deliberately ignore the new is as much an ethical choice as to wholeheartedly embrace it. Judgements may be assisted by assessing the motives behind the work, or the consequences of the action, but motives can vary or change in individuals and consequences can rarely be guaranteed. In the final analysis, negative decisions, i.e. not to do anything, are comfortable and rely on a long established status quo; a decision to introduce new methods must be made by someone, hopefully with all the foregoing complexities in mind.

EARLY DEBATES ON THE ETHICS OF FERTILIZING HUMAN EGGS *IN VITRO*

Ethical debates on fertilization *in vitro* are an extension of numerous other conflicts on standards in human reproduction: on infanticide, abortion, sterilization and contraception. Arguments and opinions from one set of debates intrudes into the others, an inevitable consequence of the development of methods for studying human embryos *in vitro*. I would like to give a brief summary of the earlier debates relevant to human conception *in vitro*, before turning to our views on the current ethical situation.

The initial work of *in vitro* fertilization of human eggs involved Patrick Steptoe, a doctor, myself, and Jean Purdy, a nurse and my assistant. My duty as a scientist was to draw attention to new possibilities in science and medicine, even if they sounded barely credible, and to apply my knowledge to the problem under study. This was, and is, my scientific ethic; to stimulate discussion on the possible development of studies on fertilization *in vitro*, to discuss their safety and ethical aspects and to apply them where appropriate. Working with Patrick Steptoe placed me directly in the realm of medical ethics, and I had to respect his ethical standards too, e.g. in consulting with the Ethical Committee of the Hospital. We had then jointly to convince others of the value of our work. During these early days, there was neither law, nor indeed any professional opinion on which to base our decisions. There was one well-tried and trusted medical rule to guide us — "Do no harm". We believed, and still believe that this was applied in our studies.

In the 1960s, ethical discussions on fertilization *in vitro* were largely restricted to the individual opinions of ourselves and a few other colleagues, and some journalists. Debate became more widespread in the early 1970s, as our work progressed. Despite contributions from politicians, theologians and lawyers, it still nevertheless failed to reach the professional bodies in science or medicine, with rare exceptions, and was certainly overlooked in any formal legal sense. It was essential for us to publish several papers on ethics, and to attend numerous conferences, where we could stimulate debate about our work. We had to elucidate the basic concepts of the work and carry out the necessary studies, pursuing the ethics and, finally, with John Maddox, then Editor of *Nature,* stimulating the formation of the first national ethical committee in the UK, composed of diverse professions and dealing with *in vitro* fertilization and other ethical topics (Jones and Bodmer, 1974).

The debates in those earlier years were often concerned with broad fundamental issues outside the clinic or laboratory: on topics such as the sanctity and meaning of life, recalling the numerous debates on abortion. There were sincere doubts about the acceptability of conception *in vitro* among many theologians. These were answered by writers such as Francouer (1972), who wrote that man should contribute to the ongoing task of creating man and nature because God had shared his creative powers with us. Many of these debates revealed the fundamental nature of ethics, and the relationship between the older concepts and the issues raised by modern science and medicine.

Some debates were less fundamental, even trivial. One such argument stated that treatment of infertility by conception *in vitro* was not a "cure", because the original derangement in the oviduct remained in the patient (Kass, 1971); the only cure was to repair the oviduct. Treating infertility by replacing embryos growing *in vitro* was held to be synonymous with treating a symptom, a "desire" to have children. Surprisingly, this view has been repeated recently (Daniel, 1982). The basis of this argument seemed worthless to me earlier (Edwards, 1974), since much medicine treats symptoms and conditions, using bypass operations or remedies such as false teeth and spectacles. It sounds equally irrelevant to me today. Presumably, the use of pacemakers, or ectopic grafts of pancreatic tissue for the treatment of diabetes is merely satisfying the "desire" of those patients to live. This "desire" must drive most of us, day and night, so that perhaps each of us can begin to understand the special problems of the infertile. Moreover, *in vitro* fertilization must at least involve a partial cure, because the uterus is "cured" and can now accept a baby, even if the oviduct remains damaged. This whole debate is a red herring, diverting attention from serious debate, and is merely about semantics: one dictionary defines "cure" as "to heal, to restore to health, to remedy", and I will leave conclusions about the "cure" of infertility by fertilization *in vitro* to my readers. In any case, it is doubtful just how many medical or surgical treatments actually "cure" a defect, i.e. leave it as it was before the disease. The debate is hardly worth pursuing.

Another semantic argument of those years criticized the cure of infertility by fertilization *in vitro* because the future child could not consent to such experimental work; conception must remain as it has always been, divine and unchangeable (Ramsey, 1972). This appeal to a received ethic has not been heeded. The theological basis of this argument was challenged by theologians and others at the time, yet it has also been received recently (Walters and Singer, 1982). Its implications are considerable. Every drug, pill, body activity etc. undertaken by a pregnant woman would be suspect, since every medicament offered during pregnancy, and perhaps even before conception, could potentially influence the fetus. The argument misunderstands the nature of medicine itself, because virtually all treatments of adults, children and fetuses alike — carry some hint of the unknown, some degree of experimentation.

Perhaps no drug or treatment is totally safe. More surprisingly, the proposer of this argument apparently believes that AID is acceptable, providing the recipient simultaneously performs sexual intercourse with her husband (Ramsey, 1970). AID is one of the most massive intrusions in human conception, and the legitimacy of the child.

There was also another widely-held related argument to counter: that "natural" conception was superior to "artificial" conception *in vitro,* because it was expressed in a loving relationship between two couples, and was in some way ordained divinely. This viewpoint was challenged by, amongst others, several theologians (Fletcher, 1971), pointing out that interference with conception for good ends is more acceptable than accepting the status quo. For me, a glance at some of the unfortunate products of natural conception – triploid and trisomic children, others suffering from genetic lesions, some ending as disordered growths in the mother's body, is sufficient to demand that some sort of intervention is essential in conception to ensure that children are born as normal as we can possibly ensure. And loving relationships between couples are perhaps expressed in greater measure in response to the clinical necessities of *in vitro* fertilization than during "natural" conception. There is no guarantee of a loving relationship in natural conception, merely a sexual relationship.

My viewpoints on numerous other debates on the outlandish consequences of fertilization *in vitro,* on cloning an individual, establishing a master race, man-animal hybrids, have been given elsewhere (Edwards, 1974, 1980). How sad it is for a scientist to discover such fears about the application of science amongst intelligent commentators. There were also short-sighted and specious arguments that the infertile should not be treated because too many children are born already, or that adoption was a better alternative than *in vitro* fertilization. Despite these and other debates on the ethics of fertilization *in vitro,* no law and virtually no standards were established in those early days, except for one Act in the UK, the Congenital Disabilities (Civil Liabilities) Act, which was not designed in any way to deal with human conception *in vitro.*

CURRENT ETHICAL

SITUATION ON HUMAN
CONCEPTION *IN VITRO*

Current ethical debates on the fertilizing of human eggs *in vitro* are more restricted in outlook, and are related to specific situations, or to the consequences of particular acts. Standards and laws have still not been established, 20 years since the work began, 4 years since the birth of Louise Brown, and more than 50 births since the opening of Bourn Hall. What a curious and prolonged delay, leaving the practitioners working in a void, compelled to make their own decisions, to be succeeded by an almost frenzied flurry of professional and governmental interest as seven or more clinical Commissions in the UK alone decided to investigate the ethics of fertilization *in vitro*. It is hard to see any serious or sudden development justifying the establishment of Commissions by several churches, the Royal College of Obstetricians and Gynaecologists, the British Medical Association, the Council for Science and Society, the Medical Research Council and, now, the Governmental Warnock Commission. This effort is all the more astonishing when we read of the mass of human disasters associated with asbestos, anti-inflammatory drugs and smoking, for none of these subjects have received such ethical attention. Many legal articles have now been written on *in vitro* fertilization, for example Hubble (1981).

There has been one major change in the situation in recent years. Many babies have now been born, and many more are on the way. Numerous clinics are opening around the world. Ethical Commissions have been established in six or more countries, and their recommendations should provide a fascinating set of documents to compare one with another. The massive increase in the clinical application of work on fertilization *in vitro* has apparently led to ethical arguments of a more practical kind, for example on embryo donation or freezing embryos. For the present, the broad sweep of ethical debate seems to have been replaced by discussions on particular situations stemming from the application of *in vitro* fertilization.

In this final part of my lecture, I would like to discuss the current ethics of human conception *in vitro* from my viewpoint as a scientist. I wish to divide the topic into three parts: the ethics of children born through the procedure, the ethics of studying the "spare" embryo and its constituent tissues, and the use of embryonic tissue for grafting into adults.

The Ethics of Children Born Through Conception *In Vitro*

The primary ethic is clear. Any child born after a conception *in vitro* must be normal, and delivered into a loving family. This rule must apply to the alleviation of infertility, where embryos are grown undisturbed *in vitro,* and also to such work as averting the birth of handicapped children by dividing embryos and using one half to identify those carrying deleterious genes. Whatever the treatment, it must not damage the normal development of the child in any way.

There can be no ethical objections to human conception *in vitro* where the mother and father desire their own child. The methods have been painstakingly developed and backed by relevant animal studies and research over a period of 15 years, with full, frequent and open discussions amongst all sections of the community. Numerous studies on animals have shown how preimplantation embryos grow normally *in vitro.* They can also tolerate massive forms of interference, such as dissecting off cells and tissues, dividing them into two or four, removing a pronucleus from a fertilized egg, and exposure to various drugs or chemicals; yet the embryo either succumbs immediately if the treatment is too harsh, or all survive normally if the treatment is tolerated.

The methods are ethically acceptable to patients. All the available evidence indicates that the incidence of anomalies in the children would be similar to those born after an unassisted pregnancy, although careful follow-up studies are needed. Medical demands on the patients are fully acceptable, even if repeated treatments are needed, and many couples earnestly desire to be offered the methods to have their own children. Most of the couples are married, their approach being taken on trust. The size of the problem is considerable. Patients who might be helped include those with tubal disorders, oligospermia, idiopathic infertility, immunological infertility and others perhaps more than one-half of all infertile couples, as discussed earlier in this lecture (Tables XIV and XV).

There are some ethical advantages in *in vitro* fertilization. At present, for example, AID is offered to couples where the husband has severe oligospermia. But fertilization *in vitro* may be successful even when very few spermatozoa are available, and a husband with a total number of 10^6 spermatozoa has a chance to conceive his own child. Doctors treating oligospermia therefore face a new ethical decision to use AID, which is undoubtedly easier, but where the baby is genetically unrelated to the husband, or to try first for conception *in vitro*. In essence, the importance of paternity within a marriage is being debated.

Concern has been expressed about some of the parental consequences of *in vitro* fertilization. It has obviously been possible to donate oocytes or embryos to recipients since 1970, when the first blastocysts were grown *in vitro,* although such donations have not yet been reported. Couples in which one, or both partners have problems in gametogenesis or the liberation of gametes, and who otherwise have no chance of pregnancy, could have their own family through oocyte and embryo donation. Would this step be a boon to the unfortunate couples, or a Pandora's box leading to all sorts of abuses? Under these circumstances, children are related genetically to only one or neither of the infertile couple, but this ethical issue is not confined to fertilization *in vitro*. It also arises after AID, adoption, and with step-mothers and step-fathers. The ethical problems associated with donating oocytes or embryos to recipients should be acceptable in those societies where AID and adoption are accepted. Indeed, the ethical problems may be less because the recipients must gestate the fetus. I believe that oocyte and embryo donation should be accepted. There is no evidence of any additional risk of malformations in the children, who will presumably be glad to be alive, like the rest of us are. Moreover, the strong desire of the recipients to establish a family should help to ensure that babies are born into responsible and loving homes.

Surrogate mothers who carry a baby for a couple who do not wish to, or cannot gestate a baby, raise different issues. By means of embryo transfer, a surrogate could gestate an embryo for another couple, and would have no genetic relationship with the baby under these circumstances. No reports have yet appeared in the literature about the adoption of this procedure. Surrogate mothers have been known to accept AID, with the intention of giving the newborn child to the donor. This situation is more extreme than with embryo transfer, because the surrogate will have to surrender her own genetic child at birth.

Surrogate motherhood is not a step to be undertaken lightly and there are various complications if embryo transfer (not AID) is indicated. The surrogate is transitory, unrelated, a temporary incubator. She has no medical reason for her treatment, no formal claim for medical attention, and the doctors have no claim on her. Her involvement exposes her to the dangers of pregnancy, and the fetus is itself exposed to any of her habits which may cause damage. I understand that the surrogate has a legal right to change her mind, abort the child, or claim it at birth. Such situations have already arisen, and averting them could lie outside the authority of the medical profession. Problems could arise of a legal familial, psychological and emotional nature for all concerned, including the doctors. We believe that, at present, the surrogate mother should not be introduced into programmes of *in vitro* fertilization until careful analysis, and perhaps legislation has been passed to provide a guide, even though evidence from the United States indicates that the problems of surrogate motherhood following AID can be avoided if careful plans are made beforehand.

Day to day ethical issues of a practical nature arise in clinics practising *in vitro* fertilization. Many of the respective rights of patients and doctors are similar to those associated with other forms of medicine, but novel situations can arise, e.g. in the number of embryos replaced in the mother. A request from a patient for four or five embryos may be unacceptable to the embryologist or doctor, who wish to avoid multipregnancy. Similar differences of opinion could involve embryos which are cleaving erratically or slowly. The embryologist has a unique responsibility to patients, for example, in taking the necessary steps ensuring the correct parentage of an embryo, and in ensuring the conditions of growth are optimal. The resolution of such issues is perhaps left to local ethical committees who can have a responsible role in such matters.

The "Spare" Embryo and Research on Human Embryology

In many programmes of *in vitro* fertilization, ovarian stimulants are used to produce three or four oocytes for fertilization. This situation arises through attempts to give infertile couples the best chance of establishing a pregnancy. Spare embryos would be avoided by limiting the number of oocytes removed from the ovary, or the number inseminated, but these actions could reduce the chance of establishing pregnancy. There is a mixed population of follicles following ovarian stimulation (Edwards, 1980), and it is essential to aspirate them all in order to ensure that the ripest oocytes are collected. Attempts must then be made to fertilize all the oocytes which are aspirated, because there have been examples where only one or perhaps two oocytes, were fertilized even though four or more were aspirated.

Inevitably, four or perhaps more embryos will be obtained from some patients. Only two or three should be replaced, depending on the age of the mother. What should happen to the others? If facilities are available for frozen storage, then the spare embryos could be frozen for an attempt at a later replacement in the mother, but this may merely delay the decision as to what to do with them, and ultimately, some spare embryos will be available in a frozen state rather than in a fresh state. Should all the embryos be replaced in the mother, even if there are five or six? There is no doubt that many gynaecologists would disapprove of such a practice. In effect, therefore, spare embryos will inevitably arise from an *in vitro* fertilization programme.

In some laboratories, preovulatory oocytes obtained from women who are not being treated for infertility are being fertilized *in vitro* for the purposes of scientific investigation; there is no intention of replacing these embryos into the mother. In effect, the embryo is being used deliberately for observational or experimental studies, and this practice raises its own ethical dilemma. I have discussed the situation earlier, and wrote then (Edwards, 1974):

> Some laboratories are prepared to develop programmes on fertilization *in vitro* and early growth of the embryo as a scientific study, thus accepting the view that human embryos can be deliberately initiated in the laboratory and then destroyed later. The situation is very different from that occurring in clinical studies where the embryos are used in attempts to cure infertility, and it cannot be justified by reference to current social practices where embryos or fetuses conceived accidentally are aborted, for example the use of IUD or menstrual aspiration for birth control. Accepting fertilization *in vitro* as a laboratory study in its own right can thus lead to the establishment of values about early human growth, including the assumption that these stages of life are expendable for scientific purposes.

This point is as relevant today as it was then, because some human embryos are established purely for experimental studies, just as animal embryos are. There are, therefore, two major sources of embryos for investigation, the occasional supernumerary ("spare") embryos arising through *in vitro* fertilization programmes, and those arising as a result of a deliberate decision to fertilize oocytes for research purposes. Embryos may also be recovered from the female reproductive tract after fertilization *in vitro,* hence a similar ethical situation will arise here too.

It may be helpful in making such decisions if the potential rewards of research are discussed, to provide an awareness of the benefits that may accrue to other embryos, or to other adults. There is no doubt that many fundamental studies of great scientific and clinical value can be carried out before organogenesis is advanced, before distinct organs have appeared in the embryo. Spare embryos could be used for improving the treatment designed to cure infertility: to test culture media, find out if growth is abnormal, and if embryos can escape from the zona pellucida. It is essential to gain evidence periodically that the embryos are capable of developing beyond the stages when they are replaced in the mother; there must be a reasonable chance of achieving implantation to justify continuing the necessary medical and scientific procedures, and to continue with such tests on the method of culture and chromosome complement in the embryos.

Spare embryos might also help to study the origin of some very disturbing clinical situations in women and their fetuses. There is still no clear idea of the true incidence of chromosomal imbalance in the embryo: investigating the chromosomal constitution of the spare embryos at a very early stage of development say up to day 8 or 9 – would provide enough evidence on the incidence and perhaps the origin of such chromosomal errors. Many mitoses may be needed, more than are present in a 5-day blastocyst, because there are indications that babies with Down's syndrome are mosaics, perhaps arising through non-disjunction in a cleavage division or by the partial reversion to diploidy of an afflicted fetus. The uniform trisomics, which almost certainly arise through a meiotic error in egg or spermatozoon, may all die in early gestation (Hassold and Matsuyama, 1978; Edwards 1980).

There are numerous other types of disordered fetal growth to be understood. Hydatidiform moles might arise through anomalies in pronuclear growth or syngamy; this condition can lead to serious illness and to fetal cancer in the mother. There is a close relationship between the antigens expressed on embryonic and cancer cells. Research on early human development could clarify how identical and conjoined twins are formed, help with new methods of fertility regulation, explain why some ova become "blighted", and clarify the relationship between the antigens of the placenta and the immune response of the mother. Each of these studies could be of direct benefit to many patients, and should not be discarded because spare embryos must be used. I believe it is ethical to use spare embryos for these purposes, that the balance of choice insists on knowledge being gained which might be essential to an understanding of the origins and development of human disorders. I have not attempted to discuss the use of human embryos in fundamental studies on the synthesis of macromolecules and membrane transport systems, on the origin of polarity and the blastocyst, or the inactivation of an X chromosome in cells of the female blastocyst. Many of these studies can be done on animal embryos, yet it might prove essential to study human embryos too. It is impossible to predict the clinical value of "pure" research and results on animals might not apply to man.

Let me turn briefly to the freezing of embryos, a topic that has raised considerable argument and debate. Our programme at Bourn Hall has not begun. What is novel about freezing, what questions and doubts arise that have not already arisen with the use of fresh embryos? In my opinion, there are very few ethically novel situations: all the issues were already raised by the use of fresh embryos. Freezing merely makes some approaches easier; a frozen embryo, when thawed, is like a fresh embryo. Let us take some examples.

Freezing embryos may help to establish a pregnancy between a husband and wife, by storing those spare for a later replacement. This must be ethically acceptable. Frozen embryos could also be replaced into a recipient mother, a simpler procedure than with fresh embryos, because there is no need to co-ordinate the menstrual cycle of donor and recipient. There is no new ethical situation because embryo donation can be achieved using fresh embryos.

Some bizarre situations could arise such as replacing a frozen embryo into its mother after she had delivered a sibling which was ovulated later. This situation could arise with embryos stored for some years. Would the date of fertilization be important in the question of inheritance, or the date of birth? Birth date is used today, when the exact time of conception of two twins, for example, cannot be determined, and the first born is accepted as the older, but it may not apply if the exact date of fertilization was known. The child, when adult, might claim an earlier conception as a right of inheritance.

Thoughts of banks of spare embryos, left alone and unwanted, have raised alarm about their possible use. Yet once again, there is nothing ethically novel, because the fresh spare embryos arising in programmes of *in vitro* fertilization raise similar moral issues. The same ethical questions arise in both situations, but are more acute with a bank of frozen embryos. Some of the frozen embryos would have been saved for a later replacement, and it should not be difficult to arrange conditions such as a time limit for their storage, acceptable to the parents, if divorce or death of the parent means they are no longer needed for this purpose. Other embryos might have been frozen for research. The disposal of such banks is the culmination of a series of earlier decisions to freeze individual embryos; decisions on what to do with them have simply been deferred until large numbers accumulate. I am not denying the size of the ethical problem after freezing; I am merely pointing out that most ethical issues are very similar to those arising with fresh embryos.

Modifying Embryos *In Vitro*

Elegant methods have been devised for the study of early embryology in mammals. The techniques of micromanipulation, the study of teratocarcinoma cells, and the study of embryo disaggregation and reaggregation have yielded experimental data of the highest order in the investigation of early mammalian growth. Should such techniques be applied to human embryos which will be replaced in the mother to develop to full term?

Various manipulations could be carried out on embryos before they are replaced into the mother, and some of these methods could be beneficial. An embryo could be divided into two, to produce identical twins for infertile patients. This procedure could help with programmes of fertilization *in vitro,* because replacing two nonidentical embryos apparently gives higher implantation rates than replacing a singleton, as discussed earlier. Identical twin transfers might also give better results. Should a single embryo be divided, to produce twins for this purpose? There should be no objection to identical twins, because enough occur naturally. But how about quadruplets? The limit here would be the willingness of the doctor to initiate a quadruple pregnancy, with its attendant risks of abortion and maternal morbidity. Two of the embryos could be frozen-stored, and replaced later in the mother, to produce a second set of identical twins which were identical to the first set. Some sort of guide seems to be needed here, perhaps embodied in legislation, to decide on how far such treatments should be carried.

Presently, with limited resources, time and manpower, decisions are easier when based on expedient common sense and basic practical medicine.   When these limits are removed, the technical possibilities may become bewildering.

There is an alternative use of dividing embryos into two. One half could be examined to type the other, especially in families known to be carrying inherited defects.   Embryos carrying a defective gene could then be "aborted *in vitro*" at 5 days of gestation, and a non-defective embryo replaced into the mother. The excision of pieces of trophoblast might provide an alternative method of typing embryos. This approach is surely preferable to the current method of aborting fetuses later in pregnancy. So far, neither our group nor any others have undertaken this programme, and we prefer to wait for higher rates of pregnancy after fertilization *in vitro* to make this approach to genetic screening more acceptable. The birth of handicapped children might be avoided by adopting this procedure, but it demands an ethical choice to be made between the rights of a child to a normal birth against those of a 5-day blastocyst growing *in vitro*. Surely, the rights of the child are greater.

New ethical issues will undoubtedly arise from the application of gene transfer techniques by embryos. At present, these have been restricted to mice, but they will undoubtedly be extended to farm animals before too long.   At present, the transferred DNA is incorporated into the recipient's genome and transmitted to offspring, but there have been varied reports about the control of the expression of the gene in the recipient. The transferred genes for growth hormone and a promoter are expressed in recipient mice, increasing their body size considerably (Palmiter *et al.,* 1982).

Some of these techniques might one day be applicable to human embryos, to avert the expression of a recessive mutant gene. There are major difficulties in technique, and, more importantly, in selecting the correct embryo for treatment.   It seems highly doubtful that such techniques will be used to modify the multifactorial quantitative characteristics of human beings for many years to come.

The Ethics of the Spare Embryo

The ethical problems arising over the "spare" embryo, perhaps raise the most acute issues that we must face. Many people hold a dual belief; that fertilization is the beginning of life, and that from henceforth the embryo is sacrosanct, untouchable. This viewpoint must be respected, although it is obvious that most of the population does not seem to share it. After all, IUDs and post-coital contraceptives destroy embryos that are probably aged up to 7, 8 or even more days after fertilization. It also goes without saying that abortion involves the destruction of a fully formed fetus, and that this method is used deliberately for family limitation in some countries. These current situations should be stressed, to put in perspective the age and size of the tiny spare embryos growing *in vitro,* embryos the size of a pinhead that have hardly begun to differentiate. Yet size alone is obviously an insufficient parameter for complex ethical decisions.

This debate raises intractable questions of when life begins and the rights and duty of scientists and doctors to study embryos. Who can grant permission to a scientist or anyone else to study an embryo which will not survive as a result of his work? Parents can give permission for medical procedures to be carried out which are designed to help their children. But the situation is very different with embryos, where any benefits accrue to others, and certainly not to the embryo itself. Even the rights of the parents to "give away" embryos or gametes might be questioned, not as a gift for a recipient to carry to birth, but as sufficient permission to carry out embryo research. A similar argument about research on mid-term fetuses was advanced by Tiefel (1976).

Can anyone give permission for analyses to be carried out on a human pre-implantation embryo, even if it is the "spare" of a set that was not replaced into the mother? The situation is even more extreme if fertilization was achieved without any intention to replace it in its mother, where a deliberate decision was taken to produce an embryo for research. Who has rights to do this? Perhaps no-one has such absolute right; responsibility can be shared by making decisions in committees, but even so, any decision to carry out such research can only be justified on strictly utilitarian grounds. Can spare embryos be avoided so that the problem does not arise? Yes, by using the natural cycle to establish test-tube babies, when only one or two eggs will ever be collected (Purdy, 1982b).

Should human embryos be used for such varied studies? Are there any grounds to strictly forbid any attempt to assess the growth and characteristics of human embryos in culture? Embryonic rights at such an early age a few days after conception — are a matter for conjecture; absolutists give full rights at fertilization, whereas others believe that rights accrue gradually throughout gestation and so accept methods of fertility control such as IUDs and abortion. Who can decide if an embryo is a "bundle of cells" and when it becomes a human being?

What are the strengths and weaknesses of the absolutist's case? The argument implies that "life" begins at fertilization, but this is not true because life is continuous and has patently begun biochemically in the oocyte long before this. This implication is also compromised by parthenogenesis, because ovulatory oocytes can be activated without fertilization, and develop into advanced fetal stages. Absolutists would not accept research on cleaving embryos after fertilization; one reason may be that once fertilization is breached, then there is no obvious point to defend during later embryology. But cleaving embryos are not sentient and are minute, so why should they be defended? Do absolutists fear that studying early human embryos would undermine the value of human life, or lead to abuses in the application of embryo research? The latter situation is the well-known "camel's nose" argument and applies to virtually every human activity, not only fertilization *in vitro,* but absolutists also deny the study of human embryos *in vitro* for medical reasons, which is basically the case made above for such studies.

There does not seem to be much intrinsically valuable in an embryo being human. It will have a human karyotype and metabolism, but it does not possess any of the higher functions or senses of older fetuses, and could only make a biochemical response to other biochemical stimuli. An embryo is an embryo, not a fetus or a child. Another related defence offered by absolutists is the need to respect the individual genotype as established at fertilization, the basis of individuality. But this argument cannot be accepted either, because genotypes might be established long after fertilization, for example in twins, mosaics and chimaeras. Moreover, a hydatidiform mole or a choriocarcinoma has a unique human genotype, but no-one can give any value to such a genotype or to the embryo before it transformed into these conditions. The absolutist's arguments are a full stop: they block any further reasoning of the balance between benefits and problems, so leaving serious clinical problems uncured.

I sometimes suspect that in all of us, and especially absolutists, there is a psychological remnant of the centuries of bitter debate, of the distressing laws and penalties associated with abortion, contraception and sterilization. There seems to be a stress on the potential rather than the actual value of an embryo, the attribution of "humanness" to embryos long before this is apparent. There is also a fear that once the dykes preventing research on embryos are breached, numerous embryos will then be deliberately initiated for research, and not for replacing into their mothers. This is a fear I partly share; it concerns the ethics of quantity, the argument that once one embryo is studied, then there is no limit to the number that can be studied. I prefer research on human embryos to be devoted to clinical needs, to the alleviation of human suffering of an obviously immediate nature, rather than to establishing scientific concepts which could also be studied in animals. There must be an immediate justification for research in human embryos, even though the practical consequencs of scientific research cannot be foreseen. Limiting research on human embryos to clinically-valuable studies should be encouraged, even though it is not mentioned in guidelines now being issued, which are permitting many laboratories to study human embryos *in vitro* without any need to replace them in the mother. Perhaps some form of licensing, or some very broad guidelines should be considered, permitting some but not total freedom for non-clinical research.

I find the benefits to be gained by studying embryos to considerably outweigh any objections to their study *in vitro*. This belief cannot be justified by quoting other practices, such as the use of IUDs or post coital contraception, or the argument that many embryos conceived *in vivo* are doomed to die anyway during early pregnancy. It is not an ethical justification to argue that I can do something because others are already doing it. There must be ongoing debate about the balance of advantages to be gained, the benefits that could accrue to other embryos and adults from the study of early human growth. There is a recognized clash of principles, and an analogy might help to clarify the situation. Most of us would accept the injunction to "love thy neighbour", but not if he was threatening injury or death to us. In these circumstances, the principle would outweigh the love of neighbour. We are in a similar position, and I believe that the need for knowledge is greater than the respect to be accorded to an early embryo. How long should embryos be grown *in vitro?* Most people would draw an arbitrary line against studying them after the neural tube and sensory systems had formed. I believe that embryos should be grown through their early stage of differentiation at least to 14 days, if there is any potential clinical value in the research. Many human disorders arise during these stages of growth, and there could be unexpected clinical opportunities in studies of differentiation and organ formation.

In concluding this lecture, I would like to outline some potentially fascinating studies on differentiating embryos which might one day be of considerable value in clinical practice. These will involve cutting embryos through their early stages of differentiation, perhaps to day 14. Such studies exemplify the potential clinical advantages of research on early human embryos.

The Spare Embryo and Tissue Grafting

Wide opportunities could arise from the use of embryonic tissue in clinical medicine. Cytodifferentiation and early organogenesis begins within 12 days after fertilization (O'Rahilly, 1973, 1982), so that the formation of organ rudiments can be studied *in vitro* and the differentiating tissues could be used clinically. One human embryo has been grown *in vitro* for 9 days (Fig. 16) (Edwards and Surani, 1977). The ectodermal and mesodermal derivatives differentiate at this time; a few days later, the neural plate would have appeared, haemopoetic cells would be present in the yolk sac, and other tissues would have formed. Obviously, many forms of defective human growth could be studied *in vitro,* raising similar issues to those described above in relation to chromosomal and other disorders. The difference now is that the embryo is older, perhaps 14 days after fertilization, at the stage recommended as the limit to growth *in vitro* by the Ethics Advisory Board of the US Department of Health, Education and Welfare (Federal Register, 1979).

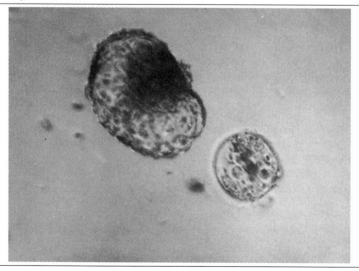

FIG. 16   Growth of a human blastocyst *in vitro* until day 9 after fertilization. The embryo in culture on day 9. The zona has been shed, but retains some inclusions; the embryo has expanded considerably. The embryonic disc can be clearly seen, together with the trophoblast and blastocoelic activity (Edwards and Surani, 1977).

Before deciding on the permitted stage to which growth *in vitro* should be permitted, it is essential to examine some of the possibilities opened up in other areas of medicine by the use of embryonic tissue. For these purposes, embryos would have to be grown to between 12 and 14 days, and their constituent tissues for longer. Such tissues would contain rapidly dividing stem cells which could theoretically be used in recipients. There is a belief that the transplantations of embryonic cells do not lead to the problems of graft rejection arising with adult tissues (Billingham and Silvers, 1964); if this belief is correct, embryonic stem cells cultured *in vitro* could be invaluable as universal donor cells, being accepted by all recipients. Unfortunately, this promise does not seem to have been fulfilled with pancreatic cells from human fetuses aged several months, because these cells are apparently rejected in recipients as the histocompatibility antigens differentiate (Sutherland, 1980). Nevertheless, there is one approach which could avert transplantation rejection, and this is based on observations that mouse embryos can be made to resemble either one of their two parents.

The principle is to induce gynogenesis or androgenesis in embryos. Such studies in mice were, indeed, part of my first research work in Edinburgh University, although the haploid androgenones and gynogenones did not develop very far (Edwards, 1957). A new approach has recently been tested successfully. One of the two pronuclei is removed from the fertilized mouse egg, and the diploid chromosomal complement is restored in the embryo by preventing cytokinesis when the first cleavage division is expected (Hoppe and Illmensee, 1977). Gynogenones can also be produced in mice by retaining the second polar body in the egg before removing the male pronucleus (Borsuk, 1982); this method may result in higher rates of embryonic development because some of the mother's heterozygosity is retained. After the removal of the male pronucleus, embryos develop with a close resemblance to the mother, whereas removal of the female nucleus results in an embryo resembling the father. Androgenetic and gynogenetic mouse embryos develop to full term, and are apparently fully normal. In effect, the mouse embryos were tailored to resemble an existing parent, and alternative methods of achieving this end include parthenogenesis and cloning to obtain an early embryo. Human embryos could presumably be treated in a similar manner, and their growth *in vitro* for 14 days could provide stem cells and tissues which were similar to, and would not be rejected by the parent; in effect, embryonic stem cells could be donated to patch up or repair a deficient organ.

This fanciful proposal should not be dismissed lightly. Several groups of oncologists have concluded that the treatment of chronic granulocytic leukaemia and other disorders by ablative chemoradiotherapy would be enhanced if an identical twin was available to donate hemopoetic tissue (Fefer *et al.,* 1982; Goldman *et al.,* 1982). Few people have identical twins, but embryonic tissue cells could perhaps be produced to match most victims of leukaemia or other disorders. The approach is theoretically possible, but the difficulties are considerable – few stem cells will be available, they may not differentiate or divide in culture, and the embryonic cells may themselves become malignant *in vitro.* Androgenetic embryos might even develop characteristics of hydatidiform moles (Kajii and Ohama, 1977). Nevertheless, some experimental work in animals has already indicated the value of this approach. Hemopoetic cells extracted from the yolk sac of mouse embryos cultured *in vitro* have been used to colonize bone marrow of lethally irradiated adults (Moore and Metcalf, 1970), and hemopoetic stem cells, including those taken from the yolk sac in mice, can be increased many-fold in culture (Dexter *et al.,* 1977, 1980; Moore and Dexter, 1978). The number of cells obtained from human embryos could presumably be increased in a similar manner.

This approach to the use of embryonic hemopoetic stem cells has advantages and disadvantages. Many clinics are now reporting good rates of survival in patients grafted with bone marrow from allogeneic donors, hence the need for syngeneic tissue may be less urgent. Stem cells from the yolk sac may not be as suitable as those taken from adult bone marrow, because they may have a restricted developmental potency (Metcalf, 1977; Loutit *et al.,* 1982). Nevertheless, fewer fetal cells than adult cells may be needed for successful grafting (Buckley *et al.,* 1976; Rieger *et al.,* 1977; O'Reilly *et al.,* 1978), and syngeneic cells are obviously simpler to use because rejection should not occur, and they might colonize the host more rapidly and so minimize post-transplantation immunodeficiency (O'Reilly *et al.,* 1978). The opportunity to graft embryonic tissue of known genetic origin could also avert a widespread search for histocompatible donors, one of the current problems and expenses of bone marrow grafting. There may be no need to make androgenones and gynogenones when using embryonic grafts. Hemopoetic stem cells from the liver of aborted fetuses can be used for grafting, especially if collected before fully competent T lymphocytes have differentiated, and liver cells from older fetuses can be used after the unwanted T lymphocytes have been removed (Good, 1982). Fetal liver cells have been transplanted with thymus tissue to correct severe immunodeficiencies in children, often without inducing graft versus host responses in the recipient, although some of these responses have occurred with grafts of liver from aborted fetuses aged as little as 5 weeks (O'Reilly *et al.,* 1978; Good, 1982).

The principle of making embryonic tissue similar to a recipient can apply to other tissues – Langerhans cells of the pancreas, myocardium, brain; tissues where there are no stem cells left, or where they no longer divide to repair damaged tissues. Pancreatic transplants using fetal tissue have been relatively unsuccessful in treating diabetics, because graft rejection occurs unless immunosuppressants are used, and even then the survival of the graft may be limited (Sutherland, 1980; personal communication). Brain grafts have proved remarkably capable of colonizing damaged brain tissue, and restoring normal function. Initial studies revealed that behavioural defects invoked by lesions in the striatal complex could be remedied by grafts of corresponding fetal tissue (Björklund *et al.,* 1980). A recent review gave other examples of successful brain grafts, and indicated that the brain might be an immunologically privileged site capable of accepting grafts from unrelated recipients *(Science,* 1982). While this manuscript was being prepared, two further reports have shown how a deficiency of LH-RH neurones in the hypothalamus of adult mutant mice can be repaired by placing grafts from the preoptic area of a normal sib into the region of the third ventricle of the recipient (Krieger *et al.,* 1982), and how the behavioural effects of induced septohippocampal regions influencing behaviour in rats were partially restored by grafts of septal tissue from embryos (Low *et al.,*

1982). Neurones from the graft can apparently infiltrate the brain of the recipient, and form synaptic connections with host neurones, although the possibility that host neurones might innervate the graft remains to be excluded (Low *et al.,* 1982).

These methods of grafting could be combined with gene transfer into embryos, as discussed earlier in this article. Stem cells from particular tissues could be obtained which have been genetically modified to avert the expression of a recessive gene. A deficiency expressed in the hemopoetic system of a child, for example, might be tailored by grafting stem cells which have been genetically modified to overcome the disorder. This method would avert the problems associated with the expression of the transferred gene in other tissues, where its expression is not needed. Obviously, there would be no need for fetal stem cells if the tissues of the child could be tailored directly, but there might be some value in the embryological approach to this kind of problem.

Could these procedures be applied to man, and would neural tissue from 14-day embryos be useful? No-one knows the answers to these questions. Perhaps embryonic tissues have not differentiated sufficiently to colonise specific areas of the brain; growth from the graft may be haphazard, and fail to restore the function of the damaged brain. If work of this kind is to be contemplated in man, it would be wise to use tissue genetically similar to the recipient, and make certain that graft rejection is avoided, but embryonic tissue might not be needed if the brain is an immunologically-privileged site, and so accepts tissue from older fetuses. Similar arguments could be applied to other tissue, e.g. myocardium. I have no knowledge of any reports about grafts of myocardial tissue.

Conclusions

In this lecture, I have described the problems that faced us when our work began on human conception *in vitro,* its development in Oldham, and later in Bourn Hall, and our current results. The ethical situation in the early years and during the current period has been assessed.

The progress of the work has been marked by a contrast

between disappointment and wonderful success, but *in vitro* fertilization must now be considered as a routine treatment for infertility. More than 100 children have been born, and there is no greater incidence of anomalies among them than during conception *in vivo*. Success rates have reached an acceptable level. There can be no reason now to withhold this treatment from infertile parents, but further improvements in success rates could make it the preferred method for alleviating several major causes of infertility.

The success of *in vitro* fertilization programmes appears to have modified the breadth of the ethical debate typical of earlier years. Much of this debate now seems to be concerned with particular situations arising in the course of the work, and it seems merely a matter of time before these ethical decisions are resolved. The other applications of the work are now emerging for discussion, including the duplication of embryos to produce identical twins, the typing of embryos for inherited defects, and perhaps the use of embryonic tissue, tailored to match a recipient, to alleviate disorders in adults. The future seems likely to be no less exciting than the past, with a steadily increasing number of rewarding scientific and clinical investigations into human conception.

Acknowledgements

I wish to thank Jean Purdy for her considerable help in the development of this work and for her contributions towards the ethics.

I wish also to thank the Reverend Dr T. C. Appleton and Dr S. B. Fishel for their comments on the manuscript.

References

Austin, C. R. (1951). Observations on the penetration of the sperm into the mammalian egg. *Australian Journal of Scientific Research,* **B, 4,** 581-596.
Batzer, F. R., Schiaff, S., Goldfarb, A. F. and Corson, S. L. (1981). Serial subunit of human chorionic gonadotrophin doubling time as a prognosticator of pregnancy outcome in an infertile population. *Fertility and Sterility,* **35**, 307-312.
Bavister, B. D. (1969). Environmental factors important for in-vitro fertilization in the hamster. *Journal of Reproduction and Fertility,* **18**, 544-545.

Bavister, B. D., Edwards, R. G. and Steptoe, P. C. (1969). Identification of the midpiece and tail of the spermatozoon during fertilization of human eggs *in vitro. Journal of Reproduction and Fertility,* **20**, 159-160.

Billingham, R. E. and Silvers, W. K. (1964). Studies on homografts of foetal and infant skin and further observations on the anomalous properties of pouch skin grafts in hamster. *Proceedings of the Royal Society, B,* **161**, 168.

Björklund, A., Dunnett, S. B., Stenevi, V., Lewis, M. E. and Iversen, S. (1980). Reinnervation of the denervated striatum by substantia nigra transplants: functional consequences as revealed by pharmacological and sensorimotor testing. *Brain Research,* **199**, 307-333.

Borsuk, E. (1982). Preimplantation development of gynogenetic diploid mouse embryos. *Journal of Embryology and Experimental Morphology,* **69**, 215-222.

Brinster, R. L. (1965). Studies on the development of mouse embryos in vitro. II. The effect of energy source. *Journal of ExperimentalZoology,* **158**, 59-68.

Buckingham, J. C., Döhler, K.-D. and Wilson, C. A. (1978). Activity of the pituitary adreno-cortical system and thyroid gland during the oestrous cycle of the rat. *Journal of Endocrinology,* **78**, 359-366.

Buckley, R. H., Whisnant, J. K., Schiff, R. I., Gilbertsen, R. B., Huang, A. T. and Platt, N. S. (1976). Correction of severe combined immunodeficiency by fetal liver cells. *New England Journal of Medicine,* **294**, 1076-1081.

Chang, M. C. (1951). Fertilising capacity of spermatozoa deposited in the Fallopian tubes. *Nature,* **168**, 697-698.

Chang, M. C. (1955). The maturation of rabbit oocytes in cultures and their maturation, activation, fertilization and subsequent development in the Fallopian tubes. *Journal of Experimental Zoology,* **128**, 379-405.

Daniel, W. J. (1982). Sexual ethics in relation to in-vitro fertilization and embryo transfer: the fitting use of human reproductive power. In *Test-Tube Babies,* edited by W. Walters and P. Singer, pp. 71-78. Melbourne: Oxford University Press.

De Kretzer, D., Dennis, B., Hudson, B., Leeton,J., Lopata, A., Outch, K., Talbot, J., and Wood, C. (1973). Transfer of a human zygote. *Lancet* **ii**, 728-729.

Dexter, T. M., Allen, T. D. and Lajtha, L. G. (1977). Conditions controlling the proliferation of haemopoitic stem cells *in vitro. Journal of Cellular Physiology,* **91**, 335-344.

Dexter, T. M., Spooncer, E., Toksoz, D. and Lajtha, L. G. (1980). The role of cells and their products in the regulation of *in vitro* stem cell proliferation and granulocyte development. Journal *of Supramolecular Structure,* **13**, 513-524.

Dunstan, G. R. (1974). *The Artifice of Ethics.* Second edition 1978. London: SCM Press.

Edwards, R. G. (1957). The experimental induction of gynogenesis in the mouse. I. Irradiation of the sperm by X-rays. *Procedings of the Royal Society, B,* **146**, 469-487.

Edwards, R. G. (1962). Meiosis in ovarian oocytes of adult mammals. *Nature,* **196**, 446-450.

Edwards, R. G. (1965a). Maturation *in vitro* of mouse, sheep, cow, pig, rhesus monkey and human ovarian oocytes. *Nature,* **208**, 349-351.

Edwards, R. G. (1965b). Maturation *in vitro* of human ovarian oocytes. *Lancet,* **ii**, 926-929.

Edwards, R. G. (1971). Problems of artificial fertilization. *Nature,* **233**, 23-25.

Edwards, R. G. (1972). Judging the social values of scientific advances. In *Genetics and the Quality of Life,* edited by C. Birch and P. Abrecht, pp. 41-49. London and Oxford: Pergamon Press.

Edwards, R. G. (1973). Studies on human conception. *American Journal of Obstetrics and Gynecology,* **117**, 587-601.

Edwards, R. G. (1974). Fertilization of human eggs in vitro: morals, ethics and the law. *Quarterly Review of Biology,* **49**, 3-26.

Edwards, R. G. (1980). *Conception in the Human Female.* London and New York: Academic Press.

Edwards, R. G. (1981). Test-tube babies, 1981. *Nature,* **293**, 253-256.

Edwards, R. G., Bavister, B. D. and Steptoe, P. C. (1969). Early stages of fertilization *in vitro* of human oocytes matured *in vitro. Nature,* **221**, 632-635.

Edwards, R. G., Donahue, R. P., Baramki, T. A. and Jones, H. W. (1966). Preliminary attempts to fertilise human oocytes matured in vitro. *American Journal of Obstetrics and Gynecology,* **96**, 192-300.

Edwards, R. G. and Fishel, S. B. (1982). The human uterus in the luteal phase and early pregnancy. In *Human Conception in Vitro,* edited by R. G. Edwards and J. M. Purdy, pp. 257-288. London and New York: Academic Press.

Edwards, R. G., Fishel, S. B. and Purdy, J. M. (1983a). *In vitro* fertilization of human eggs. Analysis of follicular growth, ovulation and fertilization. In *Fertilization of the Human Egg* in vitro, edited by H. M. Beier and H. R. Lindner, pp.l69-l88. Berlin; Springer-Verlag.

Edwards, R. G. and Gates, A. H. (1959). Timing of the stages of the maturation divisions, ovulation, fertilization and the first cleavage of eggs of adult mice treated with gonadotrophins.Journal *of Endocrinology,* **18**, 292-304.

Edwards, R. G. and Purdy, J. M. (Editors) (1982). *Human Conception in Vitro.* Proceedings of the First Bourn Hall Meeting. London and New York: Academic Press.

Edwards, R. G., Purdy, J. M. and Fishel, S. B. (1983b). *Proceedings of the Royal Society of Medicine* (in press).

Edwards, R. G. and Sharpe, D. J. (1971). Social values and new developments in human embryology. *Nature,* **231**, 87-91.

Edwards, R. G. and Steptoe, P. C. (1973). Biological aspects of embryo transfer, In *Law and Ethics of A.I.D. and Embryo Transfer,* Ciba Foundation Symposium (New Series) 17, pp. 11-40. Amsterdam: Associated Scientific Publishers.

Edwards, R. G. and Steptoe, P. C. (1975). Induction of follicle growth, ovulation and luteinisation in the human ovary. *Journal of Reproduction and Fertility Supplement,* **22**, 121-163.

Edwards, R. G. and Steptoe, P. C. (1980). *A Matter of Life.* London: Hutchinsons.

Edwards, R. G., Steptoe, P. C. and Purdy, J. M. (1970). Fertilization and cleavage in vitro of preovulatory human oocytes. *Nature,* **227**, 1307-1309.

Edwards, R. G., Steptoe, P. C. and Purdy, J. M. (1980). Establishing full-term pregnancies using embryos grown *in vitro. British Journal of Obstetrics and Gynaecology,* **87**, 737-756.

Edwards, R. G. and Surani, M. A. H. (1977). The primate blastocyst and its environment. *Uppsala Journal of Medicine,* **22**, 39-50.

Everett, J. W., Sawyer, C. H. and Markee, J. E. (1949). A neurogenic timing factor in control of the ovulatory discharge of luteinizing hormone in the rat. *Endocrinology,* **44**, 234-250.

Federal Register (1979). U.S. Department of Health, Education and Welfare. 18 June. Fefer, A., Cheever, M. A., Greenberg, P. D., Appelbaum, F. R., Boyd, C. N., Buckner, C. D., Kaplan, H. C., Ramberg, R., Sanders, J. E., Storb, R. and Thomas, E. D. (1982). Treatment of chronic granulocytic leukemia with chemoradio therapy and transplantation of tissue from an identical twin. *New England Journal of Medicine,* **306**, 63-68.

Fishel, S. B. and Edwards, R. G. (1982). Essentials of fertilization. In *Human Conception in Vitro,* edited by R. G. Edwards and J. M. Purdy, pp. 157-179. London and New York: Academic Press.

Fishel, S. B., Edwards, R. G. and Purdy, J. M. (1983a). *In vitro* fertilization of human oocytes: Factors associated with embryonic development *in vitro,* replacement of embryos and pregnancy. In *Fertilization of the Human*

Egg in Vitro, edited by H. M. Beier and H. R. Lindner, pp.25l-269. Berlin: Springer-Verlag.

Fishel, S. B., Edwards, R. G. and Purdy, J. M. (1983b). *Proceedings of the Carmel Symposium* (in press).

Fletcher, J. (1971). Ethical aspects of genetic controls. *New England Journal of Medicine,* **285**, 776-783.

Fowler, R. E. and Edwards, R. G. (1957). Induction of superovulation and pregnancy in mature mice by gonadotrophins. *Journal of Endocrinology,* **15**, 374-384.

Francouer, R. T. (1972). We can – we must: reflections on the technological imperative. *Theological Studies,* **33**, 428-439.

Frydman, R. (1982). Discussion on human conception in vitro. In *Human Conception in Vitro,* edited by R. G. Edwards and J. M. Purdy, pp. 346. London and New York: Academic Press.

Goldman,J. M., Baughan, A. S.J., McCarthy, D. M., Worsley, A. M., Hows,J. M., Gordon-Smith, E. C., Catovsky, D., Batchelor, J. R., Goolden, A. W. G. and Galton, D. A. G. (1982). Marrow transplantation for patients in the chronic phase of chronic granulocytic leukaemia. *Lancet,* **ii**, 623-625.

Good, R. A. (1982). Towards safer marrow transplantation. *New England Journal of Medicine,* **306**, 421-423.

Hassold, T. J. and Matsuyama, A. (1978). Origin of trisomies in human spontaneous abortions. *Human Genetics,* **46**, 285-294.

Hayashi, M. (1963). Fertilization *in vitro* using human ova. *VIIth Conference of the International Planned Parenthood Federation, Singapore,* p. 303. Amsterdam: Excerpta Medica.

Henderson, S. A. and Edwards, R. G. (1968). Chiasma frequency and maternal age in mammals. *Nature,* **218**, 22-28.

Hoppe, P. C. and Illmensee, K. (1977). Microsurgically produced homozygous diploid uniparental mice. *Proceedings of National Academy in Sciences, U.S.A.,* **74**, 5657-5661.

Hubble, G. C. (1981). Liability of the physician for the defects of a child caused by *in vitro* fertilization. *Journal of Legal Medicine,* **2**, 501-521.

Jacobs, P. A., Angel, R. R., Buchanan, I. M., Hassold, T.J., Matsuyama, A. M. and Manuel, B. (1978). The origin of human triploids. *Annals of Human Genetics,* **42**, 49-57.

Jagiello, G., Karnicki, J. and Ryan, R. J. (1968). Superovulation with pituitary gonodotrophins. Methods for obtaining metaphase figures in human ova. *Lancet* **i**, 178-180.

Jones, A. and Bodmer, W. F. (1974). *Our Future Inheritance: Choice or Chance?* Oxford: Oxford University Press.

Kajii, T. and Ohama, K. (1977). Androgenetic origin of hydatidiform moles. *Nature,* **268**, 633-644.

Kass, L. (1971). Babies by means of in-vitro fertilization: unethical experiments on the unborn? *New England Journal of Medicine,* **285**, 1174-1179.

Kennedy, I. and Edwards, R. G. (1975). A critique of the Law Commission Report on Injuries to Unborn Children and the proposed Congenital Disabilities (Civil Liability) *Bill. Journal of Medical Ethics,* **1**, 116-121.

Krieger, D. T., Perlo, M. J., Gibson, M. J., Davies, T. F., Zimmerman, E. A., Ferin, M. and Charlton, H. M. (1982). *Nature,* **298**, 468-471.

Kuhse, H. (1982). In *Test-Tube Babies,* edited by W. Walters and P. Singer. Oxford: Oxford University Press.

Lopata, A. (1980). Successes and failures in human in-vitro fertilization. *Nature,* **288**, 642-643.

Loutit, J. F., Marshall, M. J., Nisbet, N. W. and Vaughan, J. M. (1982). Versatile stem cells in bone marrow. *Lancet,* **ii**, 1090-1093.

Low, W. C., Lewis, P. R., Bunch, S. T., Dunnitt, S. B., Thomas, S. R., Iversen, S. D., Björklund, A. and Stenevi, U. (1982). Function recovery following neural transplantation of embryonic septal nuclei in adult rats with septohippocampal lesions. *Nature,* **300**, 260-262.

Menkin, M. F. and Rock, J. (1948). In-vitro fertilization and cleavage of human ovarian eggs. *American Journal of Obstetrics and Gynecology,* **55**, 440-452.

Metcalf, D. (1977). *Hemopoietic Colonies.* Berlin: Springer-Verlag.

Moore, M. A. S. and Metcalfe, D. (1970). Ontogeny of the haemopoietic system: yolk sac origin of *in vivo* and *in vitro* colony-forming cells in the developing mouse embryo. *British Journal of Haematology,* **18**, 279-296.

Moore, M. A. S. and Dexter, T. M. (1978). Stem cell regulation in continuous hematopoietic cell culture. In *Immuno biology of Bone Marrow Transplantation,* edited by R. P. Gale and G. Opels, pp. 9-20. New York: Grune & Stratton.

Nichols, D.J. and Chevins, P. F. D. (1981). Plasma corticosterone fluctuations during the oestrous cycle of the house mouse. *Experientia,* **37**, 319-320.

O'Rahilly, R. (1973). *Developmental Stages in Human Embryos.* Washington, D.C.: Carnegie Institute.

O'Rahilly, R. (1982). *IPPF Wall Chart on Early Human Development.* London:
International Planned Parenthood Federation.

O'Reilly, R. J., Pahwa, R., Dupont, B. and Good, R. A. (1978). Severe combined immunodeficiency: Transplantation approaches for patients lacking an HLA genotypically identical sibling. In *Immunobiology of Bone Marrow Transplantation,* edited by R. P. Gale and G. Opels, pp. 187-199. New York: Grune & Stratton.

Palmiter, R. D., Brinster, R. L., Hammer, R. E., Trumbauer, M. E., Rosenfeld, M. G. Birnberg, N. C. and Evans, R. M. (1982). Dramatic growth of mice that develop from eggs microinjected with metallothionein – growth hormone fusion genes. *Nature,* **300**, 611-615.

Pincus, G. and Enzmann, B. V. (1935). The comparative behaviour of mammalian eggs *in vitro* and *in vivo*. I. The activation of ovarian eggs. *Journal of Experimental Medicine,* **62**, 665-675.

Purdy, J. M. (1982a). Methods for fertilization and embryo culture *in vitro*. In *Human Conception in Vitro,* edited by R. G. Edwards and J. M. Purdy, pp. 135-148. London and New York: Academic Press.

Purdy, J. M. (1982b). Comment, p. 365. In *Human Conception in Vitro,* edited by R. G. Edwards and J. M. Purdy. London and New York: Academic Press.

Psychoyos, A. (1973). Endocrine control of egg implantation. In *Handbook of Physiology,* Section 7. Endocrinology, Vol. II, Part 2. Washington, D.C.: American Physiological Society.

Ramaley, J. A. (1974). Differences in serum corticosterone patterns in individual rats: relationship to ovulatory cycles. *Journal of Endocrinology,* **66**, 421 -426.

Ramsey, P. (1970). *Fabricated Man. The Ethics of Genetic Control.* New Haven, Connecticut: Yale University Press.

Ramsey, P. (1972). Shall we "reproduce"? I. The medical ethics of in-vitro fertilization. *Journal of the American Medical Association,* **220**, 1346-1350.

Rieger, H. L., Rieger, M. D., Lustig, J. V., Hirschhorn, R. and Rothberg, R. M. (1977). Reconstitution of T-cell function in severe combined immunodeficiency disease following transplantation of early embryonic liver cells. *Journal of Paediatrics,* **90**, 707-712.

Science (1982). Transplants as guides to brain development; grafts correct brain damage. *Science,* **217**, 340-344.

Shettles, L. B. (1955). A morula stage of human ova development *in vitro*. *Fertility and Sterility,* **6**, 287-289.

Steptoe, P. C. and Edwards, R. G. (1981). Laparoscopic recovery of pre-ovulatory human oocytes after priming of ovaries with gonadotrophins. *Lancet* i, 683-689.

Steptoe, P. C. and Edwards, R. G. (1976). Reimplantation of a human embryo with subsequent tubal pregnancy. *Lancet,* **i**, 880-882.

Steptoe, P. C. and Edwards, R. G. (1978). Birth after the reimplantation of a human embryo. *Lancet,* **ii**, 366.

Steptoe, P. C., Edwards, R. G. and Purdy, J. M. (1971). Human blastocysts grown in culture. *Nature,* **229**, 132-133.

Steptoe, P. C., Edwards, R. G. and Purdy, J. M. (1980). Clinical aspects of pregnancies established with cleaving embryos grown *in vitro. British Journal of Obstetrics and Gynaecology,* **87**, 757-768.

Steptoe, P. C. and Webster, J. (1982). Laparascopy of the normal and disordered ovary. In *Human Conception in Vitro,* edited by R. G. Edwards and J. M. Purdy. London and New York: Academic Press.

Sutherland, D. E. R. (1980). International human pancreas and islet transplant registrary. *Transplantation Proceedings,* **12**, Supplement 2, 229-236.

Thibault, C. (1969). *In vitro* fertilization of the mammalian egg. In *Fertilization Comparative Morphology, Biochemistry and Immunology,* Vol. II, edited by C. B. Metz and A. Monroy, pp. 405-435. London and New York: Academic Press.

Tiefel, H. O. (1976). The cost of foetal research: ethical considerations. *New England Journal of Medicine,* **294**, 85-90.

Trounson, A. O., Leeton, J. F., Wood, C., Webb, J. and Wood, J. (1981). Pregnancies in humans by fertilizing *in vitro* and embryo transfer in the controlled ovulatory cycle. *Science,* **212**, 681-682.

Walters, W. and Singer, P. (1982). *Test-Tube Babies.* Oxford: Oxford University Press.

Wood, C., Trounson, A. 0., Leeton, J., Talbot, J. Mc., Buttery, B., Webb, J., Wood, J. and Jessup, D. (1981). A clinical assessment of nine pregnancies obtained by *in vitro* fertilization and embryo transfer. *Fertility and Sterility,* **35**, 502-508.

Yanagimachi, R. and Chang, M. C. (1964). *In vitro* fertilization of golden hamster *ova. Journal of Experimental Zoology,* **156**, 261-376.

Appendix: Galton Lectures 1914 to 2006

1914   Sir Francis Darwin: **Francis Galton, 1822-1911**

1915   Prof. J Arthur Thomson: **Eugenics and War**

1916   Prof. E B Poulton: **Eugenic Problems after the Great War**

1917   Discussion, opened by Major Leonard Darwin: **The Disabled Sailor and Soldier and the Future of our Race**

1919   Dean Inge: **What Nations and Classes will Prevail?**

1920   Prof. Arthur Keith: **Galton's Place Among Anthropologists**

1921   Mr W Bateson: **Commonsense in Racial Problems**

1922   **Speeches for the Galton Centenary**

1923   Prof. A C Pigou: (no title given)

1924   Dr G Elliot-Smith: **Problems of Race**

1925   Dr F C S Schiller: **The Ruin of Rome and its Lessons for Us**

1926   The Rt Rev Bishop of Birmingham: **Some Reflections on Eugenics and Religion**

1927   Dr A F Tredgold: **Mental Disease in Relation to Eugenics**

1928   Dr C J Bond: **Causes of Racial Decay**

1929   Major Leonard Darwin: **The Society's Coming of Age: The Growth of the Eugenic Movement**

1930   Prof. S J Holmes: **Natural Selection in Man and the Evolution of Human Intelligence**

1931   Prof. Sir J Arthur Thompson: **Warnings from Nature or Seven Red Flags from Biology**

1932 E J Lidbetter: **The Social Problem Group as Illustrated by a Series of East London Pedigrees**

1933 Mr Justice McCardie: **My Outlook on Eugenics**

1934 Sir Josiah Stamp: **Eugenic Influences in Economics**

1935 Prof. A M Carr-Saunders: **Eugenics in the Light of Population Trends**

1936 Dr Julian S Huxley: **Eugenics and Society**

1937 Mr J M Keynes: **Some Economic Consequences of a Declining Population**

1938 Dr John A Ryle: **Medicine and Eugenics**

1939 Dr C G Darwin: **Positive Eugenic Policy**

1940 The Lord Horder: **Eugenic Policy**

1941 Informal discussion, opened by Lord Horder: **Eugenics in Wartime**

1942 Prof. J D Bernal: **The Need for a Social Sciences Research Council**

1943 Sir William Beveridge: **Eugenic Aspects of Children's Allowances**

1945 Dr C P Blacker: **Eugenics in Retrospect and Prospect**

1946 Prof. Godfrey Thomson: **The Trend of National Intelligence**

1947 Dr W Norwood East: **The Non-sane Non-insane Offender**

1948 Sir Russell Brain: **Some Reflections on Genius**

1949 The Rt Rev Bishop of Birmingham: **The Mixing of Races and Social Decay**

1950 Dr A S Parkes: **The Primrose Path – Some Aspects of the Population Problem**

1951 Dr G C L Bertram: **Eugenics and Human Ecology**

1952 Dr J A Fraser Roberts: **The Genetics of Mental Deficiency**

1953   Prof. T H Marshall: **Social Selection in the Welfare State**

1954   Prof. F A E Crew: **A Eugenic Appraisal of the Welfare State**

1955   Prof. Sir Cyril Burt: **The Meaning and Assessment of Intelligence**

1956   Mr Frederick Osborn: **Galton and Mid-century Eugenics**

1957   Prof. Tage Kemp: **Genetic-Hygienic Experiences in Denmark in Recent Years**

1958   Prof. Aubrey Lewis: **Fertility and Mental Disorder**

1959   Mrs Mary Stocks: **Reflections on a Changing Class Structure**

1960   Dr Eliot Slater: **Galton's Heritage**

1961   Sir Robert Platt: **Inherited Disease in Man**

1962   Sir Julian Huxley: **Eugenics in Evolutionary Perspective**

1963   Mrs Margaret Pyke: **Family Planning: An Assessment**

1964   Prof. Jan A Böök: **Some Mechanisms of Chromosome Variations and their Relation to Human Malformations**

1965   Dr Howard B Newcombe: **The Study of Mutation and Selection in Human Populations**

1966   Dr J M Tanner: **Galtonian Eugenics and the Study of Growth**

1967   Dr A H Halsey: **The Changing Relations between Biological and Social Science**

1968   Dr G Ainsworth Harrison: **The Race Concept in Human Biology**

1969   Dr Kathleen Kenyon: **Women in Academic Life**

1970   Professor Sir Dugald Baird: **The Obstetrician and Society**

1971   Dr C O Carter: **The New Eugenics?**

1972   Prof. J E Meade: **Economic Policy and the Threat of Doom**

1973   Mr P R Cox: **Population Prospects and the New Biology**

1974   Prof. W H G Armytage: **The Docimological Dilemma: Quality Control or Quantity Surveying?**

1975   Sir John Brotherston: **Inequality, Is It Inevitable?**

1976   Dr Alex Comfort: **Sexuality in Later Life** (read by W.H.G. Armytage)

1977   Prof. Margaret Sutherland: **Educating Girls – To Repair the Ruins of our First Parents**

1978   Prof. Paul Gebhard: **Sexuality in the Post-Kinsey Era**

1979   Dr Peter Laslett: **The Centrality of Demographic Experience**

1980   Mr Peter Diggory: **The Long-term Effects upon the Child of Perinatal Events**

1981   Prof. Bernard Benjamin: **Variation of Mortality in the United Kingdom**

1982   Dr R G Edwards: **Human Embryos in Vitro**

1983   Prof. Hans J Eysenck: **Intelligence: New Wine in Old Bottles?**

1984   Prof. N R Butler: **The Way Ahead: Lessons from Cross-Disciplinary Studies of Health, Development, Behaviour, Education and Family Life**

1985   Prof. A F Shorrocks: **Inequality and Economic Opportunity**

1986   Prof. Roger Short: **The Enigma of Human Fecundity**

1987   Prof. Sir Andrew Huxley: **Julian Huxley – A Family View**

1988   Prof. David Robinson: **Controlling Legal Addictions: 'Taking Advantage of What's There'**

1989 Prof. Trefor Jenkins: **Genetics and Medicine: Sharing the Benefits**

1990 Prof. D F Roberts: **The Pitcairn Islanders**

1991 Prof. J H Edwards: **Francis Galton – Numeracy and Innumeracy in Genetics**

1992 Mr S L Barron: **The Changing Status of the Fetus**

1993 Prof. Alan S McNeilly: **Breastfeeding and the Baby: Natural Contraception**

1994 Prof. Peter Parsons: **From Energy Budgets to Adaptive Limits under Stress**

1995 Prof. Thomas J Bouchard, Jr: **Behaviour Genetic Studies of Intelligence, Yesterday and Today: The Long Journey from Plausibility to Proof**

1996 Prof. Richard Soloway: **Marie Stopes, Eugenics and the Birth Control Movement**

1997 Dr A W F Edwards: **The Eugenics Society and the Development of Biometry**

1998 Prof. Pauline Mazumdar: **Eugenics: The Pedigree Years**

1999 Prof. Arthur Jensen: **Galton's Legacy to Research on Intelligence**

2000 Mr Robert Resta: **Genetic Counselling: Its Scope and Limitations**

2001 Dr Allan Bradley: **The Human Genome Project**

2003 Prof. J D Y Peel: **Spencer in History: The Second Century**

2005 Prof. Robin Dunbar: **Taking Social Intelligence Seriously**

2006 Prof. Marcus Pembrey: **Human Inheritance, Differences and Diseases: Putting Genes in their Place**

Between 1914 and 1967 the Galton lectures were published in the *Eugenics Review*. Subsequent lectures were incorporated in the proceedings of the annual conferences at which they were presented and published successively by *The Journal of Biosocial Science* (1969-71), Academic Press (1972-85), Macmillan (1986-94), *The Journal of Biosocial Science* (1995) and the Galton Institute (1996-98 and 2000-05). No conference volume was produced in 1999 but the Galton Lecture was published in *The Journal of Biosocial Science*.

Index

ALSO AVAILABLE

HUMAN ABILITY
GENETIC AND ENVIRONMENTAL INFLUENCES
Edited By ROBERT PEEL and MAZIN ZEKI

Proceedings of the 2005 Conference of the Galton Institute

CONTENTS

ISBN 0954657004

Available post paid from the Institute's General Secretary, price
£5.00

HERBERT SPENCER

THE INTELLECTUAL LEGACY

Edited By GRETA JONES AND ROBERT PEEL

Proceedings of the 2003 Conference of the Galton Institute

CONTENTS

ISBN 0950406686

Available post paid from the Institute's General Secretary, price £5.00

A CENTURY OF MENDELISM

Edited by ROBERT PEEL and JOHN TIMSON

Proceedings of the 2000 Conference of the Galton Institute

CONTENTS

ISBN 095040666X

Available post paid from the Institute's General Secretary, price £5.00

EUGENICS IN AUSTRALIA:

Striving for National Fitness

by

Diana Wyndham

CONTENTS

ISBN 0950406678

Available post paid from the Institute's General Secretary, price £5.00

HUMAN PEDIGREE STUDIES

Edited by ROBERT PEEL

Proceedings of the 1998 Conference of the Galton Institute

CONTENTS

ISBN 0950406643

Available post paid from the Institute's General Secretary Price
£5.00

ESSAYS IN THE HISTORY OF EUGENICS

Edited by ROBERT PEEL

Proceedings of the 1997 Conference of the Galton Institute

CONTENTS

ISBN 0950406635

Available post paid from the Institute's General Secretary Price
£5.00

MARIE STOPES, EUGENICS AND THE ENGLISH BIRTH CONTROL MOVEMENT

Edited by ROBERT PEEL

Proceedings of the 1996 Conference of the Galton Institute

CONTENTS

ISBN 0950406627

Available post paid from the Institute's General Secretary Price
£5.00

POPULATION CRISES AND POPULATION CYCLES

by

CLAIRE RUSSELL AND W M S RUSSELL

CONTENTS

ISBN 0950406651

Available post paid from the Institute's General Secretary Price
£5.00